James Earl of Kildare.
Master General of the Ordnance in Ireland.
and Colonel-in-Chief of the Royal Irish Regiment of Artillery
Reproduced from the painting at Carton. (by Ramsay)
by permission of the Duke of Leinster.

HISTORY

OF THE

Royal Irish Regiment of Artillery

BY

J. J. CROOKS (Major)

Author of
"A HISTORY OF THE COLONY OF SIERRA LEONE"
AND "THE GOLD COAST ARTILLERY CORPS, 1851-63"

THE ORDNANCE ARMS OF IRELAND

BROWNE AND NOLAN, LIMITED
DUBLIN, BELFAST, CORK, WATERFORD :: 1914

[ALL RIGHTS RESERVED]

CONTENTS

PAGE

INTRODUCTORY CHAPTER 1

1755.

Augmentations to the Army in Ireland—Military Stores from England—Artillery Detachment from Woolwich—The Old Artillery Traine in Ireland—Gun Yard and Butt at Royal Hospital—Garrisons and Magazines in Ireland—Establishment of Office of Ordnance—Instructions to March a Field Traine—Inferior Officers of the Traine—Guns and Ammunition—Distribution of the Traine—Traine of Artillery reduced—Warrant to Bombardiers—Fitting out a Field Traine—Troops Encamped at Thurles—Artillery Drills—Brass Cannon Proved—Accidents in Firing—Detachment Inspected 7

1756

Enlistment Regulations—Artillery Company Formed—Inspection of the Company—Artillery to Kilkenny Camp—Artillery Drills—Battalion Guns to Regiments of Foot—Establishment of the Company . . . 28

1757

Brass Mortars Proved—Ammunition for Battalion Guns—Artillery Quartered in Barracks—Regulations for Pay, Subsistence, Arrears, Stoppages, Clothing, and Arms—Dates of Appointment of Non-Commissioned Officers, and Days on which the Privates were Inlisted—List of Cheques signed by the Muster Master General—Estimate for Arms and Accoutrements—Recruiting for the British Establishment—Army on the Irish Establishment 36

1758

Reward for Deserters—Artillery Mounting the Garrison Guards—Regulated Form of Furlough—Ammunition for Artillery Practice—Deductions for the Infirmary—Appointment of Commandant—Accident in Firing Salute—Target Practice—Surgeon to the Company—Earl of Kildare, Master of the Ordnance . . . 53

1759

Artillery Company to Encamp—Allowance for Bat Horses—Report on Hats 66

PAGE

1760

Raising a Regiment of Irish Artillery—Establishment of Four Companies — Arms, Accoutrements, and Clothing—Recruiting—French Fleet off Carrickfergus—Detachment to Cahir—Butt of Earth in Phœnix Park—Regiment to Encamp—The King's House at Chapel-Izod—Regiment Reviewed—Head Quarters at Chapel-Izod—Earl of Kildare, Colonel in Chief . . 63

1761

The King's House at Chapel-Izod—Contract for Clothing—Company at Leixlip—Recruiting—Honours to Master General of Ordnance—New Piece of Artillery—Company at Maynooth 79

1762

Major Chenevix Promoted Lieut.-Colonel Commandant—Riots and Disturbances—Reward for Deserters—Gentlemen Cadets—Hired Houses at Chapel-Izod . 87

1763

Englishmen Allowed to Enlist in Irish Artillery—Officers to Reside at Chapel-Izod and Maynooth—Chapel-Izod Parish Church—Company Pay Lists—Orders to Officers in Writing—Forts and Fortifications . . 95

1764

Artificers' Payment for Places—A New Barrack for Artillery—Drum Major's Dress—Orders for Gunpowder Magazine—Laboratory at Chapel-Izod . . . 106

1765

Infirmary at Chapelizod—Regimental Magazine—Marquis of Kildare Resigns Post of Master General—Riots and Disturbances—Political Demonstration . . . 116

1766

The Earl of Shannon appointed Master General—Reductions in the Regiment—Detail of the Guards—Reduction of Gunners to Mattrosses—Discharged Men Recommended for Admission to Royal Hospital—Sedan Chair for the Sick 124

1767

Band Instruments—Pistols Supplied—Alterations in Clothing and Accoutrements 136

v

1768

Mattross Tried by General Court Martial—Deserters Pardoned—Officers to Reside at Chapel-Izod . . 140

1769

Men's Measure to be taken for Clothing—Artillery Practice —The Regimental Band 147

1770

The Earl of Shannon Resigns Post of Master General—The Earl of Drogheda appointed in Succession—Laboratory Tent for Church Service—Estimate for a New Artillery Barrack—Lodging Money to Married Men—Detached Commands—Men wanted to Attend the Guns 150

1771

Augmentation to the Regiment—Memorial from the Superior Officers—Muster of Invalid Pensioners—Admittance to Storehouses—Muster of Detachments 157

1772

Hired House for Barracks at Chapel-Izod . . . 165

1773

Cost of Regimental Clothing—New Accoutrements—Cess on Old Barrack at Chapel-Izod 168

1774

"Record" Review and Sham Fight—Rank of Fireworkers Abolished 171

1775

Volunteers to Serve in America—Recruiting in Cork . . 176

1776

Discharged Men for Garrison Duty—Death of Lieut.-Colonel Chenevix—Promotion of Major Straton—Invalids Unfit for Garrison Duty—Coals for Guard Houses—Proof House at Salute Battery—Shortage of Duty Men—Allowance to Invalids. 179

1777

Draft for North America—Recruiting for the Regiment—Return of Recruits Raised—Gallant Behaviour of Draft sent to America 186

vi

PAGE

1778

Volunteers for North America—Detachments to Charlesfort and Duncannon Fort—A Return of the Regiment—Augmentation to the Regiment—Barrack Accommodation—Detachments to Cork and Clonmel—Return of Recruits Enlisted—Detachment to Belfast—Floating Batteries for Dublin Harbour—Ordnance Cast in Ireland 194

1779

Floating Batteries for Dublin Harbour—Detachments to Carrickfergus, etc.—The Magazine Guard—Augmentation to the Regiment—Detachment to Limerick—The Salute Battery 211

1780

Floating Batteries in Dublin Harbour—Lieut.-Colonel Straton Promoted 216

1781

Detachment to Cork—Company of Invalids—Board of Ordnance—Detachment to Castlebar—Improvement in the Method of Firing 218

1782

Augmentation to the Regiment—Floating Batteries in Dublin Harbour—Detachments in Cork Harbour . 222

1783

A Return of the Regiment—Batteries in Cork Harbour, etc.—The Invalid Company—Detachment to Carlow—Reduction of the Regiment—Petition from the Discharged Men—Enlistments in East India Company's Service 225

1784

Burial Expenses—Recruiting for the Regiment. . . 237

1785

Memorial from the Captains relative to Sundry Expenses of their Companies 242

1786

Guard at the Magazine—The Invalid Company. . . 250

PAGE

1787
Funeral Procession of Late Lord Lieutenant—Irish Artillery Band—State Kettle Drums . . . 253

1788
Reported Removal of Regiment from Ireland—Increased Pay to General Straton 259

1789
Barrack Accommodation at Chapel-Izod—The Earl of Carhampton appointed Colonel *en Seconde* . . . 261

1790
The Regiment Reviewed—The Establishment . . . 262

1791
Changing the Artillery Quarters 263

1792
Grant of Bread Money—The Regiment Reviewed by Lieut.-General Pattison 264

1793
Augmentation to the Regiment—Three Companies Embark for the West Indies—The Companies on the Continent—A Flying Six Pounder Gun 269

1794
Three Companies Embark for the Continent—Recruiting to Continue—Drafts for Foreign Service—Augmentation of Two Companies—Beating Orders to Raise Men — Additional Lieutenant-Colonel and Major — Augmentation of Eight Companies— Monthly Return for August—Companies in West Indies—Recruits Drafted to Great Britain 274

1795
Drafts Embark for England—Bounty Money for Recruits—Three Companies from the Continent—The Regiment formed into Two Battalions—Camp at Laughlinstown—Detachments for West Indies—Monthly Return for August—Presentation of Swords to Two Officers . . 284

1796
Detachments to Kildare and Cork—Monthly Return for August—Brass Cannon from England—Review at Laughlinstown—The French Fleet off Bantry Bay . 294

PAGE

1797

Detachment to Hillsboro'—Commissions in Irish Artillery—Increased Pay to Soldiers—Draft for the West Indies—Appointments of Colonel-in-Chief and Colonel *en Seconde*—Court-Martial on an Officer—Forming a Corps of Drivers—Arrival of British Artillery in Ireland—Repository of Artillery 299

1798

British Artillery Reviewed—Detachment at Chatham—Monthly Returns for January and July—Subscriptions to Carry on the War—The Army Undisciplined—Companies on Foreign Service—Plan to take Dublin Castle—The Rebellion in Ireland—The Irish Artillery in the Field—Cannon Captured by the French—Artilleryman Executed for Disloyalty—Formation of the Artillery into Brigades 308

1799

Monthly Returns—Militia Gunners Discontinued—Detachments to West Indies 323

1800

Appointment of Brigade Major—Monthly Return—Invalid Company Augmented 327

1801

Union of Great Britain and Ireland—Union of Irish Artillery with British Artillery—Companies of British Artillery from England—Disposal of Supernumerary N. C. Officers and Gunners—Reduction of the Regiment—Ten Companies transferred to British Artillery and numbered the "Seventh Battalion"—The Invalid Company—The Band of the Regiment—Dress, etc., of the Regiment 332

APPENDICES.

A.—SUCCESSION OF COLONELS AND LIEUTENANT-COLONELS 343

B.—ROLL OF OFFICERS WHO ENTERED THE IRISH ARTILLERY 345

C.—ROLL OF OFFICERS TRANSFERRED TO BRITISH ARTILLERY 354

INDEX 361

INTRODUCTORY CHAPTER

BEFORE giving this book to the public, I am anxious to explain, in a few prefatory words, how I came to write it.

When a school-boy in Dublin, I heard a good deal about the Irish Artillery Regiment, which had its Head-Quarters, during the second half of the eighteenth century, in the village of Chapel-Izod, near Dublin City.

Later, I served with a Battery of the Royal Regiment, which was originally a company of the Irish Artillery. The incorporation of ten Irish companies with the older corps in 1801, when the Act for the Union between England and Ireland came into force, will be dealt with in its proper place further on.

Chapel-Izod is the scene of the well-known novel, *The House by the Churchyard*, by J. S. Lefanu. The book is full of exciting military episodes in the palmy days of the village, and it was to me at least fascinating reading.

A trial for murder is the chief sensation in the work. The novelist, when a little boy, professes to have seen a skull turned up in Chapel-Izod churchyard, and to have heard from the lips of an old pensioner of the Irish Artillery, the story of a Mattross who was shot through the head for striking his Captain.

Shortly after reading the novel I paid a visit to the old church and the burial-ground attached to it, and viewed the tombs commemorative of the Officers and Soldiers of the Irish Artillery.

I was greatly interested, too, in *A History of the Royal Regiment of Artillery*, by Captain F. Duncan, R.A., published in the Eighteen-eighties. The account of the Artillery on the Irish Establishment, given in Chapter XIV. of that admirable work, is, however, necessarily brief, owing to limits of space. It whetted my thirst for a fuller record of the services of the Corps, and I was in hopes that in course of time a writer, possessing manuscript material, letters, diaries, etc., concerning the Irish Artillery, and qualified to deal with its history, would place such a book before the public.

Then, one day in my rambles along the Quays of Dublin, I bought at a book-shop a Pamphlet,* published in 1768, containing particulars of the trial by Courts-Martial of a Mattross of the Irish Artillery,

---

* Under the title, "A Mirror for Courts-Martial," by C. Lucas, M.D., a citizen of Dublin in Parliament.

stationed at Chapel-Izod. The perusal of this Pamphlet turned my interest strongly in the direction of the Dublin Press, and suggested to me the idea of wading through the newspapers of the period in quest of military events and other subjects of interest.

After looking over half a century's pages of the *Dublin Gazette*, the *Dublin Journal*, and the *Freeman's Journal*, I was led to attempt the History of the Royal Irish Regiment of Artillery.

In due course I visited the Departments of Records, etc., and consulted books and papers bearing on Artillery matters, and I avail myself of this opportunity of thanking the authorities at the Record Offices in Dublin and London, the Chief Secretary's Library, Dublin Castle, and the Royal Artillery Record Office and Royal Artillery Institution at Woolwich, for their ready and useful help.

At the Public Record Office, Dublin, the books and documents in relation to the Irish Artillery, open to inspection, are few, and nothing there of an early date could be afforded me. I mention, as an instance, the Regimental Returns. The earliest available Monthly Statement showing the effective Strength and Distribution of the Corps, is for the month of February, 1788—some twenty-seven years after its formation.

The London Record Office contains the Pay Lists

and Muster Rolls of the Irish Artillery on service in England and abroad only. It may be mentioned in passing that all Companies serving out of Ireland were paid on the British Establishment, wherever employed, and came under the head of "Foreign Service" in the Regimental Returns.

The Journals of the Irish House of Commons, deposited at the Chief Secretary's Library, Dublin Castle, contain Returns furnished from time to time by the Muster Master-General, showing the numbers of officers and men in the several Regiments of Horse, Dragoons, and Foot, on the Military Establishment in Ireland, but I failed to trace therein any Return furnished by the Principal Officers of Ordnance showing the Establishment of the Royal Irish Regiment of Artillery earlier than that for the year 1767.

At the Royal Artillery Record Office, Woolwich, there is deposited a Record Book, containing manuscript notes connected with the History of the Royal Irish Artillery. Evidence that these notes were written subsequent to the incorporation of the Irish Companies, is apparent from the Remarks in the Record Book that "the Monthly Return Books* and other Documents, from May, 1789, to October, 1794, having been sent to Dublin Castle, and never having been

* I failed to trace these books.—AUTHOR.

forthcoming since, the means of following up the progressive augmentation is imperfect."

The valuable manuscript books connected with the Board of Ordnance in Ireland, deposited at the Royal Artillery Institution, Woolwich, deserve special mention, as to that Institution I am indebted for most of the information contained in this history. But, unfortunately, there is a gap in the Records after the year 1789.

I have derived no aid from private letters or diaries, and, owing to the absence of official documents already mentioned this book, has no claim to completeness. Some day, perhaps, the task may be taken up by abler hands with more perfect results and this work help to contribute to that end.

I need scarcely add that there has been no attempt at descriptive writing; and although this work has been compiled mainly for military readers, and as a contribution to military affairs in the days when Ireland had a Parliament of its own and Dublin was one of the gayest capitals in Europe, it is hoped that some of the particulars narrated may be of interest to the general reader.

The works which were most useful to the author were: Cleaveland's *History of the Royal Artillery;* Browne's *England's Artillerymen;* Duncan's *History of the Royal Artillery;* Askwith's *List of Officers of the Royal Artillery; Army Lists (The)*, Years 1756 to 1801; *Journals* of the Irish House of Commons.

In looking over the pages of this history, one cannot but be struck with the growth of the Irish Artillery Corps in its career of less than half a century. From a Subaltern's party of twenty-four Non-Commissioned Officers and Men of the British Artillery sent from Woolwich in the year 1755, the Regiment was increased to two Battalions, consisting of twenty Marching Companies and an Invalid Company. In 1800, the strength of the Regiment reached its maximum, 2,132 of all ranks.

Major J. J. Crooks.
Colonial Secretary of Sierra Leone.

1755

Augmentations to the Army in Ireland.

It was not until 1755, the year preceding the commencement of the Seven Years' War, and some forty years after the formation of a fixed Artillery Regiment for Great Britain, that it was proposed to create an Artillery Corps on the Irish Establishment.

After a recess extending over eighteen months, the Marquis of Hartington, Lord Lieutenant, opened the Session of the Parliament of Ireland, on Tuesday, the 7th October, 1755, and His Excellency's references to the Augmentations to be made in the Army Establishment of the Kingdom, is contained in the following sentences:

"The King's service having required several Regiments to be taken off this Establishment, His Majesty, always attentive to the safety of this Kingdom, has been pleased to Order a proper augmentation to be made in the remaining Regiments of Foot.

"By His Majesty's Commands, I have provided seven thousand stands of new arms, which have been delivered to the Troops, together with some additional Military Stores, such particularly as are provided for a Field Train of Artillery, Tents and other Necessaries for a Camp have likewise been provided, so that a considerable Body of Troops may on any emergency march and encamp on the shortest warning."

Military Stores from England.

For the information of the general reader it may be stated that the Accounts of the Irish and British Departments of the Ordnance, were kept perfectly distinct.

The following Treasury Letter, dated 26th April, 1755, shows that the Military Stores furnished from England to the Irish Board of Ordnance were issued on payment of the full value thereof.

Copy of Treasury Letter for Landing Stores.

GEORGE R.,

Whereas we have thought fit for Our Service that the Arms and Military Stores specified in the List hereunto annexed should be issued out of Our Stores of Ordnance within Our Tower of London for the Use of Our Kingdom of Ireland, Our Will and Pleasure is that Out of Our Stores of Ordnance under your Charge You forthwith cause the said Arms and Military Stores to be sent to Ireland on board a Vessel which you are to provide for that Purpose and to be delivered to Our Right Trusty and wellbeloved Councillor William Lord Cavendish of Hardwick commonly called Marquis of Hartington Our Lieutenant General and General Governor of Our said Kingdom of Ireland or to any Person or Persons whom He shall appoint to receive the Same on Payment of the full value thereof in Sterling Money of Great Britain together with all the Expenses attending the same.

And for so doing, etc.

Given at Our Court at St. James's, the 26th day of April, 1755, in the 28th year of Our Reign.

To Our Right Trusty and wellbeloved Councillor Sir John Ligonier, Knight of the Bath, Lieut.-General of Our Ordnance and to the Rest of the Principal Officers of the same.

By His Majesty's Command,

T. ROBINSON.

Artillery Detachment from Woolwich.

That effective action had already been taken in regard to a Train of Artillery, the following will indicate:—

May.—A detachment of a First Lieutenant and twenty-four Non-Commissioned Officers and private Men were this year sent from Woolwich to Ireland, at the request of the Lord Lieutenant towards the forming a battalion of Artillery for that Kingdom. (*Macbean's MSS. in Royal Artillery Institute.*)*

10th June.—The *Koningsburgh*, Edward Bryan, Commander, from London, with 7,000 stand of Arms, and a large quantity of Military Stores from the Tower, and a Detachment from the Royal Regiment of Artillery at Woolwich, arrived here under the convoy of the *Albany* man of War, Captain Longdon, Commander. The Arms, etc., are deposited in His Majesty's Stores at the Castle, and the men billetted on the public houses in the city.—(*Dublin Gazette.*)

The date of arrival in Ireland (June the 10th, 1755), of the Subaltern's party from Woolwich, which formed the nucleus of the Irish Artillery Corps, may, accordingly, be taken as the starting point for any *Records* of that Regiment.

---

* The Official Catalogue of the Artillery Museum in the Rotunda, Woolwich, 1906 (page 13), says, Captain-Lieutenant Forbes Macbean, R.A., was selected in 1755, to command the Detachment of the Royal Artillery sent in that year to Ireland to form the nucleus of the Royal Irish Artillery, but the Adjutancy falling vacant at that time, he purchased it, under the system then in force, and held it until his promotion to a Company in 1759.

The Old Artillery Traine in Ireland.

But before entering into details regarding the new Artillery Corps, the Old Traine may be conveniently referred to here, and for the purpose of this history we begin at the seventeenth century.

Charter of the Royal Hospital, 1684.

Towards the end of the seventeenth century we find mention of " The Gunners of Our Traine of Artillery in Ireland."

The Charter, dated 19th February, 1684, of the Royal Hospital, built on the site of the Priory of Kilmainham, near Dublin, for the Relief and Maintenance of antient and maimed Officers and Soldiers of the Army of Ireland, contains the following :

> And Lastly, Our Will and Pleasure is, and We do hereby further for Us, Our Heirs and Successors, Ordain and Declare, that the Master Gunner, and other Officers of the Ordnance in Our said Army, in Our said Kingdom of Ireland, shall and may from Time to Time, make such Use of the Gun-Yard, House, and Butt, lately erected on Part of the aforesaid Sixty-four Acres of Land, and the Ground staked out, lying East from the said Gun-Yard, containing from thence about Two Thousand Six Hundred Foot in Length, and about One Hundred Feet in Breadth, to Exercise the Gunners of Our Train of Artillery there, in such manner as by the chief Governor or Governors of Our said Kingdom of Ireland, shall be thought fit.

Reorganisation of the Garrisons and Magazines in Ireland.

24th August, 1684.—In Colonel Cleaveland's notes on the early " *History of the Royal Artillery* " * he

---

* Published by the Royal Artillery Institution, Woolwich.

quotes His Majesty's Warrant, dated 24th August, 1684, for the Reorganisation of the Garrisons and Magazines in Ireland, and also the following

Rules and Orders.

It being for your Majesty's profit as well as security to have such rules and orders established in Ireland, as may best preserve the ordnance, ammunition, and habiliaments of war, under a cheque, that your Majesty from time may know the state and condition of your magazines, and stores in that Kingdom :—

It is humbly proposed

1st. That some Officers of his Majesty's Ordnance in England may be commanded into Ireland to take a remain of all the Ordnance, ammunition, and other habiliaments of war that are in any town, garrison, castle, or fort in that Kingdom.

2nd. That the Master of the Ordnance in Ireland may be directed to appoint persons to attend taking of the remain, that they as his deputies seeing the account taken, the Master of the Ordnance may be charged therewith.

3rd. The remain being so taken, a copy to be delivered to the Duke of Ormond, your Majesty's Lieutenant, and another copy brought over and lodged in your Majesty's Office of the Ordnance in the Tower, to remain for a cheque to future account.

4th. That the Master of the Ordnance in Ireland do annually transmit a general remain into England to shew all the expense, decays or wants of the year preceding, to the end your Majesty may be truly informed of the condition of the magazines.

5th. That the most proper places for the making of magazines being resolved upon, they be reduced to as few as may be with safety for the lessening of the charge, and other considerable reasons.

6th. That all ordnance and arms, where there is no established garrison, be removed to the magazines.

Whereas at present your Majesty's stores of war are dispersed unproportionally into thirty-four garrisons, as may appear by the last remain, many of which are not only an unnecessary charge, but unsafe, for your Majesty's magazine to be continued longer in, it is humbly proposed that those garrisons may be reduced to as few as may be with conveniency and safety, and that such as shall be adjudged fit to be continued be well garrisoned and put in a better condition for your Majesty's service, and the defence of your Majesty's Kingdom of Ireland, either against foreign invasions or other hostile attempts whatsoever, and that each province may be usefully provided for, it is humbly offered That in

*Leinster,**

Dublin may be continued the chief magazine . . .

*Connaught **

Athlone, Galloway, ...

*Munster **

Duncannon, Limerick, Charles Fort, Kinsale, Castle Park . . . .

*Ulster **

Charlemont, Londonderry, Culmore Castle, Carrickfergus . . . .

* The full particulars are too long for reproduction here.

These are the places most considerable to be garrisoned according to the best information that I have hitherto received; but it is humbly desired that His Grace the Lord Duke of Ormond, Lieutenant, and your Majesty's Council may judge if any other forts are absolutely necessary.

(Signed)   DARTMOUTH.

ESTABLISHMENT OF THE OFFICE OF ORDNANCE AND TRAIN OF ARTILLERY.*

22nd March, 1687.—His Majesty's Warrant, directing that instead of the old establishment of the Office of Ordnance and Train of Artillery in Ireland, the following should take place from this date:—

			£	s.	d.
Master of the Ordnance			500	0	0
Lieutenant of the Ordnance			300	0	0
Surveyor or Comptroller			200	0	0
Clerk of the Ordnance and Deliveries			100	0	0
Storekeeper			100	0	0
Chief Engineer			200	0	0
Master Gunner			50	0	0
His Mate			25	0	0
Armourer			25	0	0
30 other Gunners at 9d. a day each			410	12	6
6 Clerks of Stores at £28 per annum each			168	0	0
1 more at £26 5s. 0d.			26	5	0
1 Gunner at Dungannon			16	16	0
1 Do.	Cork		16	16	0
1 Do.	Kinsale		16	16	0
1 Do.	Charles Fort		16	16	0
1 Do.	Mate there		14	0	0
1 Do.	Limerick		16	16	0
1 Do.	Galloway		16	16	0
1 Do.	Athlone		16	16	0
1 Do.	Londonderry		16	16	0

* From Cleaveland's History.

1	Gunner at	Carrickfergus	.	.	.	£16 16 0
1	Do.	Mate Culmore	.	.	.	14 0 0
1	Do.	Mate Passage	.	.	.	14 0 0
1	Do.	Mate Waterford	.	.	.	14 0 0

INSTRUCTIONS TO MARCH A FIELD TRAINE.

23rd March, 1718-9.—Board of Ordnance.

As a sample of the Instructions to the Officer appointed to Command the Field Traine on their march in Ireland, the following may be taken:—

By the Master General of the Ordnance.

Their Excellencies the Lords Justices of Ireland having by their Order of the 21st of this Instant March, thought fit to direct that a Field Traine Consisting of twelve Guns with all necessarys thereunto belonging (for his Majesties Service) be ordered to march from this Towne to Athlone there to remain till further Order.

1*stly*. You are therefore hereby required to take care that the Ammunition and other Stores and Habiliments of War mentioned in a paper hereunto annexed, be loaded in the several Bumcarts, Waggons, and Tumbrills etc. (ordered to attend the said Guns) in the most convenient manner and to take ye said Traine of Artillery with all things thereunto belonging under your care.

2*ndly*. You are to take care that the Officers, Artificers, Gunners, Mattrosses, horses and Drivers attending ye said Traine, and under your Command, do observe a strict Discipline and Order, both on their march and in Camp or Quarters.

3rdly. You are to take care that no embezzlement of any kind whatsoever be made of his Majesties Ammunition or other Stores of War, and that none be delivered out but what is by Order of the Commander in Chief of the Army in the Field, and that due receipts be taken on the back of such Orders for the Stores you shall so deliver.

4thly. You are not to suffer any money to be laid out but where the necessity of the Service requires, and to take care that upon any Expenditure of any of his Majesties Costs for the Contingencies of the said traine, and that the several persons Employed do give receipts for whatever sums of money you shall order them, at the foot of their bills expressing the work so done by them for which the money is paid, of which you are to take care that exact Entry's be kept and a just and true Account thereof remitted to the Office when and as often as you are therewith required by my Self or the Principal Officers of the Ordnance.

Lastly. You are to take care as you proceed in your Journey from place to place to returne an Account to this Office where you take up from time to time, and what other Occurrences shall happen in your March, that such further Instructions may be sent you as is necessary for his Majesties Service.

Ordnance Office, Dublin, the 23rd day of March, **1718-9.**

MOUNTJOY.

To James Wybault, Esqre.,
    Major to the Traine.

Report of the Board of Ordnance about the Inferior Officers of the Traine.

2nd November, 1734.

To their Excellencies the Lords Justices General and General Governors of Ireland.

May it please Your Excellencies,

In obedience to Your Excellencies Commands signified to us by Mr. Secretary Tickell's letter of the 25th day of October last, Requiring us forthwith to lay before Your Excellencies, a Return of the Names of all the Inferior Officers and Artificers belonging to His Majesties Ordnance and Traine in this Kingdom, Distinguishing the time when each of them was Appointed and by what Authority, and which of them have been Approved by the Chief Governor or Governors of Ireland for the time being.

We have in pursuance to Your Excellencies Commands, hereunto Annexed a List of the Inferior Officers and Artificers belonging to the Traine, with the date of their Several Warrants, which said Inferior Officers and Artificers are, and have always been appointed by Warrant under the hand and seal of the Master of the Ordnance, but how many of them have been approved by the Government we cannot take it upon us to say, which is humbly submitted to Your Excellencies consideration.

Signed by four Principal Officers of the Ordnance.

Office of Ordnance,*

Dublin Castle, the 2nd November, 1734.

---

* The Ordnance Office, in the Lower Courtyard of Dublin Castle, a brick building ornamented by the Irish Ordnance Arms carved on the entrance archway, is now the official residence of the Master of the Horse.

A List of the Inferior Officers, Artificers, Gunners and Mattrosses, belonging to his Majesties Traine of Artillery in Ireland.

EMPLOYMENTS	PERSONS NAMES	DATE OF WARRANT

Garrison of Dublin.

EMPLOYMENTS	PERSONS NAMES	DATE OF WARRANT
Storekeeper	Brent Smyth	2 April, 1706
Paymaster	George Boyd	1 July, 1734
Gent of ye Ordnance	Robert Leeson	10 April, 1716
Ditto	John Fowles	15 Nov., 1727
Firemaster	William Gilbert	4 Aug., 1725
Ditto	Charles Terrot	1 July, 1728
Bombardier	George Alston	1 Dec., 1701
Ditto	John Deane	2 Aug., 1726
Armorer	James Willson	31 Dec., 1715
Assistant Armourer	Joshua Baker	1 Jan., 1717
Ditto	John Skamon	26 June, 1727
Ditto	Michael Ramsford	11 July, 1727
Ditto	William Truelock	17 Mar., 1728-29
Waggon and Carriage Maker	Joseph Mirfield	31 Dec., 1715
Smith	Robert Greenway	24 Aug., 1717
Harness Maker	Peter Vanderleur	24 Aug., 1717
Wheelright	Richard Richardson	17 April, 1728
Master Gunner	Jacob Fenner	17 March, 1715
Master Gunner's Mate	Edward Fenner	1 Sep., 1733
Gunner	William Morris	24 Aug., 1717
Ditto	Samuel Morgan	7 May, 1720
Ditto	Robert Willson	20 May, 1724
Ditto	Thomas Potts	2 Aug., 1726
Ditto	Robert Daman	26 June, 1727
Ditto	John Pearson	11 April, 1928
Ditto	John Hartwell	11 April, 1728
Ditto	Hugh McFaran	11 April, 1728
Ditto	William Beckson	24 Mar., 1728-29
Ditto	Francis Allesien	1 April, 1729
Ditto	William Elrington	24 May, 1729
Ditto	John Logan	25 Feb., 1731
Mattross	James Newell	16 Feb., 1715-16
Ditto	Henry Picknoll	2 Aug., 1726
Ditto	Joseph Wright	26 Aug., 1726
Ditto	Robert Kent	26 Aug., 1726
Ditto	John Mauze	11 April, 1728
Ditto	John Hand	11 Sep., 1728
Ditto	Samuel Kilburne	11 Sep., 1728
Ditto	Henry Armstrong	24 May, 1729
Ditto	Richard Monnely	15 Oct., 1729
Ditto	Charles Daman	26 Feb., 1732-33

List of Officers, etc.—*continued.*

EMPLOYMENTS	PERSONS NAMES	DATE OF WARRANT

Garrison of Dublin—continued.

Mattross	Richard Homan	1 Aug., 1733
Ditto	Samuel Bullock	23 May, 1734
Comptroller's Clerk	William Johnson	1 April, 1734

Garrison of Athlone.

Gunner	John Roberts	9 Aug., 1712
Mattross	John Wheland	10 Jan., 1728-29

Garrison of Charlemont.

Gunner	John Stewart	7 July, 1719
Mattross	Gust McGusty	14 Feb., 1717-18

Garrison of Londonderry.

Storekeeper	Michael Hewettson	31 Dec., 1715
Gunner	Stephen Husbands	9 Jan., 1709-10
Ditto	James Husbands	27 April, 1733
Mattross	John Wright	Sometime in 1695
Ditto	William Browne	27 April, 1733

Garrison of Gallway.

Storekeeper	Robert Cooke	1 April, 1734
Gunner	George Thomas	11 April, 1728
Ditto	Simon Trulock	29 Jan., 1733-34
Ditto	Richard Hudson	25 Nov., 1733
Mattross	Austin Swanwick	25 Nov., 1733
Ditto	Richard Irwyn	29 Jan., 1733-34

Garrison of Limerick.

Storekeeper	Cornelius Parker	18 June, 1722
Gunner	George Peaseley	17 May, 1721
Ditto	Isaac Patten	4 March, 1725-26
Ditto	Joseph Edgar	11 Sep., 1728
Ditto	John Jones	1 Sep., 1733
Mattross	John Collins	10 Jan., 1724-25
Ditto	Edward Wood	19 Dec., 1725

Garrison of Duncannon.

Storekeeper	William Darby	10 Dec., 1724
Master Gunner	Adam Jenkins	13 Oct., 1716

List of Officers, etc.—continued.

EMPLOYMENTS	PERSONS NAMES	DATE OF WARRANT
Garrison of Duncannon—continued.		
Gunner	Michael Chapman	31 Dec., 1715
Ditto	David Bone	24 Aug., 1717
Mattross	John Stephens	2 June, 1708
Ditto	Thomas Chapman	25 Feb., 1730-31
Garrison of Waterford.		
Storekeeper	William Darby	10 Dec., 1724
Garrison of Carrickfergus.		
Storekeeper	Henry Gill	5 Oct., 1733
Gunner	John Davis	1 March, 1711-12
Mattross	John Kerneghan	14 April, 1729
Garrison of Kinsale.		
Storekeeper	John Houghton	14 Dec., 1717
Master Gunner	Edward Brinn	16 Mar., 1715-16
Gunner	John Wiltshire	23 July, 1709
Ditto	Robert Hart	1 Sep., 1712
Ditto	James Crawford	1 Jan., 1719-20
Ditto	Henry Kary	27 April, 1725
Ditto	William McDaniell	26 May, 1733
Ditto	Edward Stowards	26 Oct., 1733
Ditto	Edward Place	10 Dec., 1733
Ditto	Marks Jane	1 April, 1734
Mattross	Joseph Deane	7 Feb., 1730-31
Ditto	John Rowe	26 Oct., 1733
Ditto	John Stowards	10 Dec., 1733
Ditto	John Walton	1 April, 1734

In the foregoing Report of the Board it will be noticed that the Inferior Officers and Artificers belonging to the Ordnance and Traine in Ireland held their Appointments under a Warrant signed by the Master of the Ordnance.

In the Memorial to the Lord Lieutenant, dated 29th December, 1770 (*vide* events of that year further on), it is stated " that the Men of the Old Establishment were continued for Life in consideration of their having purchased their Employments."

We cannot trace any scale of prices for Employment in the Artillery Train, but if we may judge by the following Extract from a Letter to be found among the Ordnance Records for the year 1755 the fee payable for a Mattross' Warrant was a moderate one.

Extract from Letter.

". . . would it be worth your while to accept a Mattrosses place in the Ordnance Department, I mean one on the Irish Establishment.

"The Duty is but Trifling and you may attend Office till something better Offers.

"The Nett Money of the Pay is about Ten Pounds Yearly; you must attend all Firing Days and now and then at the Stores, and one week in twelve at the Office, or pay a Man for Doeing Duty there.

"In a Little Time a Gunner's place may be vacant which would be very comfortable as to Duty and the Salary about £13 a year.

"If this any way suits your conveniency I hope to be able to get it done."

REPORT OF THE BOARD OF ORDNANCE ABOUT GUNS AND AMMUNITION.

28th February, 1754.—The *matèriel* provided for a new Field Train of Artillery in Ireland, is detailed in the following Report :—

The Report of the Master
and Principal Officers of the Ordnance.

Humbly Representeth,

That by His Excellency the Earl of Harrington's Order bearing date the 27th day of March 1750, we were empowered to carry into Execution a Scheme for providing a new Field Train of Artillery for the Service of this Kingdom and were also directed to give an Account from time to time of the progress made in this work.

That by a Memorial bearing date the 17th day of March 1752, we informed Your Grace how far we had proceeded thereunto to which Memorial we Humbly refer.

We further beg Leave to acquaint Your Grace that since that time there have been Nine 6-Pounders cast proved and Lodged in his Majesty's Stores, which with Twelve before provided make up Twenty-one, that being the Number of Guns ordered to be made and are now completed for their Carriages.

That there are also Sixty Mortars now mounted, Forty of $4\frac{1}{2}$ Inches and Twenty of 6 Inches, besides Four of 8 Inches ready for proving that there remains but Two Mortars of 10 Inches to make up the full Number intended.

That there is likewise lodged in His Majesty's Stores One Thousand Shot for 6-Pounders, Six Hundred Charges of Grape Shot, Two Hundred Shells for 6 Inch Mortars, One Thousand Shells for $4\frac{1}{2}$ Inch Mortars, and the Founder is now at work to compleat the Number Contracted for.

Which is humbly submitted to Your Grace's Consideration.

Ordnance Office

the 28th day of February, 1754.

MOLESWORTH   J. BROWNRIGG
EDW: HILL   J. DAVYS
JOHN CORNEILLE
THOMAS GOOLD.

THE ESTABLISHMENT OF THE TRAIN IN THE YEAR 1755.

The Establishment and the Distribution of the Train this year, was the same as in the year 1734. (See Report of the Board for 1734, already mentioned.)

The following are the rates of pay of the Artillery element.

	Per Diem s. d.	Per Annum £ s. d.
1 Major of the Train of Artillery, Henry Brownrigg, Esqre.	—	200 0 0
2 Firemasters . . . each	4 0	146 0 0
1 Master Gunner to attend the Train	—	50 0 0
1 Master Gunner's Mate ditto	—	25 0 0
2 Bombardiers . . . each	2 0	73 0 0
1 Master Gunner at Kinsale	2 0	36 10 0
1 Master Gunner at Duncannon Fort	2 0	36 10 0
34 Gunners to attend the Train each	1 0	620 10 0
27 Mattrosses ditto each	0 9	369 11 3

TRAIN OF ARTILLERY REDUCED.

On the formation (1st April, 1756) of the "Artillery Company in Ireland," Major Brownrigg of the Train of Artillery, and 34 Gunners and 27 Mattrosses, were struck off the Ordnance Establishment, and incorporated with the new Company. (See Events for 1756-7 further on.)

The Firemasters, Master Gunners, and Bombardiers with the Train, were placed upon Half Pay, and struck off the Irish Establishment at the same time, (*vide* Appendix, 24th October, 1757, to Journals of the Irish House of Commons, and Annual Army List), for the following :—

ON THE IRISH HALF PAY.

Train of Artillery reduced, 1755.

	s.	d.	
Matthew Young—late Firemaster	2	0	per Day
George Gonne— Ditto	2	0	,,
James Wall—late Master Gunner in Dublin	1	4¼	,,
Samuel Fenner—late Mate to the said James Wall	0	8½	,,
John Chambers—late Bombardier	1	0	,,
Matthew Peters— Ditto	1	0	,,
Edward Heard—late Master Gunner at Charles Fort	1	0	,,
Robert Patterson—late Master Gunner at Duncannon Fort	1	0	,,

WARRANT OF APPOINTMENT TO BOMBARDIERS.

It is of interest to note that Bombardiers,* the name given to the lowest rank of Non Commissioned Officers in the Artillery, are included in the foregoing Half Pay List.

The wording of the Warrant signed by the Master General of the Ordnance in Ireland, dated the first day

---

"* Formerly in the French Army, the duty of the Bombardier was to serve Mortars and Howitzers only, which were bombarding arms, and hence has been derived the word Bombardier "—(*Military Dictionary*).

of December, 1745, appointing John Chambers Gent.*
to be one of the Bombardiers, is as follows :—

To John Chambers, Bombardeer.

By Virtue of a Power and Authority by the King's Most
Excellent Majestie Given, I do (upon the Good Testimony and
Assurance which I have received of the Abillitie of you the
said John Chambers Gent), Nominate, Constitute and Appoint
you to be one of the Bombardeers belonging to his Majesties
Traine of Artillery in Ireland, in the Room and place of John
Chaignean Resigned. You are therefore carefully and diligently to attend the duty of that employment by doing and
performing all and all manner of things thereunto belonging,
and to observe and obey all such orders and directions as shall
from time to time be given or sent you, either by my Self,
the Lieutenant and the rest of the Principal Officers of the
Ordnance or any other your Superior Officers according to
the Rules and Discipline of War.

FITTING OUT A FIELD TRAIN.

28th June.—The Lord Lieutenant's Warrant to the Master General of the Ordnance, directing him to furnish an Estimate of the expense of fitting out a Field Train of Artillery, consisting of six light 6-pounders, two Royal, and two Cohorn mortars complete with their proper Furniture and all necessaries relative thereto, allowing one hundred Rounds for each Gun, and fifty Rounds for each Royal and Cohorn, together with a proportion of Intrenching Tools, wheelbarrows, etc., for Two hundred Men.

Also an Establishment of Officers and Men to attend the said Train, together with an Estimate of the daily expense of such Establishment and of the Quantity of Forage, Bread, Firing, and Straw that will be

---

* *Re* designation " Gent," see purchase of Employments by Old Establishment, in previous pages.

wanting for the same, for the space of Forty-two days.

Also an Estimate of the expense of Transporting to and from the Camp, supposed at about the distance of Fifty or Sixty Miles from Dublin, the said Train (including Horses and Drivers), together with the Camp Equipage and Necessaries mentioned on the other side belonging to Twenty-one Troops or Four-hundred and ninety-two Cavalry, and Eight Regiments of Foot.

Troops Encamped at Thurles.

17th July.—Board of Ordnance.

Warrant sending a List* of the Camp Equipage and Necessaries provided and approved of for the number of Troops proposed to be encamped at Thurles, and directing the Board of Ordnance to cause the Articles mentioned in the said List to be packed up and sent to Thurles by the 25th July, and to be lodged in the Barracks there.

Artillery Drills in Phœnix Park.

18th August.—Two Pieces of Ordnance were carried to His Majesty's Park, the Phœnix, where the Gunners, Mattrosses, and Bombardiers lately arrived from England, every day go through their Exercises, and a Guard is regularly kept.—(*Dublin Gazette.*)

---

* The List is too long for reproduction here.

Brass Cannon Proved.

22nd August.—Board of Ordnance.

The Board directed to cause the Twenty Brass Guns, Six Pounders, lately cast in this Kingdom by John Pounder, and now in His Majesty's Stores, to be proved again according to the Rules observed on the like Occasion at Woolwich.

30th August.—This week twenty Pieces of Brass Cannon cast in this Kingdom, were tried in His Majesty's Park, the Phœnix, which stood the Proof Fire very well.—(*Dublin Gazette*).

12th December.—A new light Brass Six Pounder was fired three hundred times in less than three hours with a serviceable charge of powder and ball, and stood the fire perfectly well, which was oftener than any Cannon of the same Dimension was ever fired in the same Time.—(*Dublin Gazette.*)

Accidents in Firing.

23rd September.—At the Firing the Guns in the Phœnix Park, on the joyful news of His Majesty's safe arrival in England, a Serjeant of Lieutenant General Handyside's Regiment of Foot who was formerly a Gunner abroad, had his arm torn off with the rammer, the Gun going off before he could ram down the charge, and one of the Mattrosses had his Eye beat out with a splinter of the said rammer. They were both taken care of at the Infirmary in James's Street, but it's feared the Serjeant cannot recover.—(*Dublin Gazette.*)

Detachment Inspected by Lord Lieutenant.

13*th October.*—His Excellency the Lord Lieutenant, attended by a great number of General and Field Officers, reviewed (the term used at that period for "inspection"), in His Majesty's Park, the Phœnix, the Detachment from the Royal Regiment of Artillery, lately arrived here from England, when they went through their Firings and Evolutions, entirely to the satisfaction of His Excellency and the Officers present. (*Dublin Gazette.*)

1756

Enlistment Regulations.

27th February.—Down to 1755, no Irishman was allowed to be enlisted for the Army serving in Ireland, as may be gathered from the following extract from the *Dublin Journal* of that year:—

> Many of the English news-writers are most invidious, false and ignorant in their accounts of the Irish Regiments in the late Battle in America, as they are in many facts relating to this most loyal and brave nation; it being a truth too well known, that although 12,000 Troops are maintained at the charge of Ireland, yet the unhappy natives of this Kingdom, are deprived of the liberty of serving their King and Country, there being a Military Law made without any Act of Parliament that no Irishman whatever can be admitted into the Foot Service or other Soldiery of Ireland as a common man, the Army of Ireland being always recruited and filled up by men from England or Scotland.

What led the Government to act thus?

The answer is that the Test Act of 1673, directed against Catholics was then in force. It was also part of the Government policy to promote every measure that would tend to strengthen the Protestant religion in Ireland, and one of the means employed to ensure this end, was the recruiting His Majesty's Army on the Irish Establishment from English Protestants.

But in order to raise men for the Battalions of Foot in Ireland, ordered to be augmented, a partial relaxation of the stringent Enlistment conditions that had previously been required was deemed expedient, and "Able-Bodied Protestants" of the Province of Ulster were permitted to "take the shilling," as appears from the following —

27th February.—Board of Ordnance.

Warrant signifying His Majesty's pleasure that the several Battalions of Foot in this Kingdom be Augmented in Manner following . . . which Augmentations are to be made by Able Bodied Protestants to be raised in the several Counties of the Province of Ulster . . . and directing the Board of Ordnance to cause to be delivered to the said Additional Men, the best and most serviceable Regimental Arms now remaining in His Majesty's Stores.

AN ARTILLERY COMPANY TO BE FORMED.

1st April.—His Majesty's Warrant* directing certain Allowances for an Artillery Company to be formed in Ireland.

13th October.—His Majesty's Warrant adverting to the Warrant of the 1st April, 1756, directing certain Allowances for an Artillery Company to be formed in Ireland.

GEORGE R.

Right Trusty and Right entirely beloved Cousin and Councellor We greet you well. Whereas by Our War-

---

* Not reproduced here. See later Warrant, dated 13th October, 1756, augmenting the Numbers in that Company, and making the Pay the same as that of Officers and others of the like rank in the British Artillery.

rant bearing date the 1st day of April, 1756, We were pleased to Order and direct certain Allowances to be placed upon the Establishment of Our Kingdom of Ireland for an Artillery Company to be formed there amounting in the whole to the sum of Two thousand Seven hundred thirty seven pounds ten shillings per Annum which said Allowances were to commence and be accounted payable from the 31st day of March last 1756, And Whereas We have thought fit to augment the Numbers in that Company and to add so much to their pay so as to make it of more utility and in General nominally the same with that of Officers and others of the like Rank in Our Regiment of Artillery in England in Order to encourage a Service so Essentially necessary, Our Will and pleasure therefore is and We do hereby Direct and Command that the said several Officers of the said Artillery Company with their said Allowances amounting to the sum of Two thousand Seven hundred thirty seven pounds ten shillings per annum be struck off the said Establishment from the said 31st day of March, 1756, And that in lieu thereof an Artillery Company to consist of the Officers and others with the Allowances following be formed in Ireland and placed upon the said Establishment from the said 31st day of March, 1756, that is to say :—

	Per Diem		Per Annum		
	s.	d.	£	s.	d.
One Major	15	0	273	15	0
One Captain	10	0	182	10	0
One First Lieutenant	5	0	91	5	0
One Second Lieutenant	4	0	73	0	0
Three Lieut. Fireworkers, each at	3	8	200	15	0
Five Sergeants, each at	2	2	197	14	2
Ten Bombardiers, each at	1	8	304	3	4

	Per Diem		Per Annum		
	s.	d.	£	s.	d.
Five Corporals, each at	1	10	167	5	10
Thirty-four Gunners, each at	1	4	827	6	8
One hundred and two Mattroses, each at	1	0	1,861	10	0
Two Drummers, each at	1	0	36	10	0
			£4,215	15	0

Amounting in the whole to the sum of Four thousand Two hundred fifteen pounds fifteen shillings per Annum, And we do hereby Authorise and require you to give the necessary Orders and Directions not only for discontinuing the said former Allowances amounting to Two thousand Seven hundred thirty seven pounds ten shillings but also for inserting the said new Allowances of Four thousand Two hundred fifteen pounds fifteen shillings per Annum clear of all the usual deductions for Poundage, Hospital, and Pells from the said 31st day of March, 1756, on the said Military Establishment of Our Kingdom of Ireland accordingly to be paid and payable in like manner as other Forces in that Our Kingdom are paid. And for so doing this shall be as well to you as to all other Our Officers and Ministers who shall or may be concerned in making the said payment in pursuance hereof or allowing the same upon Account a sufficient Warrant. And so We bid you very hearty farewell.

Given at Our Court at Kensington the 13th day of October, 1756, in the 30th Year of Our Reign.

By His Majesty's Command

HOLLES NEWCASTLE.
R. NUGENT.
P. WYNDHAM O'BRIEN.

To Our Right Trusty and Right entirely beloved Cousin and Councellor William Duke of Devonshire Our Lieutenant General and General Governor of Our Kingdom of Ireland and to Our Lieutenants Deputy or other Chief Governor or Governors of that Our Kingdom for the time being.

List of Officers.

List of the Officers of the Artillery Company in Ireland, their Commissions being dated the 1st of April, 1756.

    Major—Henry Brownrigg.
    Captain—John Straton.
    First Lieutenant—George Skipton.
    Second Lieutenant—William Gray.
    Lieutenant Fireworkers—William Brady.
      Do.   John Ratcliffe.
      Do.   Robert Graham.

According to their Commissions, the Officers were commanded " to exercise the Officers, Bombardiers, Gunners, and Mattrosses, belonging to the said Regiment in the use of Mortars and the Art of Gunnery, and to keep them in good Order and Discipline."

The Officers were appointed from the following sources.

(1.) *Major in Command*,
  from Major for the Train of Artillery in Ireland.

(2.) *Captain,*
  from the Captain Lieutenant of British Artillery, who organised the Company.

(3.) *First Lieutenant,*
  from Lieutenant Fireworker, British Artillery.

(4.) *Second Lieutenant,*
  from Lieutenant Fireworker, British Artillery.

(5, 6, & 7.) *Lieutenant Fireworkers.*

  The Fireworkers were generally chosen from Cadet Gunners or Cadet Mattrosses, but we could not ascertain the previous rank (if any) of these Officers, as the records of Woolwich Academy do not extend to the years 1755-56.

INSPECTION OF THE COMPANY.

16th July.—The Right Hon. the Earl of Rothes reviewed the Artillery Company of this Kingdom in the Lower Castle-yard, who made a very grand and pleasing appearance.—(*Dublin Gazette.*)

ARTILLERY TO KILKENNY CAMP.

3rd August.—About seven o'clock in the morning, twelve Pieces of Brass Ordnance with the like number of Bomb-carts, with Ammunition and other Military

stores, escorted by a party of the Royal Regiment of
Artillery and an Officer's Guard of Soldiers, set out
from the Arsenal in the Castle for the Camp forming
near Kilkenny.—(*Dublin Gazette.*)

ARTILLERY DRILLS IN THE PHŒNIX PARK.

31st August.—The new-raised Company of Artillery, with the Detachment of the Royal Regiment from
Woolwich, have for some time past been daily exercised in the Park, and Saturday several of them were
billetted in different parts of the City and Suburbs.
(*Dublin Journal.*)

INSPECTION OF THE ARTILLERY COMPANY.

12th October.—Yesterday the Battalions together
with the Train of Artillery were reviewed in His
Majesty's Park, Phœnix, by the Right Hon. the
Earl of Rothes.—(*Dublin Journal.*)

BATTALION GUNS TO REGIMENTS OF FOOT.

25th October.—Board of Ordnance.
Warrant directing that the Battalion Guns which
were assigned to the respective Regiments of Foot
during the late Encampment do remain with the said
Regiments, and be kept at their respective Head
Quarters, and that the Ammunition, etc. . . .
thereunto belonging be likewise kept with the said
Guns. . . .

Establishment.

The strength of the Company on 31st December was as follows :

Major	1
Captain	1
First Lieutenant	1
Second Lieutenant	1
Firemasters	3
Serjeants	2
Corporals	3
Bombardiers	4
Gunners	33
Mattrosses	67
Drummers	2
Total of all ranks	118

Only 5 Men were Enlisted for the Company during the year. For further Details see Memorial of the Principal Officers of the Ordnance dated 19th September, 1757, in events of year 1757.

1757

Brass Mortars Proved.

2nd May.—Board of Ordnance.

Warrant directing the Board to cause 32 of the 64 Brass Mortars which were cast in Ireland to be again proved, taking to assistance such Officers of the Artillery Company as the Major and Captain thereof shall think necessary.

16th May.—Report that the said Mortars were proved in the presence of the Board and the Officers of Artillery, and stood their proof extremely well.

Ammunition for Battalion Guns.

16th May.—Board of Ordnance.

Warrant directing the issue out of His Majesty's Stores of War in Dublin, the Quantity of Ammunition, Tubes, and Portfires necessary for the Two Battalion Guns of each Regiment to practise twice before the next Review, and to perform their Firings at the Review, as specified in the annexed Copy of a Calculation thereof made by the Captain of the Artillery Company.

. . . . . .

The Quantity of Ammunition necessary for Two Battalion Guns to practice twice before the Review, and to perform their Firings at the Review.

	Cartridges containing 8 ounces each	Tubes
For 64 Rounds, 1st Practice ..	128	140
For 64 Rounds, repeat	128	140
Total for Practice ..	256	280

	Cartridges containing 12 ounces each	Tubes
For 64 Rounds at the Review ..	128	140
Portfires for the Two Practices and the Review		72

The above Calculation for One Battalion only.

JOHN STRATON,
Captain of Artillery.

ARTILLERY QUARTERED IN BARRACKS.

31st May.—This day the Artillery Company who have been billetted on the Publicans of the City for some time past, marched into the Barracks * there to take up their quarters for the future.—(*Dublin Gazette.*)

REGULATIONS TO BE OBSERVED IN THE ARTILLERY COMPANY.

29th July.—*Board of Ordnance.*

Warrant sending Three Papers, viz.:—

No. 1. Containing an Account of the Daily and

---

* The Royal Barracks, the largest and oldest in Dublin, situated on an eminence overlooking the River Liffey, and a little east of the entrance to the Phœnix Park, comprised only the Royal Square in 1757. Since that year the Palatine, Cavalry, and Clock Squares have been added.

Annual Full Pay, Subsistence and Arrears, together with the Annual Stoppages for Agency and Clothing of the Royal Regiment of Artillery.

No. 2. Containing an Account of Clothing for one of the Companies of the said Regiment when first raised, also an Account of Clothing after the first year.

And *No.* 3. Containing an Account of the Arms of the said Regiment.

And signifying His Majesty's Royal Pleasure that the same Regulations be observed with respect to the Pay, Subsistence, Arrears, Stoppages, Clothing and Arms of His Company of Artillery in this Kingdom, as are mentioned in the said Papers.

.   .   .   .   .   .

Given at His Majesty's Castle of Dublin,
the 29th day of July, 1757.

By their Excellencies Command

HENRY MEREDYTH.

To the Board of Ordnance.

[TABLE.

ROYAL REGIMENT OF ARTILLERY (REGULATION No. 1).

ONE COMPANY CONSISTING OF	Full Pay per Diem each	Subsistence per Diem each	Arrears per Diem each	Full Pay per Annum each	Subsistence per Annum each	Arrears per Annum each	Stoppages for Agency per Annum each	Stoppages for Clothing per Annum each
	s. d.	s. d.	s. d.	£ s. d.	£ s. d.	£ s. d.	£ s. d.	£ s. d.
1 Major	15 0	11 3	3 9	273 15 0	205 6 3	68 8 9	The Officers pay three pence in the Pound out of their full Pay	
1 Captain	10 0	7 6	2 6	182 10 0	136 17 6	45 12 6		
1 Captain Lieutenant	6 0	4 6	1 6	109 10 0	82 2 6	27 7 6		
1 First Lieutenant	5 0	3 9	1 3	91 5 0	68 8 9	22 16 3		
1 Second Lieutenant	4 0	3 0	1 0	73 0 0	54 15 0	18 5 0		
3 Lieutenant Fireworkers	3 8	2 9	0 11	66 18 4	50 3 9	64 14 7		
3 Serjeants	2 0	1 7¾	—	36 10 0	30 0 8¾	—	0 9 1½	6 0 1¾
3 Corporals	1 10	1 6½	—	33 9 2	28 2 8½	—	0 8 4½	4 18 1
8 Bombardiers	1 8	1 4½	—	30 8 4	25 1 10½	—	0 7 7½	4 18 10½
20 Gunners	1 4	1 1¼	—	24 6 8	20 3 0¼	—	0 6 1	3 17 6¾
64 Mattrosses	1 0	0 9½	—	18 5 0	14 8 11½	—	0 4 6¾	3 11 5¾
2 Drummers	1 0	0 9½	—	18 5 0	14 8 11½	—	0 4 6¾	3 11 5¾
108 TOTAL								

ROYAL REGIMENT OF ARTILLERY

Clothing one of the Companies of the Royal Regiment of Artillery when first raised.

3 Serjeants, each
- Coat and Breeches
- Waistcoat
- Shirt and Neckcloth
- Pair of Shoes
- Pair of Stockings
- Cloth for Spatterdashes

3 Corporals
8 Bombardiers
———
11 each
- Coat and Breeches
- Waistcoat
- Shirt and Neckcloth
- Pair of Shoes
- Pair of Stockings
- Cloth for Spatterdashes

20 Gunners
63 Mattrosses
———
83 each
- Coat and Breeches
- Waistcoat
- Shirt and Neckcloth
- Pair of Shoes
- Pair of Stockings
- Cloth for Spatterdashes

2 Drummers, each
- Coat and Breeches
- Waistcoat
- Shirt and Neckcloth
- Pair of Shoes
- Pair of Stockings
- Cloth for Spatterdashes
- A Cap
- Belt and Sling

One Fifer
- Coat and Breeches
- Waistcoat
- Shirt and Neckcloth
- Pair of Shoes
- Pair of Stockings
- Cloth for Spatterdashes
- A Cap
- Belt and Sling
- Cord and Tassel

---

79 Waistcoats to be made out of Old Coats for each Captain. The saving goes to buy Arms, Buff. and defray-

* HEAD-DRESSES

In above Regulations the head-dresses worn by the It is stated, however, in the Minutes of the Board of Company for year ending 16th August, 1758.
For Serjeants .. .. 5 Carline hats
For Corporals and Bombardiers, 15 }
For Gunners and Mattrosses, 136 } Felt hats laced
For Drummers .. .. 2 Caps and 2

(REGULATION No. 2.)

Clothing a Company of the Royal Regiment of Artillery after the first Year.

3 Serjeants, each
{ Coat and Breeches
Shirt and Neckcloth
Pair of Shoes
Pair of Stockings
Cloth for Spatterdashes

3 Corporals
8 Bombardiers
——
11 each
{ Coat and Breeches
Shirt and Neckcloth
Pair of Shoes
Pair of Stockings
Cloth for Spatterdashes

20 Gunners
63 Mattrosses
——
83 each
{ Coat and Breeches
Shirt and Neckcloth
Pair of Shoes
Pair of Stockings
Cloth for Spatterdashes

2 Drummers, each . . The same one year as another

1 Fifer . . The same one year as another.

Broad Gold Lace for 3 Serjeants' Waistcoats, each 3½ yards = 10½ yards.
Narrow Gold Lace for 3 Serjeants' Waistcoats, each 6 yards = 18 yards.

Worsted for Lace
{ 3 Corporals
8 Bombardiers
20 Gunners
63 Mattrosses
——
94
} Waistcoats, each 10 yards
13 Gross 4 Dozen
= 10 yards

Metal Buttons for
{ 3 Serjeants
3 Corporals
11 Bombardiers
——
17
} Waistcoats
each 16
22 Dozen 8

Brass Buttons for
{ 20 Gunners
63 Mattrosses
——
83
} Waistcoats
each 16
110 Dozen 8.

Company for which the Board pay 1s. 6d. each to the ing various Contingencies.

FOR THE COMPANY.

Non-Commissioned Officers and Men are not included. Ordnance, that the following Articles were provided for the

laced with gold.
with gold.
Plain Hats.

(No. 2A.)

REGULATIONS IN REGARD TO CLOTHING.

The Agent charges the Board of Ordnance five pence in the pound upon the Effective, i.e., according to the Muster Roll.

A stoppage of two pence for every twenty-eight days is made from each Man and paid Monthly to the Surgeon, by the Captains, and no other stoppage is made by the Captains.

The stoppage for Clothing the Regiment remains in Hands of the Board of Ordnance, and by them paid to the Contractor.

The Standard for the English Artillery is the finest and best Men Europe produces.

Sixty-one Days' Subsistence of a Mattross, amounting to £2 8s. 3½d., is allowed the Captain for Levy Money for each Man.

When a vacancy happens it is ordered to be Kept Open sixty-one Days in order to make good what is allowed for Levy Money.

No Warrant Men allowed, nor any Allowance in lieu thereof.

ROYAL REGIMENT OF ARTILLERY (REGULATION No. 3) OF THE ARMS.

1. *The Officers* are allowed Fuzees with Slings and Bayonets, a Cartouch Box (holding nine Cartridges) and Belt, they find their own Swords, which are not confined to any Pattern.

2. *The Serjeants* have Halberts, Brass Hangers and a Stich'd Waist Belt.

3. *The Corporals* have the same Arms as the Serjeants.

4. *The Bombardiers* have Carbines with Slings, Bayonets, Waist-Belts and Cartouch Boxes (which hold nine Cartridges) and Brass Hangers.

5. *The Gunners* have Carbines with Slings, Bayonets, and Brass Hangers, they have also Powder Horns with Slings and Four Priming Wires each, and Waist-Belts and Cartouch Boxes.

6. *The Mattrosses* have Carbines with Slings, Bayonets, Cartouch Boxes and Waist-Belts.

7. *The Drummers* have Hangers and Waist Belts.

8. There is *one Fifer* allowed to each Company, he is Mustered as one of the sixty-four Mattrosses, has the same Arms as the Drummers, and is allowed one large and one small Fife, in a brass case painted with His Majesty's Arms, which he carries in a worsted sling.

9. *The Buff and Arms* allowed as often as His Grace the Master General shall judge necessary.

CLOTHING FOR THE COMPANY.

31st August.—Board of Ordnance.

The Memorial of the Principal Officers of the Ordnance to defray the Expense of the Off-reckonings of the Company of Artillery, with a Schedule of Clothing for the year 1756.

That the Several Particulars of Clothing, etc., mentioned in a Schedule hereunto annexed, were contracted for by Major Brownrigg of the Company of Artillery, and that the same were accordingly provided and delivered to the several Non-Commissioned Officers and private Men of the said Company being 112 in number, and have since been worn by them.

SCHEDULE OF CLOTHING FOR THE YEAR 1756.

For 2 Sergeants' Clothing :—

    2 Coats and Breeches.
    2 Waist Coats.
    2 Laced Hats.
    2 Shirts and Neck Cloths.
    2 Pair of Shoes.
    2 Pair of Stockings.
    Cloth for 2 Pair of Spatterdashes.

For 3 Corporals and 4 Bombardiers :—

    7 each of above-named Articles.

For 34 Gunners and 67 Mattrosses :—

    101 each of above-named Articles.

For 2 Drummers' Clothing :—

    2 Coats and Breeches.
    2 Waist Coats.
    2 Caps.
    2 Plain Hats.
    2 Slings and Belts.
    2 Pair of Shoes.
    2 Pair of Stockings.
    Cloth for 2 Pair of Spatterdashes.

NUMBER OF MEN IN THE COMPANY.

19th September.—Board of Ordnance.

The Memorial of the Principal Officers of the Ordnance.

That His Majesty by His Royal Letter bearing date

the 18th day of October, 1756, was pleased to Establish a Company of Artillery in this Kingdom from the 1st day of April, 1756, consisting of

1 Major, 1 Captain, 1 First Lieutenant, 1 Second Lieutenant, 8 Lieutenant Fireworkers, 5 Serjeants, 5 Corporals, 10 Bombardiers, 84 Gunners, 102 Mattrosses, and 2 Drummers, that the said Company not having been completed till very lately Subsistence has been issued to them only upon Account.

That Your Memorialists have hereunto annexed a List (as given to us by the Commanding Officer of the Company) of the Commission and Non-Commission Officers and Privates Effective Men of said Company from the 1st day of April, 1756, to the 30th day of June, 1757, specifying the dates of the Officers Commissions, the appointments of the Non-Commission Officers, and the days on which the private Men were enlisted: and humbly pray that Your Excellencies will be pleased to order the said Company to be Cleared for that Period according to the said List, allowing sixty-one days Subsistence as Levy Money for Fifty-two Mattrosses who were enlisted, besides the number draughted from the several Regiments.

Your Memorialists also hereunto annex a List of Cheques signed by the Muster Master General.

Ordnance Office, Dublin Castle,
the 19th day of September, 1757.

A LIST OF THE COMMISSION AND NON-COMMISSION OFFICERS AND PRIVATES OF THE COMPANY OF ARTILLERY IN IRELAND, FROM THE 1ST DAY OF APRIL, 1756, TO THE 30TH OF JUNE, 1757, SPECIFYING THE DATES OF THE OFFICERS' COMMISSIONS, THE APPOINTMENTS OF THE NON-COMMISSION OFFICERS, AND THE DAYS ON WHICH THE PRIVATE MEN WERE INLISTED.
(All the Officers' Commissions are dated the 1st April, 1756.)

Month			Serjeants	Corporals	Bombardiers	Gunners	Mattrosses	Drummers	Total of Non-Com. Officers and Private Men
1756 April	1st	From the Old Establishment	—	—	—	34	27	—	
	28th	Inlisted	—	—	—	—	1	—	
		Total Numbers in April	—	—	—	34	28	—	62
May	1st	Drafted	—	—	—	—	5	—	
	1st	Inlisted	—	—	—	—	1	—	
		Total Numbers in May	—	—	—	34	34	—	68
June	1st	Drafted	3	3	4	—	—	1	
	1st	Inlisted	—	—	—	—	—	1	
		Total Numbers in June	3	3	4	34	34	2	80
July	1st	Drafted	—	—	—	—	31	—	
		Total Numbers in July	3	3	4	34	65	2	111
Aug.	1st	One Serjeant promoted to an Officer							
	1st	One Gunner discharged							
	1st	Inlisted	—	—	—	—	1	—	
		Total Numbers in August	2	3	4	33	66	2	110
Sept.		Total Numbers in Sept.	2	3	4	33	66	2	110
Oct.	1st	Inlisted	—	—	—	—	1	—	
		Total Numbers in October	2	3	4	33	67	2	111
Nov.		Total Numbers in Nov.	2	3	4	33	67	2	111
Dec.		Total Numbers in Dec.	2	3	4	33	67	2	111

A LIST OF THE COMMISSION AND NON-COMMISSION OFFICERS, ETC.—*Con.*

Month		Serjeants	Corporals	Bombardiers	Gunners	Mattrosses	Drummers	Total of Non-Com. Officers and Private Men
1757 Jan.	1st One Gunner promoted to an Officer							
	Total Numbers in January.	2	3	4	32	67	2	110
Feb.	1st Died, One 1st Drafted 1st Inlisted	3 — 2	2 — —	6 — —	2 — —	1 2 —	— — —	
	Total Numbers in February	5	5	10	34	69	2	125
Mar.	Total Numbers in March .	5	5	10	34	69	2	125
April	1st Two Mattrosses discharged 1st Inlisted	—	—	—	—	2	—	
	Total Numbers in April .	5	5	10	34	69	2	125
May	Total Numbers in May .	5	5	10	34	69	2	125
June	6th One Mattross discharged 16th One Mattross discharged 6th to 29th Inlisted	—	—	—	—	14	—	
	Total Numbers in June .	5	5	10	34	81	2	137
Since June to the present, 13th September, 1757, Seven men have been discharged, One died, and Twenty-Nine have been Inlisted, which completes the Company, and our Numbers are now		5	5	10	34	102	2	158

JOHN STRATON,
Captain of Artillery.

19th September.—CHEQUES ON THE ARTILLERY COMPANY.

For three Months ending 30th June, 1756.

    3 Serjeants . . vacant
    2 Corporals . . ditto
    6 Bombardiers . ditto
    68 Mattrosses . ditto

JOHN LYONS, Dy.
Mr. Mr. General.

For three Months ending 30th September, 1756.

3 Serjeants	. .	vacant
2 Corporals	. .	ditto
6 Bombardiers	. .	ditto
1 Gunner	. .	discharged
36 Mattrosses	. .	vacant

JOHN LYONS, Dy.
Mr. Mr. General.

For three Months ending 31st December, 1756.

3 Serjeants	. .	vacant
2 Corporals	. .	ditto
6 Bombardiers	. .	ditto
1 Gunner	. .	ditto
35 Mattrosses	. .	ditto

JOHN LYONS, Dy.
Mr. Mr. General.

For three Months ending 31st March, 1757.

1 Gunner	. .	absent
1 Mattross	. .	dead
1 Mattross	. .	on furlough
32 Mattrosses	. .	vacant

JOHN LYONS, Dy.
Mr. Mr. General.

For three Months ending 30th June, 1757.

1 Bombardier	. .	dead
1 Bombardier	. .	discharged
1 Bombardier	. .	prisoner at Armagh
1 Gunner	. .	absent
2 Mattrosses	. .	absent
4 Mattrosses	. .	discharged
19 Mattrosses	. .	vacant

JOHN LYONS, Dy.
Mr. Mr. General.

ARMS AND ACCOUTREMENTS.

19th September.—Board of Ordnance.

The Memorial of the Principal Officers of the Ordnance, representing that the several particulars of Arms and Accoutrements mentioned in a Schedule hereunto annexed, will be necessary to be provided for the Company of Artillery in this Kingdom, patterns of which Arms and Accoutrements have been viewed by us and are agreeable to the Arms and Accoutrements made use of by the Royal Regiment of Artillery in England.

ESTIMATE FOR PROVIDING ARMS AND ACCOUTREMENTS FOR THE COMPANY OF ARTILLERY.

Arms.

			£	s.	d.
7 Carbines for Officers, Brass Mounted, at	50/–	17	10	0
146 Ditto private men	34/–	246	4	0
10 Halberts for Serjeants	9/–	4	10	0
158 Hangers	6/6	51	7	0

Accoutrements.

7 Cartouch Boxes and Belts for 7 Officers	15/6	5	8	6
7 Slings for 7 Officers	3/–	1	1	0
5 Stitched Waist-belts for 5 Serjeants	7/6	1	17	6
5 Ditto for 5 Corporals	7/6	1	17	6
10 Ditto for 10 Bombardiers	5/–	2	10	0
10 Slings for ditto	2/–	1	0	0
10 Cartouch Boxes with straps for ditto	2/4	1	3	4

For 34 Gunners.

34 Shoulder-belts with horns and wires	12/3	20	16	6
34 Waist-belts	5/–	8	10	0
34 Slings	2/–	3	8	0
34 Cartouch Boxes with Straps	2/4	3	19	4

For 102 Mattrosses.

102 Waist-belts	5/–	25	10	0
102 Cartouch Boxes with Straps	2/4	11	18	0
102 Slings	2/–	10	4	0
2 Drums with Cases	34/1	3	8	2
TOTAL		£422	2	4

Officers at Dinner.

22nd November.—The Gentlemen of the Board of Ordnance, and the Officers of the Royal Regiment of Artillery, met at the Phœnix Tavern in Werburgh Street, where an elegant entertainment was provided for them. After Dinner among many loyal toasts expressive of their Loyalty and Attachment to the Illustrious House of Hanover, was drunk success to the Prussian Arms, etc.; and the evening concluded with ringing Bells, Fireworks, and all other Demonstrations of joy on account of the News of a complete victory being gained over the Combined Army by the King of Prussia.—(*Dublin Gazette.*)

Watch Ammunition.

7th December.—Board of Ordnance.
Warrant notifying that in the opinion of a Board of Officers, the Quantity of Watch Ammunition to be allowed for the Annual Consumption of the Artillery Company for Twelve Months, should be Six Barrels and three Quarters of Gunpowder, and Twenty-five Pounds of Ball.

Recruiting for the British Establishment.

23rd December.—Recruiting in the Province of Ulster met with such success, that Recruiting Parties from Great Britain arrived in Ireland to enlist men for the Royal Regiment of Artillery and for other Regiments on the British Establishment.

The following Proclamation on the subject appeared in the *Dublin Gazette* :—

DUBLIN CASTLE, 23rd *December*, 1757.

Whereas information hath been laid before the Lord Lieutenant, That several Officers with Recruiting Parties are lately arrived in this Kingdom from Great Britain; and that they have raised, and are, at this Time raising Men in different parts of Ireland, for the Royal Regiment of Artillery and for other Regiments on the British Establishment, all which Proceedings are entirely without the Consent or Privity of the Government here; His Grace doth hereby signify his Pleasure to all such Officers and their Parties, that they do immediately desist from raising any Men in this Kingdom, and doth strictly charge and command them, that they do on no Account whatever presume to take away any Men from hence, whom they have already inlisted but that they do discharge all such Men forthwith as they will answer the Contrary at their Peril. Whereof all Justices of the Peace, and all other His Majesty's Officers Civil and Military, whom it may concern, are to take notice.

RICHARD RIGBY.

THE IRISH ESTABLISHMENT.

Mr. Fortescue's summing up of the Irish Establishment in his admirable *History of the British Army*, may be quoted here.

He says : " Until 1800, all the cumbrous machinery which hampered the progress of the Army at home had been duplicated in the sister Kingdom. Ireland had her own Sovereign, the Lord Lieutenant, her own Commander-in-Chief, her own War Office, her own Paymaster-General, her own Board of Ordnance, her own Artillery, her own establishment for the strength of Regiments, and her own rates of Pay. For years this arrangement had been the distraction of Administrators, as it still is of historians, giving rise to endless jobbery and incredible financial confusion. The transfer even of a single Officer from the British to the Irish Establishment signified a troublesome adjustment of differences of pay, and the transfer of a Regiment meant not only change of emoluments and position, but the choice of a new Agent and subjection to new and extremely capricious patronage. Every Lord Lieutenant was bound to submit to the King his periodical lists of promotions and vacancies, on which George the Third would write minutes in his own hand, occasionally exposing and checking some flagrant job."

1758

Reward for Deserters.

4th March.—The following is from the *Dublin Gazette* :—

Deserted.

From the Royal Company of Artillery in Dublin, commanded by Henry Brownrigg, Esquire, Major.

>   A—— B——, Mattross.
>   C—— D——

Twenty shillings Reward for each Deserter, besides the Allowance by Act of Parliament.

Camp at Wicklow.

18th May.—There is a Camp of several Companies of Foot, formed on the Murrough of Wicklow, which, with the Artillery, etc., make a very fine appearance. —(*Dublin Journal.*)

Artillery Mounting the Garrison Guards.

20th May.—Thursday the Company of the Royal Train of Artillery mounted the several Guards to relieve the Infantry on Duty; and yesterday there was a Field Exercise in the Phœnix Park, where it is said there will be an Encampment this summer.— (*Dublin Journal.*)

Regulated Form of Furlough.

1st June.—Board of Ordnance.

The following is given here to show the regulated Form of Furlough granted, in 1758, to Non-Commissioned Officers and Soldiers of the Artillery Company, when going on Leave of Absence.

License to pass to Great Britain.

By the Honble. the Principal Officers
    of His Majesty's Ordnance.

Permit the bearer hereof A—— B——, Mattross in the Artillery Company, to pass from Charles Fort to Great Britain upon his Lawfull Business for the space of three Months he behaving as becometh and then to Return to his Quarters at Charles Fort or where he may be Ordered, this Furlough being good for Ninety days from the date hereof.

Given under Our hands at the Ordnance Office this first day of June, 1758.

        Signed by Four Officers of the Ordnance.

To all Civil and Military Officers
    whom this may Concern.

Ammunition for Artillery Practice.

5th June.—Board of Ordnance.

Warrant directing the Board to issue from Time to Time to the Commanding Officer of the Artillery Company, such Quantities of Stores and Ammunition as shall be necessary for the said Company to practise their Exercises with the long Gun and Mortar this Season, taking the receipt of the said Commanding Officer for the same.

DEDUCTIONS FOR THE INFIRMARY.

4th August.—Board of Ordnance.

Warrant authorizing the Board to allow the following Weekly Deductions out of the Monthly Subsistence of the Non-Commissioned Officers, Gunners and Mattrosses of the Company of Artillery, in Order to entitle them to the Benefit of an Infirmary for the cure of Sick and wounded Soldiers of His Majesty's Army in this Kingdom (they not being included in the Establishment made during the Government of Lord Carteret for said Infirmary) to commence from 1st day of August last.

From each Serjeant,	one penny per week	
Do.	Corporal and Bombardier,	one halfpenny do.
Do.	Gunner,	one farthing do,
Do.	Mattross and Drummer, their Pay being equal	half a farthing do.

APPOINTMENT OF COMMANDANT.

24th August.—On Major Brownrigg resigning the command of the Artillery Company, he was succeeded by Captain Daniel Chenevix from 14th Dragoons.

Accident in Firing Salute.

24th August.—When firing the Guns from the Salute Battery in the Phœnix Park, a Mattross had the misfortune to have one of his arms broke, when recharging a Piece, by some powder which lodged in a chamber or honeycomb therein, and died on 26th.—(*Dublin Gazette.*)

Target Practice in the Park.

2nd September.—The Company of the Royal Regiment of Artillery performed the quick firing of the Cannon, and shooting at the Target in His Majesty's Park the Phœnix, before the Right Hon. the Earl of Rothes and several other General Officers.—(*Dublin Gazette.*)

Surgeon to the Artillery Company.

15th September.—*Board of Ordnance.*

Warrant by the Principal Officers of H.M. Ordnance, appointing Arthur Winter, Surgeon to the Artillery Company.

You are hereby required to Attend the Artillery Company at their Respective Musters, and you are likewise to be particularly careful in Attending the Sick of the said Company, and follow such Directions, as shall be from time to time given you by the Commanding Officer of the said Company.

Signed by Three Officers of H.M. Ordnance.
Ordnance Office,
   15th September, 1758.

Target Practice at Ringsend.

14th October.—In the morning several Pieces of Ordnance, under a Guard of the Artillery Company, were carried from the Arsenal to Ringsend-strand, where said Company exercised the quick Firing of the Cannon and shooting at the Target.—(*Dublin Gazette.*)

Royal Warrant to James Earl of Kildare.

2nd November.—Letters Patent were signed at Dublin, containing a Grant from His Majesty unto James Earl of Kildare, of the Office and Place of Master of the Ordnance in the Kingdom of Ireland, in the Room of Richard Viscount Molesworth deceased.

Earl of Kildare, Master of the Ordnance.

George the Second, by the Grace of God, of Great Britain, France, and Ireland, King, Defender of the Faith and so forth.

To All unto whom these presents shall come Greeting.

Whereas We are well satisfied of the Loyalty, Integrity, and Ability of Our Right Trusty and Right well beloved Cousin and Councillor James Earl of Kildare, and his fitness to execute and Discharge the Office and Place of Master of Our Ordnance in Our said Kingdom of Ireland, Know ye therefore that We of Our special Grace, certain knowledge and meer Motion by and with the Advice and Consent of the Most Reverend Father in God Our Right Trusty and Right intirely beloved Councillor George Archbishop of Armagh Primate of All Ireland, Our Right Trusty and Right well beloved Cousin and Councillor Henry Earl of Shannon, and our Right Trusty and well beloved Councillor John Ponsonby Esquire, Speaker of our House of Commons in our said Kingdom of Ireland, Our Justices General and General Governors of our said Kingdom of Ireland and according to the Tenor and Effect of Our Letters under Our privy Signet and Sign Manual bearing date at Our Court at Kensington the 18th day of October 1758, in the thirty second year of Our Reign and now enrolled in the Rolls of Our High Court of Chancery in Our said Kingdom of Ireland, Have given and granted and by these presents for Us Our Heirs and Successors We do give and grant unto the said James Earl of Kildare, the said Office and Place of Master of all and all manner of Ordnance of Us Our Heirs and Successors in Our said Kingdom of Ireland together with all and singular Salaries, Allowances, Stipends, Fees, profits, Rights, Perquisites, Benefits, Privileges, and Advantages whatsoever to the said Office belonging incident or in any manner appertaining and him the said James Earl of Kildare Master of all and all manner of Ordnance of Us, Our Heirs and Successors in Our said Kingdom of Ireland, We have made constituted and Ordained and by these presents We do make Constitute and Ordain To have hold, enjoy, exercise, and Occupy the said Office together with all and singular the Salaries, Allowances, Stipends, Fees, Profits, Benefits, Privileges, and Advantages whatsoever to the said Office belonging incident or in any Manner appertaining unto the said James Earl of Kildare for and during Our pleasure to be exercised by himself or his sufficient Deputy or Deputies for and during Our Pleasure as fully, freely and entirely and in as beneficial manner and form to all Intents and Purposes as Richard Viscount Molesworth Deceased, or any other Person or Persons heretofore having exercising or occupying the said Office hath or have had received, perceived or enjoyed or ought to have had received, perceived or enjoyed in and for the exercise and execution of the said Office. And moreover of Our like special Grace, certain knowledge and meer motion by and with the Advice and Consent aforesaid and according to the Tenor and Effect of Our aforesaid Letters We have given and granted and by these Presents for Us Our Heirs and Successors We do give and grant unto the said James Earl of Kildare all and all manner of Salaries, Allowances, Stipends, Fees, Profits, Rights, Perquisites, Benefits, Privileges, and Advantages whatsoever to the said Office belonging, incident or in any manner appertaining to be received, perceived and enjoyed by him during Our Pleasure. And further We have given and granted and by these Presents We do give and grant unto the said James Earl of Kildare that these Our Letters Patent or the emolument of them shall be in all things good, firm, valid, sufficient and effectual in the Law unto the said James Earl of Kildare against Us Our Heirs and Successors according to the Tenor of Our aforesaid Letters in all the Courts of Us, Our Heirs and Successors in Our said Kingdom and elsewhere wheresoever without any other Confirmation, Lycence, Warrant or Toleration from Us Our Heirs and Successors hereafter, by the said James Earl of Kildare or his Deputy or Deputies to be Obtained or procured anything Cause or matter whatsoever to the contrary thereof notwithstanding Provided always that these Our Letters patent be enrolled in ye Rolls of Our High Court of Chancery in Our said Kingdom of Ireland within the space of Six months next ensuing the date of these Presents.

In Witness whereof We have caused these Our Letters to be made patent. Witness Our aforesaid Justices General and General Governors of Our Kingdom of Ireland at Dublin, the Second day of November in the thirty second year of Our Reign.

DOMVILL.

Artillery Company at Leinster Lawn.

7th November.—The Company of the Train of Artillery marched to the Right Hon. the Earl of Kildare's,[*] to compliment him on his being appointed Master of the Ordnance, and went thro' their Exercise in his Lordship's courtyard to the entire satisfaction of his Lordship and many gentlemen present.— (*Dublin Gazette.*)

Establishment.

The Establishment continued this year at 165 of all ranks.

---

[*] The historical interest of the Kildare town house rests altogether with Lord Edward Fitzgerald, son of the Earl, who was implicated in the Rebellion in Ireland of 1798. After the Act of Union (1800) was passed, the mansion shared the fate of the old houses in Dublin belonging to its resident nobility, being now occupied by the Royal Dublin Society.

1759

THE ARTILLERY COMPANY TO ENCAMP.

4th May.—Board of Ordnance.

Warrant directing the Board to issue the necessary Orders for one Lieutenant, one Serjeant, two Bombardiers, one Drummer, and twenty private Men of the Artillery Company to hold themselves in readiness to march on the shortest notice from Dublin Barracks to His Majesty's Phœnix Park in order to be encamped with His Majesty's other Forces which are to be encamped there during the time the Foot Barracks of Dublin will be repairing, as also for having Six Field Pieces and Three Mortars with their proper Ammunition, complete, in readiness to be sent with the said Detachment, and to remain under their care during the time of the said encampment.

ALLOWANCE FOR BAS HORSES.

26th June.—Board of Ordnance.

Warrant directing an advance of the Sum of £80 to the Board, to be by them paid to the Commanding Officer of the Artillery Company to enable him to purchase Eight Bas Horses for the use of the said Company, that is to say, one for the Major, one for the Captain, three for the five Subalterns, two for the

Non-Commissioned Officers and private Men, and one for the Surgeon.

Also £25 upon Account towards defraying the Expense of maintaining the said Horses at the Rate of nine-pence per day for each Horse.

Also £10 upon Account towards defraying the extraordinary Expense of purchasing Bread for such of the Non-Commissioned Officers and private Men of the said Company as shall be encamped this Summer.

Also an Allowance of 4s. 8d. per day to be computed from the 26th May past to be by them paid over to the Officer who was appointed to act as Quarter Master to the said Company during the Encampment, the same to be continued until further Order.

Breaking up Camp.

22nd October.—The Camp was broke up in His Majesty's Deer Park, Phœnix, which consisted of . . . Regiments of Foot and a Company of the Train of Artillery, several Great Guns, Waggons, etc.

The Soldiers marched directly to the Barracks, and the Artillery, etc., were laid up in the Arsenal at the Castle.—(*Dublin Journal.*)

Report on Hats Supplied.

24th October.—Board of Ordnance.

Received the Report of the Master and Wardens of the Corporation of Hatters, setting forth that having viewed and examined the 110 Hats of the Artillery Company, they are of Opinion the said Hats are of the size of the Pattern, but that 81 are not Equal in goodness to it.

CARTRIDGES FOR BATTALION GUNS.

6th November.—Board of Ordnance.

An Order signed by the Board to Lieutenant Ratcliff of the Artillery Company directing him to cause to be made up for the use of Twelve Battalions, the number of Cartridges, Tubes, and Portfires, that was at first delivered to the several Regiments of Infantry for the use of their Battalion Guns.

ESTABLISHMENT.

The Establishment continued this year at 165 of all ranks.

1760

RAISING A REGIMENT OF ROYAL IRISH ARTILLERY.

15th January.

By the Lord Lieutenant General and General Governor of Ireland.

BEDFORD.

A Proposal having been laid before the King for raising in this Kingdom a Regiment of Royal Irish Artillery to consist of four Company's instead of the present subsisting Company of Artillery, We send you, herewith, an Establishment for such a Regiment of Artillery, which having been laid before the King, His Majesty hath been graciously pleased to approve thereof, the present Artillery Company being intended to be Incorporated into the said Regiment of four Companies towards forming the same : And We do hereby direct and require you forthwith to consider and Report unto Us what Particulars of Arms, Accoutrements and Extraordinary Clothing, etc., are Necessary to be provided for the use of the said Regiment specifying the several sums which will be wanting as well for Levy Money as to Defray the Expense of such Particulars and in what manner the same is to be provided : As also to report unto Us on what Day you think it will be proper to place the said Regiment on the Establishment and at what Times the Commission and Non-Commission Officers and Private Men shall respectively enter into Pay and likewise what Disposition is to be made with Respect to Off-reckonings agreeable to the Established Rules of the Royal Regiment of Artillery in Great Britain, Copies whereof have already been sent to you.

> Given at His Majesty's Castle of Dublin
> the 15th Day of January, 1760.
>
> By His Grace's Command.
>
> RICHARD RIGBY.

To the Master and Principal Officers
of His Majesty's Ordnance
or any three of them.

A SCHEME OF ESTABLISHMENT OF A REGIMENT OF FOUR COMPANIES OF ROYAL IRISH ARTILLERY, PROPOSED TO BE RAISED IN LIEU OF THE PRESENT COMPANY.

	Full Pay per Diem for each. £ s. d.	Full Pay per Diem for the whole. £ s. d.	Full Pay per Annum for the whole. £ s. d.
1 Colonel in Chief, Master General of the Ordnance, for the time being		Without Pay	
1 Colonel *en Seconde*, Lieutenant of the Ordnance, for the time being		Without Pay	
1 Lieutenant Colonel Commandant	1 0 0	1 0 0	365 0 0
1 Major	0 15 0	0 15 0	273 15 0
4 Captains	0 10 0	2 0 0	730 0 0
4 First Lieutenants	0 5 0	1 0 0	365 0 0
4 Second Lieutenants	0 4 0	0 16 0	292 0 0
8 Lieutenant Fireworkers	0 3 8	1 9 4	535 6 8
12 Serjeants	0 2 0	1 4 0	438 0 0
12 Corporals	0 1 10	1 2 0	401 10 0
24 Bombardiers	0 1 8	2 0 0	730 0 0
72 Gunners	0 1 4	4 16 0	1,752 0 0
268 Mattrosses	0 1 0	0 13 8	4,891 0 0
8 Drummers	0 1 0	0 8 0	146 0 0
4 Fifers	0 1 0	0 4 0	73 0 0

A Scheme of Establishment.—&c. *continued.*

		£	s.	d.	£	s.	d.	£	s.	d.
1	Adjutant	0	5	0	0	5	0	91	5	0
1	Chaplain	0	6	8	0	6	8	121	13	4
1	Surgeon	0	4	0	0	4	0	73	0	0
427	Total				30	18	0	11,278	10	0
8	Gentlemen Cadets on Gunner's Pay	0	1	4	0	10	8	194	13	4
					£31	8	8	11,473	3	4

An Abstract of Arms, Accoutrements, and Extraordinary Clothing that will be wanting to complete the new Establishment of the Artillery with an Estimate of the Expense thereof.

Arms.

			£	s.	d.	£	s.	d.
25	Carbines for Officers and Cadets, brass mounted	at £2 10s. 0d.	62	10	0			
218	Private mens ditto	at £1 15s. 0d.	381	10	0			
14	Halberts for Serjeants and Corporals	at 11s. 6d.	8	1	0			
24	Hangers	at 6s. 6d.	78	13	0			
						530	14	0

Accoutrements.

			£	s.	d.	£	s.	d.
25	Slings for Officers and Cadets	at 3s. 0d.	3	15	0			
364	Ditto private men	at 2s. 0d.	36	8	0			
25	Cartouch Boxes with straps for Officers and Cadets	at 2s. 6d.	3	2	6			
25	Stitch'd Waist Belts for ditto	at 15s. 0d.	18	15	0			
1	Ditto for Adjutant	at 7s. 6d.	0	7	6			
7	Ditto for Serjeants	at 7s. 6d.	2	12	6			
7	Ditto for Corporals	at 7s. 6d.	2	12	6			
364	Cartouch Boxes with straps for private Men	at 2s. 4d.	42	9	4			
14	Waist Belts for Bombardiers	at 5s. 0d.	3	10	0			
38	Shoulder Belts with Horns and Wires for Gunners	at 12s. 3d.	23	5	6			
38	Waist Belts for ditto	at 5s. 0d.	9	10	0			
166	Ditto for Mattrosses	at 5s. 0d.	41	10	0			
6	Drums with Cases	at £1 14s. 1d.	10	4	6			
2	Cases with one large and one small Fife, each	at £1 2s. 7½d.	2	5	3			
						200	7	7

Clothing.

		£	s.	d.
7	Extraordinary Gold laced Waistcoats for Serjeants at £2 6s. 6d.	16	5	6

An Abstract of Arms, &c.—*continued.*

				£	s.	d.	£	s.	d.
7	Extraordinary Waistcoats for Corporals	at 18s. 0d.		6	6	0			
14	Ditto for Bombardiers	at 18s. 0d.		12	12	0			
38	Ditto for Gunners	at 12s. 8d.		24	1	4			
168	Ditto for Mattrosses	at 12s. 8d.		106	8	0			
8	Ditto for Drummers and Fifers	at 12s. 8d.		5	1	4			
28	Non-Commissioned Officers half mounting	at 15s. 0d.		21	0	0			
214	Privates ditto	at 10s. 0d.		107	0	0			

	£	s.	d.
The Amount of Extraordinary Clothing	298	14	2
The Amount of Ordinary ditto	921	19	3¼
Total Amount of the Extraordinary and Ordinary Clothing of the Augmentation of Artillery	1,220	13	5¼
The Amount of off-reckonings from 1st January inclusive the Day the said Augmentation was placed on the Establishment to the 16th August inclusive, the Day the whole Regiment is to be settled	575	18	3¼
Deficiency in the off-reckonings for said Augmentation to be provided in the same manner as the Arms and Accoutrements	644	15	2
Total Expense	£1,375	16	9

Augmentation to Artillery Company.

On opening the first Parliament in 1760, the Lord Lieutenant acquainted the Commons that His Majesty had been pleased to order a considerable augmentation to be made to his forces upon the Irish Establishment.

Following upon this announcement, Official Notifications on the subject were published in the *Dublin Gazette*, viz.:—

No. 985, Dublin Castle, 18th February, 1760.

His Majesty having been pleased to order a Regiment of Royal Irish Artillery to be raised in this Kingdom, in Lieu of the present Company, the following Commissions are come over for Officers in that Corps accordingly.

Colonel in Chief,	Earl of Kildare.
Colonel *en Seconde*,	Bernard Hale.
Lieut. Colonel Commandant	John Rutter.
Major,	Daniel Chenevix.
Captain,	John Straton.
Ditto	Richard Bettesworth.
Ditto	Thomas Desbrisay.
Ditto	George Skipton.
First Lieutenant,	William Gray.
Ditto	John Ratcliffe.
Ditto	William Brady.
Ditto	Robert Graham.
Second Lieutenant,	Thomas Jarratt.
Ditto	Robert Parks.
Ditto	William Brady.
Ditto	Thomas Burgh.
Lieutenant Fireworker,	Delany George.
Ditto	Andrew Buchanan.
Ditto	Richard H. Cradock.
Ditto	John Handcock.
Ditto	Thomas Atkinson.
Ditto	John Salt.
Ditto	Alexander Burrowes.
Ditto	Richard Nugent.

No. 986, *Dublin Castle,* 23rd *February,* 1760.

His Majesty having been pleased to order a Royal Irish Regiment of Artillery to be forthwith formed, under the command of the Earl of Kildare, Master General of the Ordnance ; If any person not under the size of five feet eight inches, nor under Eighteen years of Age, nor exceeding twenty-five, being strong and well made, and are willing to serve his Majesty in the said Regiment, they may repair to Captain John Straton in Dublin, where (having produced a genuine Certificate of their being Protestants and born of Protestant Parents, signed by the Minister or Curate of the Parish, or a Justice of the Peace for the County from whence they come,) they will be immediately entertained, and receive Subsistence as follows :—

		s.	d.		s.	d.
As Mattross, per day		0	9	per week	5	6 half p.
When promoted to Gunner	,,	1	1 far.	,,	7	8 3 far.
Bombardier	,,	1	4 half p.	,,	9	7 half p.
Corporal	,,	1	6 half p.	,,	10	9 half p.
Serjeant	,,	1	7 3 far.	,,	11	6 farthing.

N.B.—No man will be entertained who does not produce a Certificate as above, upon his offering to enlist.

By the Lieutenant General and General Governor of Ireland,

BEDFORD.

Thus was formed a distinct Regiment of Royal Irish Artillery, consisting of four Companies. The Establishment of each Company was

>   1 Captain,
>   1 First Lieutenant,
>   1 Second Lieutenant,
>   2 Lieutenant Fireworkers,
>   3 Serjeants,
>   3 Corporals,
>   6 Bombardiers,
>   18 Gunners,
>   67 Mattrosses,
>   2 Drummers,
>   1 Fifer,

making 420 of all ranks, and 4 Officers without Com panies.

The Colonelcy *en Seconde* of the Regiment was conferred upon a Lieutenant-Colonel from 3rd Foot Guards; and the Lieutenant-Colonelcy upon a Major from 3rd Regiment of Horse.

The Commissions of the Officers added and promoted by this augmentation, bore date the 8th February, 1760.

Later in the year
>   1 Chaplain,
>   1 Surgeon,
>   1 Adjutant,*

were added to the Establishment.

---

* This Officer acted as Adjutant before the date of his Commission. He was appointed to be one of the Lieutenant Fireworkers in 1762.

Guns for the Quarantine Vessel.

19th February.—Board of Ordnance.

Received from Captain Straton of the Artillery Company, a Return of the Proof of the six Iron 3 Pounders lately provided for the Quarantine Vessel, whereof one is deemed unserviceable and three burst in the proving.

The French Fleet off Carrickfergus.

23rd February.—Accounts were received at Dublin Castle, that three French Frigates under the command of Admiral Thurot arrived off Carrickfergus, and having disembarked about 1,000 Men, attacked the town.

On the 24th two Regiments of Infantry with two Pieces of Ordnance each, began their march from Dublin for the North, and on the following day a Train of Artillery commanded by Major Chenevix, with sixteen Pieces of Cannon and upwards of forty cars laden with Military Stores, took the same route.

Carrickfergus Castle surrendered, and the French embarked their Troops and sailed away, before the arrival of the forces from Dublin.—(*Dublin Gazette* and *Dublin Journal.*)

Detachment to March to Cahir.

21st May.—Board of Ordnance.

Warrant to Board directing that a Detachment of the Regiment of Artillery do hold themselves in Readiness to march to the Camp near Cahir, in Order to instruct the Regiments which are to be encamped there in the Exercise of the Battalion Guns. Two Pieces of Cannon, a proper quantity of Entrenching Tools, Ammunition, Flints, and Cartridge Paper to be held in Readiness to be sent with the said Detachment for the Use of the Troops to be encamped.

BUTT OF EARTH FOR ARTILLERY PRACTICE.

9th June.—Advertisement.

Whereas a Butt for the Artillery Regiment to fire at, is to be immediately raised in his Majesty's Park Phœnix, The Principal Officers of H.M. Ordnance, do give this public Notice, that they will treat with such Persons as are willing to Contract for the same.— (*Dublin Journal.*)

SUPPLY OF FELT HATS.

14th June.—Advertisement.

Whereas a number of Felt Hats such as the Dragoons wear, will be wanting for the Artillery Regiment on 20th Instant, The Principal Officers of H.M. Ordnance do give this public Notice that they will treat with Hatters for the same. Pattern Hats with the triangular Cock to be laid before the Principal Officers of H.M. Ordnance.—(*Dublin Journal.*)

5th July.—Advertisement.

Whereas the Royal Irish Regiment of Artillery are soon to be new-clothed, The Principal Officers of H.M. Ordnance, will Contract for supply of good Felts with the Sugar-loaf Crown for the use of the said Regiment. Patterns to be left at the Office of H.M. Ordnance.— (*Dublin Journal.*)

The Regiment Marched into Camp.

8th July.—The Royal Regiment of Artillery have marched into Camp at the back of the Magazine, in His Majesty's Park the Phœnix.

Artillery Mounting the Garrison Guards.

Yesterday morning, part of the Royal Artillery Regiment mounted the Castle and Main Guards, to let the Dragoon and Foot Regiments prepare for a Review.—(*Dublin Journal.*)

The King's House at Chapel-Izod.

16th September.—Board of Ordnance.

The Memorial of the Master General of H.M. Ordnance.

That your Memorialist has been informed that His Majesty has been graciously pleased to grant His Royal Letter for converting and applying the House of Chapel-Izod near Dublin, commonly called the King's House, and all the Houses and Offices thereunto belonging into a Barrack or Barracks for the Regiment of Royal Irish Artillery, and also for converting and applying the Garden and Ground thereto belonging adjoining to the said House to the Use of erecting thereon such Buildings as may from Time to Time be found necessary and wanting for the Accommodation of the said Regiment and for the Reception of Military Stores.

Your Memorialist therefore prays Your Excellencies to grant your Order on the said Letter for having the said House, and all the Houses, Offices, Ground and Gardens thereunto belonging delivered up to the

Master General and Principal Officers of His Majesty's Ordnance for the Uses in the said Letter mentioned.

All which is humbly submitted to Your Excellencies,

by KILDARE.

Ordnance Office, 16th September, 1760.

THE REGIMENT REVIEWED.

18th September.—The Royal Regiment of Artillery, commanded by the Right Hon. the Earl of Kildare, was reviewed in the Phœnix Park by his Lordship, when they went through their Evolutions and quick Firing to the entire satisfaction of his Lordship and a great number of spectators. After which his Lordship dined with the Officers of the Regiment in the Park upon a very elegant Dinner provided by them on that occasion.—(*Dublin Journal*.)

HEAD QUARTERS AT CHAPEL-IZOD.

29th September.—The Royal Regiment of Artillery marched out of Camp for their cantonments at Chapel-Izod, Maynooth, etc.—(*Dublin Gazette*.)

Thenceforward, Chapel-Izod became the Head Quarters of the Regiment.

The village is pleasantly situated, three miles from Dublin, on the Banks of the Liffey, adjoining the Phœnix Park, and has some historic associations. It is supposed to have derived its name from *La Belle Isolde*, a daughter of one of the ancient Irish Kings who had a Chapel here.

William III., when returning from his expedition to the south, shortly after the battle of the Boyne, spent several days at Chapel-Izod. The mansion which he occupied was frequently used as the country residence of the Viceroys of Ireland, previous to the purchase and improvement of the present Vice-regal Lodge.

The following particulars concerning the village, taken from the interesting novel *The House by the Church-yard*, alluded to in the Introductory Chapter, may be of interest to the reader.

Chapel-Izod about a hundred years ago.

In those days Chapel-Izod was about the gayest and prettiest of the outpost villages in which old Dublin took a complacent pride. . . .

There was the village church, with its tower, dark and rustling, from base to summit, with thick piled, bowering ivy. The royal arms cut in bold relief in the broad stone over the porch—where, pray, is that stone now, the memento of its old viceregal dignity? Where is the elevated pew, where many a lord lieutenant, in point, and gold lace, and thunder-cloud periwig, sate in awful isolation, and listened to orthodox and loyal sermons, and took French rappee; whence, too, he stepped forth between the files of the guard of honour of the Royal Irish Artillery from the barrack over the way, in their courtly uniform, white, scarlet, and blue, cocked hats and cues, and ruffles, presenting arms—into his emblazoned coach and six, with hanging footmen, as wonderful as Cinderella's, and out-riders outblazing the liveries of the troops, and rolling grandly away in sunshine and dust.

As for the barrack of the Royal Irish Artillery, the great gate leading into the parade ground, by the river side, and all that, I believe the earth, or rather that grim giant factory, which is now the grand feature and centre of Chapel-Izod, throbbing all over with steam, and whizzing with wheels, and vomiting pitchy smoke, has swallowed them up.

Firing and Candles.

21st October.—Board of Ordnance.

The Memorial of the Principal Officers of the Ordnance,

That the Commanding Officer of the Royal Regiment of Artillery hath laid before your Memorialists a Memorial setting forth the Great Distress the said Regiment labours under for want of Coals and Candles in their different Cantonments, with an Estimate of the Quantity per 8 Days Agreeable to the allowance granted in England, amounting to 8 Tons 5 Barrels and 2 Bushels of Coals, and 185½ pounds of Candles.

Office of Ordnance
    Dublin Castle,
        the 21st October, 1760.

The Memorial of the Commanding Officer of Royal Irish Regiment of Artillery,

That the said Regiment labour under very great difficulties in their Cantonments for want of Firing and Candles light.

That the quantity of Firing and Candles hereafter mentioned for the aforesaid Regiment, is the Allowance granted to the Royal Regiment of Artillery in England.

Your Memorialist therefore most humbly prays for relief.

Numbers to be provided for.	No. of Rooms.
25 Commissioned Officers	25
1 Orderly Room and Regimental Office	1
400 Non-Commissioned Officers, Privates, etc.	66—4 odd Men
Total	92—4

Note.—92 Rooms and 4 odd Men at One peck and a half per day, makes for 8 Days, 3 Bushels per Room for the Winter Allowance, and for the whole Regiment for said time, amounts to 8 Tons 5 Barrels and 2 Bushels.

92 Rooms and 4 odd Men, at 2 lbs. of Candles each Room per Week, amounts to 185½ lbs.

Daniel Chenevix,
Major.

Note.—£350 ordered to be Advanced on Account of Coal and Candles.

Lodging Money.

21st October.—Board of Ordnance.

The Memorial of the Commanding Officer of Royal Irish Regiment of Artillery,

That the sum of £616 12s. 9d., is due to the Officers and Men of the late Artillery Company and said Regiment for their lodging in Dublin for want of Room in the Barracks, to the 1st day of July, 1760.

Due to the late Company.

	£	s.	d.
1 Major, 27 weeks 4 days at 8s. per week			
1 Captain ditto at 8s. "			
1 First Lieutenant, ⎫			
1 Second Lieutenant ⎪ at 7s. "			
3 Fireworkers, ⎬			
1 Surgeon, ⎭			
	204	2	2
Captain Straton's Company	65	12	0
Do. Bettesworth's do.	58	2	0
Do. Desbrisay's do.	57	8	0
Do. Skipton's do.	61	15	0
Officers of the Royal Irish Regiment of Artillery ending 1st July 1760	169	13	7
Total	£616	12	9

Note.—£616 12s. 9d. Ordered to be Advanced on Account.

Earl of Kildare, Colonel-in-Chief.

27th November.—His Majesty's Warrant appointing James Earl of Kildare, to be Colonel in Chief of the Royal Irish Regiment of Artillery, the first Officer holding that situation.

GEORGE R.

George the Third by the Grace of God, King of Great Britain, France and Ireland, Defender of the Faith, etc.

To Our Right Trusty and Right Well Beloved Cousin and Councillor James Earl of Kildare, Greeting. We reposing especial Trust and Confidence in your Loyalty Courage and Good Conduct do by these Presents Constitute and appoint you to be Colonel in Chief of Our Royal Irish Regiment of Artillery in Our Army in Ireland You are therefore to take Our said Regiment as Colonel in Chief into your Care and Charge and duly to exercise and well discipline the Officers, Bombardiers, Gunners and Mattrosses belonging to the said Regiment in the use of Mortars and the Art of Gunnery and they are hereby required to obey you as their Colonel in Chief and you are to observe and follow such Orders and Directions as you shall from Time to Time receive from Us Our Chief Governor or Governors of Our said Kingdom for the Time being or any other your Superior Officer according to the Rules and Discipline of War in pursuance of the Trust hereby reposed in you; And tho' We do hereby appoint you to be Colonel in Chief of Our said Regiment Our Pleasure nevertheless is that you do not take Rank as Colonel in Our Army by Virtue of this Commission.

Given at Our Court at St. James's the 27th day of November 1760 in the first Year of Our Reign.

By His Majesty's Command

BEDFORD.

In 1741, the Earl of Kildare entered the Irish House of Commons as Member for Athy. He took an active part in Irish politics, and was one of the most popular noblemen in Ireland. He presented a Memorial to the King relative to the disposition of the surplus in the Irish Exchequer, and a Medal was struck in 1755 to commemorate the Memorial, representing the Earl, sword in hand, guarding a heap of money on a table from a hand which attempted to take it, with the motto,

"Touch not, says Kildare."

The King's House at Chapel-Izod.

24th December.—Board of Ordnance.

The Board met at the Office of Ordnance and went to Chapel-Izod and took Possession of the House commonly called the King's House, together with the Out Houses, Offices and Gardens thereunto belonging, for building a Barrack for the Royal Regiment of Artillery and erecting Store houses for the Use of the Ordnance, from thence they went to Mr. Johnston's adjoining the said King's House but were refused Admittance on which they from the Out Side demanded Possession as part of the King's Ground, but were answered by a Woman from within that it was not the King's property, and that therefore they would not deliver Possession of it.

1761

The King's House at Chapel-Izod.

Board of Ordnance.

Dublin Castle, 12th January, 1761.

Met at the Office of Ordnance, and from thence went to Chapel-Izod House to lay out the said House, for the Reception of as many Officers and Private Men of the Artillery Regiment as the same can contain; the Major reported to the Board that Lord Kildare had assigned Mrs. Humphrey's House for the Reception of a Major and one Captain, on which the Board viewed the King's House and came to the following Resolutions :—

Resolved it is the Opinion of the Board that the King's House may with some few Repairs be converted into a Barrack for the Reception of part of said Regiment as follows :—

On the Ground Floor.

No. 1, next to Mrs. Humphrey's for the Adjutant.
    2, adjoining said Room for an Office for the Adjutant.
    8, for an Orderly and Court Martial Room.
    4, large and cold, unfit for lodging Men in, may serve as kitchen to
    5, The Infirmary Room.

Above Stairs.

No. 1, over the Infirmary and Kitchen will contain
     2, 15 Beds for accommodating 80 Men.
     3, The Door between this and the Men's Room No. 2 being brick'd up, may accommodate One Officer, there being a passage to it by other stairs.
     4,   Ditto
     5,   Ditto

The Attic Story is unfit for lodging Men in, the Rooms being too low and small, and the fire-places too little, and therefore will serve for Store Rooms.

Only one of the Out Houses is fit for the reception of Men, and it will contain 50 Men. The full complement the House will contain is 80 Men.

HORSE ALLOWANCE FOR ADJUTANT.

20th January.—Board of Ordnance.

Received a Memorial from Adjutant Robison of the Royal Irish Regiment of Artillery, praying an Allowance of Ten pounds a year for maintaining a Horse, that sum being allowed the Adjutants of the Royal Regiment of Artillery in England for that purpose.

Resolved that it is the Opinion of this Board that the sum of £10 be allowed yearly to the said Adjutant Robison for keeping a Horse.

CONTRACT FOR CLOTH AND SERGE.

10th February.—Advertisement.

The Principal Officers of His Majesty's Ordnance

give this public Notice, that on Friday next they will treat with such persons as are willing to supply them with blue and scarlet cloth and serge (agreeable to the patterns now lying in the Ordnance Office) for the use of the Royal Regiment of Artillery.—(*Dublin Gazette.*)

COMPANY AT LEIXLIP.

17th February.—A Company of the Royal Regiment of Artillery quartered at Leixlip, is to remove to Chapel-Izod, and this day two covered wagons set out from the Arsenal in the Lower Castle-yard for Leixlip, to carry the Baggage of the Company.—(*Dublin Gazette.*)

RECRUITING FOR THE REGIMENT.

7th March.—Advertisement.

Any Man not under the size of five feet nine inches, nor above five feet eleven inches, nor under eighteen years of age, or exceeding twenty-three, being strong and well made, and are willing to serve in the Royal Irish Regiment of Artillery, commanded by the Earl of Kildare, they may repair to Captain Burgh of said Regiment at Lisburn in Downpatrick, or to the Commanding Officer of the Regiment at the Ordnance Office in the Lower Castle-yard on Tuesdays and Fridays, where having produced a genuine Certificate of their being Protestants, and born of Protestant Parents, signed by the Minister or Curate of the Parish, or a Justice of the Peace for the County from whence they come, they will be immediately entertained, and receive Subsistence as follows:—

	s.	d.		s.	d.
As Mattross per Day	0	9 ha.	per Week	5	6 ha.
When promoted to Gunner	1	1 far.	,,	7	8·3 far.
Ditto Bombardier	1	4 ha.	,,	9	7 ha.
Ditto Corporal	1	6 ha.	,,	10	9 ha.
Ditto Serjeant	1	7·8 far.	,,	11	6 far.

N.B.—No Man will be entertained who does not produce a Certificate as above, upon his offering to enlist.—(*Dublin Gazette*.)

BUTT IN THE PHŒNIX PARK.

14th April.—Board of Ordnance.

Received a Memorial from the Commanding Officer of the Artillery Regiment, representing that the Butt lately raised for the long Gun Practice in His Majesty's Phœnix Park, is not of sufficient Length and Height, and that there is a rising Ground between the Batteries and Butt prejudicial to said Practice, and praying the said Butt may be enlarged half the present Dimensions in Length and eight Feet higher, as also that the rising Ground may be removed.

REGULATIONS AND HONOURS TO BE PAID TO THE MASTER GENERAL OF THE ORDNANCE.

10th July.—Downing Street.

MY LORDS,

Having moved the King that the same Regulations and Honours may be paid to the Master General of the Ordnance in Ireland as are paid to the Master General of the Ordnance in Great Britain, And His

Majesty having been pleased to agree thereto, I herewith enclose a Copy of those regulations and Honours.

I desire your Lordships will sign the proper Orders accordingly.

I am, etc.,

DUNK HALIFAX.

GEORGE R.

Whereas by Our Warrants, bearing date the 30th Day of April, 1729, the 27th day of June, 1734, and the 20th day of May, 1736, We were pleased to appoint several Regulations of Honours to be paid by Our Forces to the General Officers of Our Armies and Admirals of Our Fleet, agreeable to the respective Ranks they bear, by Virtue of the Commissions they hold from Us : And Whereas we have thought fit to order, that the Master General of Our Ordnance shall have upon all Occasions the same respects paid to him from Our Troops, as the Admirals of Our Fleet, bearing Flags on the Main Top, have paid them from Our Forces ; Our Will and Pleasure is that the following rule be duly observed and put into Execution, That the Master General of Our Ordnance shall have the same respects from the Troops with Generals of Horse or Foot, that is, upon all Occasions to have the March beat to him ; and is to be saluted by all Officers the Colours excepted.

Given at Our Court at Kensington, this 5th day of October 1745 in the 19th Year of Our reign.

By His Majesty's Command

WILL YONGE.

Dublin Castle, 27th July, 1761.

His Majesty hath been pleased to direct, and Their Excellencies the Lords Justices have accordingly issued Orders, that the same Regulations and Honours be paid to the Master General of the Ordnance in this Kingdom, as are paid to the Master General of the Ordnance in Great Britain, that is to say, That he shall have the same respects paid to him by His Majesty's Troops with General of Horse and Foot, which are upon all Occasions to have the March beat to him, and to be saluted by all Officers, the Colours excepted.—(*Dublin Gazette.*)

The Regiment to Encamp.

17th July.—Board of Ordnance.

Received a Letter from Secretary Waite, signifying their Excellencies pleasure that the Board give the necessary Orders for the Royal Irish Regiment of Artillery to encamp in His Majesty's Phœnix Park for three months.

An Order to the Commanding Officer to cause the said Regiment to march to the Phœnix Park on Monday next 20th.

25th July.—Several Pieces of Ordnance, a number of Pontoons and several other Military Implements were escorted from the Arsenal in the Lower Castleyard to the Phœnix Park by a Detachment of the Royal Irish Artillery for the use of that Corps encamped at that Place.—(*Dublin Gazette.*)

Artillery Practice in the Park.

25th August.—Advertisement.

Whereas the Royal Irish Regiment of Artillery are now daily at the Practice of Guns, Howitzers, and Mortars in the Phœnix Park, All persons are cautioned to avoid going near or in rear of the Butt erected for that purpose, when they see a Flag on the said Butt.—(*Dublin Journal.*)

The Regiment Reviewed.

12th September.—The Royal Irish Regiment of Artillery encamped in His Majesty's Park the Phœnix, was reviewed by the Marquis of Kildare, and made a very fine appearance, and went through their Evolutions and the Firing of the Great Guns and Small Arms, with most surprising exactness, to the entire satisfaction of his Lordship, and a number of Officers present.—(*Dublin Gazette.*)

New Piece of Artillery Tried.

25th September.—A new Piece of Artillery invented by Captain Vallancey, Engineer, after the manner of Marshal Saxe's Amusette, was tried at the Phœnix Park. It carries a ball of lead of half a pound, is loaded at the breech by a chamber; its bore is two-thirds of the diameter of the shot; and its point blank range is about 800 yards. It has a stock and lock, and is fired from the shoulder like a common musket, resting on its carriage, which serves as a parapet to fire over. It is drawn by one Man on all occasions, and its carriage is so contrived, that in case of bogs, brooks, ditches, etc., the shafts slide back, and it is carried by two Men like a sedan chair. It is thought this Piece will be of infinite service in the Field and Garrison.—(*Dublin Gazette.*)

Camp Broke Up.

13*th October.*—The Royal Irish Regiment of Artillery broke up their Camp in the Phœnix Park; the Artillery Pontoons, etc., were lodged in the Arsenal in the Lower Castle-yard, and the Regiment is to be cantoned at Manooth, Leixlip, etc.—(*Dublin Gazette.*)

Company at Manooth.

27*th November.*—Board of Ordnance.

The Commanding Officer of the Artillery Regiment applied to the Board for Horses and Drivers to carry the Baggage of Captain Skipton's Company to Manooth on 30th Instant, and the Baggage of Captain Bettesworth's Company from Manooth to Chapel-Izod on 1st December.

An Order signed to provide Horses and Drivers.

Establishment.

The Establishment continued this year at 427 of all ranks.

1762

Major Chenevix promoted Lieut.-Colonel Commandant.

8th January.—Major Chenevix was promoted Lieutenant-Colonel Commandant of the Regiment, in succession to Lieutenant-Colonel Rutter, retired, and the Senior Captain J. Straton, was advanced to the Majority.

Commission to Daniel Chenevix, Esquire.

GEORGE R.

George the Third by the Grace of God King of Great Britain, France and Ireland, Defender of the Faith, etc.

To Our Trusty and well beloved Daniel Chenevix Esquire Greeting. We reposing especial Trust and Confidence in your Loyalty Courage and good Conduct do by these Presents constitute and appoint you to be Lieutenant Colonel Commandant of Our Royal Irish Regiment of Artillery whereof Our Master General of Our Ordnance for the Time being is Colonel Commander in Chief. You are therefore to take Our said Regiment as Lieutenant Colonel Commandant into your care and Charge and carefully and diligently to discharge the duty of Lieutenant Colonel Commandant in the said Regiment by duly exercising and well disciplining the Officers, Bombardiers, Gunners and Mattrosses belonging to the said Regiment in the use of Mortars and the Art of Gunnery and to Keep them in good Order and Discipline and they are hereby required to obey you as their Lieutenant Colonel Commandant and you are to observe and follow such Orders and Directions as you shall from Time to Time receive from Us Our Chief Governor or Governors of Our Kingdom of Ireland now and for the Time being Our Master General of the Ordnance in Our said Kingdom for the Time being Our Lieutenant General and Principal Officers of the same or any other your Superior Officer according to the Rules and Discipline of War in Pursuance of the Trust hereby reposed in you.

Given at Our Court at St. James's the 8th day of January 1762 in the Second year of Our Reign.

By His Majesty's Command

DUNK HALIFAX.

RIOTS AND DISTURBANCES.

9th January.—Cases of riot and disturbance between Soldiers and Civilians in Ireland's capital, were not uncommon, and some ugly conflicts took place. An account of the outrages committed on 31st December, 1761, is chronicled as follows in the *Dublin Gazette* :—

The Most Hon. The Marquis of Kildare, Master General of the Ordnance, being informed that the Right Hon. the Lord Mayor, hath received information upon Oath, that in the night of the 31st December last, several Men of the Royal Irish Regiment of Artillery, armed with swords and cutlasses, most outrageously and unlawfully went through several Parishes of the City of Dublin, and cruelly and inhumanly beat, cut and mangled several of the City Watch, without any provocation whatsoever, of which treatment one Man is since dead, and others in great danger of their lives, The Marquis of Kildare does hereby promise any person or persons concerned in said Riot and Murder, who within the space of three months from the Date hereof, shall discover any person or persons of said Regiment concerned in the above offence, and prosecute him or them to conviction shall receive twenty Guineas Reward.

And if any person of said Regiment concerned in the said offence (except the person or persons who actually committed the said Murder, or by whose ill usage any of the said Watchmen may hereafter die,) will make a full discovery of his accomplice or accomplices, so as he or they may be convicted thereof, the person so discovering shall not only be entitled to the above Reward, but application will be made for His Majesty's most gracious Pardon.

Kildare House, 6th January, 1762.

And as a further encouragement, Major Chenevix Commanding Officer of said Regiment, does hereby promise a Reward of ten Guineas to be paid by him on conviction of one or more of the Criminals of said Regiment, except as above excepted.

And as a further encouragement, the Officers of the said Regiment do hereby promise a Reward of twenty

Guineas to be paid by them on conviction of one or more of the Criminals of said Regiment, except as above excepted.—(*Dublin Gazette.*)

REWARD FOR APPREHENSION OF DESERTERS.

10th January.—Advertisement.

Deserted from Chapel-Izod on the 9th January, four Mattrosses of the Royal Irish Regiment of Artillery suspected to have been concerned in the Riot* against the City Watch in the night of 31st December.

Ten Guineas Reward for each Deserter above the Reward by Law.

If any of said Deserters will return to the Head Quarters of the Regiment at Chapel-Izod, within the space of One Month, they will be treated with great Lenity.—(*Dublin Gazette.*)

OFFICERS AND MEN ON LEAVE TO JOIN.

23rd January.—Advertisement.

The Master General of the Ordnance hereby directs and requires all Officers of the Royal Irish Regiment of Artillery who are now absent by License of Government, or otherwise, and Men upon Furlough, do forthwith join said Regiment.—(*Dublin Journal.*)

---

* The author was not able to trace in the Dublin Newspapers any mention of the trial of Artillerymen for taking part in the riot referred to.

The Gentlemen Cadets.

Dublin Castle, 22nd January, 1762.

Mr. Brady attended, and the Board agreed with him for Educating, Lodging, and Boarding the Eight Gentlemen Cadets of the Royal Regiment of Artillery, on the following Terms for each, to commence from the first day of February next, viz. :—

For Board, Lodging, and instructing them in Writing and Arithmetick, and every Branch of the Mathematicks, from Seven in Summer and in Winter from Eight till Two, allowing from Nine to Ten for Breakfast, Twenty Guineas per Annum with Four Guineas Entrance at First.

For Fencing, to be taught by Mr. Kelly three Times a Week at One o'Clock on Tuesdays, Thursdays, and Saturdays, Half a Guinea per Month and Half a Guinea Entrance.

For French to be taught by Mr. Bellieu, at One o'Clock on Mondays, Wednesdays, and Fridays, One Guinea per Quarter, and One Guinea Entrance.

Hours of Exercise, viz. :—

In Summer, from 21st March to 21st September, at Five in the Evening.

In Winter, from 21st September to 21st March, at Nine in the morning part of the Time allowed for Breakfast.

An Order signed by the Board directing the Paymaster to stop the Cadets' Pay from 1st February next towards defraying the aforesaid Charges.

WARRANT TO GENTLEMAN CADET.

James Marquess of Kildare, Master General of the Ordnance in Ireland, Major-General of His Majesty's Forces, and One of His Majesty's Honourable Privy Council in Ireland, etc., etc.

To A—— B——, Gentleman Cadet by virtue of the Authority to me by the King's Most Excellent Majesty in this behalf given, I do hereby nominate Constitute and Appoint you the said A—— B—— to be one of the Gentlemen Cadets in the Royal Irish Regiment of Artillery.

You are therefore carefully and Diligently to Discharge the Duty of a Gentleman Cadet in the said Regiment by doing and performing all manner of things thereunto belonging likewise to Observe and follow such Orders and Directions as you shall from time to time receive from the Master-General your Lieutenant-Colonel Commandant Captain or any other your Superior Officers according to the Rules and Discipline of War.

Given at the Office of Ordnance under my hand and Seal this   day of   in the   year of His Majesty's Reign.

KILDARE.

THE REGIMENT REVIEWED.

10th March.—The Royal Regiment of Irish Artillery, commanded by the Most Noble the Marquis of Kildare, Master General of the Ordnance, was reviewed in His Majesty's Park the Phœnix, by His Excellency the Lord Lieutenant. During the Review, one of the Mattrosses had his hand terribly wounded by the sudden discharge of one of the Pieces of Ordnance.—(*Dublin Gazette.*)

THE BUTT IN PHŒNIX PARK.

26th March.—Board of Ordnance.

An Order signed by the Board directing Captain Vallancey to proceed in enlarging the Butt in the Phœnix Park to 150 Feet, agreeable to the Plan approved by the Master General.

An Order directing the Lieut.-Colonel Commandant of the Royal Irish Regiment of Artillery to give the proper Orders that forty men or more, with as many Non-Commissioned Officers as may be thought necessary, to attend on this Service under the Direction of Captain Vallancey.

Ordered that Sixpence per Diem be allowed each private Man for his work, and one shilling per Diem be paid each Non-Commissioned Officer for his Attendance.

Hired Houses at Chapel-Izod.

26th March.—Board of Ordnance.

Lieutenant Robison informed the Board that the undernamed Housekeepers are willing to lodge the Subaltern Officers and Surgeon of the three Companies of Royal Irish Regiment of Artillery at Chapel-Izod at the following Rates per Annum, viz. :—

Widow Dawson's House, for	3	£21
John Dawson's	4	27
Clem : Dawson's	3	21
Robt. MacMullen's	2	14
Mr. Tarrant's	1	7

Ordered that Lieutenant Robison do agree with the said Persons.

Battalion Guns.

13th August.—Board of Ordnance.

A Memorial to their Excellencies representing that the Regiments in Great Britain never have Cannon with them but when they are encamped or ordered to take the Field, and then an Officer and a Party of the Regiment of Artillery with two Pieces of Cannon are ordered to join them which as soon as the Regiment goes into Quarters the Cannon is again returned into

Stores and the Detachment of Artillery return to their Head Quarters: That many of the Regiments in this kingdom have their Battalion Guns constantly with them at their Quarters which is not the case in England, and should Detachments of Artillery be sent to remain with the Regiments at all Times it would be hurtful to the Regiment of Artillery and cannot be of any service to the Regiments, as a Detachment could join them in a few Days and everything necessary for the said service would be kept in such Order as to be ready to march at a Moment's Warning to any part of the Kingdom, and submitting the same to their Excellencies consideration.

Payments Made in the Treasury.

In the Account of Payments made for Ordnance Services during the year, the following appear :—

For a Quarter's teaching the Band of Music of the Artillery Regiment	£37 8 7
To Adjutant Robison for Old Coats and Hats purchased from Men discharged out of the Artillery, to save the providing new	£7 19 3
To James Ramsay, late Mattross, an Allowance granted him of £20 per Annum, from the 10th March, 1762, the day he lost his arm at the Review	£16 3 10

Establishment.

The Establishment continued this year at 427 of all ranks.

1763

Pay of Gentlemen Cadets.

1st March.—Board of Ordnance.

Received a Memorial from the Gentlemen Cadets of the Royal Irish Regiment of Artillery, praying the Board will order them the Balance of their Pay from 1st February, 1762.

An Order directing the Paymaster to pay unto the said Cadets eleven Months' arrears from 1st February to 31st December, 1762, at the Rate of £6 1*s.* 8*d.* per Annum for Clothing etc.

Fire at Carton House.

4th March.—A fire broke out at Carton, the Marquis of Kildare's seat, but by the assistance of a Party of the Royal Irish Regiment of Artillery quartered at Maynooth, was soon extinguished.—(*Public Gazetteer.*)

Reductions in Regiments.

At the conclusion of the Peace this year, a number of Infantry Regiments on the Irish Establishment were disbanded.

Englishmen Allowed to Join Irish Artillery.

23rd April.—It was duly notified in the *Dublin Gazette,* that Men discharged from the Army and who were born in Great Britain would be allowed to enlist in the Irish Regiment of Artillery.

The Official Notification is as follows:—

Royal Irish Regiment of Artillery.

Any Men who have been in his Majesty's Service, and are not under the size of 5 Feet 9 Inches, nor above 5 Feet eleven, and do not exceed thirty years of Age, being strong and well made, will be entertained in the above Regiment, provided they bring the usual Certificates ; and those Men who were born in Great Britain, if they bring a Certificate of their good behaviour from the Commanding Officer of the Regiment they served in, no other Certificate will be required.—(*Dublin Gazette.*)

SERJEANT MAJOR AND DRUM MAJOR ADDED TO ESTABLISHMENT.

17th May.—Board of Ordnance.

Ordered that the Hatter do provide a Serjeant Major's Hat at the Price of 11*s.* 4½*d.* and a Drum Major's at 3*s.* 6*d.*—the Lace of the Drum Major's to be the same as the Serjeant's, and the Serjeant Major's lace broader.

15th July.—The Adjutant of the Royal Irish Regiment of Artillery represented that he had subsisted the Serjeant and Drum Majors of said Regiment from 1st May, 1763, no Allowance having been made from the Agent for them, and prays that the Board will give directions in this matter.

Ordered that the Agent of said Regiment be directed to place the Serjeant and Drum Majors on the Establishment from 1st May last, and that they receive Pay accordingly.

21st October.—The Commanding Officer of the Artillery reported that the Serjeant and Drum Majors and one Serjeant of the Regiment, have not received new clothing for the present year, and that a Serjeant's sash is wanting occasioned by the desertion of a Serjeant.

Ordered that the Commanding Officer of the said Regiment be acquainted that the Serjeant and Drum Majors cannot be allowed Clothing till the Regiment is supplied next year, and that a sash be provided.

BARRACKS AT CHAPEL-IZOD.

31st May.—Board of Ordnance.

Ordered that the House taken at Chapel-Izod of Mr. John Dawson, for Lodging four Officers of the Royal Irish Regiment of Artillery, be converted into an Infirmary, and that Lodgings be taken by the Quarter Master for four Officers in other parts of the Town of Chapel-Izod.

That the Quarter Master also hire a Lodging for the Surgeon's Mate of the Regiment, and that he report to the Board the Rent of the Lodgings he hires for the four Officers and Surgeon's Mate.

OFFICERS TO RESIDE AT CHAPEL-IZOD AND MAYNOOTH.

7th June.—Board of Ordnance.

It is the Marquess of Kildare's Orders that all Officers after the 30th of this Month are to reside at Chapel-Izod (the Head Quarters of the Royal Irish Regiment of Artillery) or at Maynooth, without they have leave from the Master General of the Ordnance or in his absence from the Lieutenant General of the Ordnance or in his absence from the Board of Ordnance to be Absent.

No Officer residing in Dublin tho' with leave shall do any Duty or be deemed at Quarters but shall be returned Absent.

No Lodgings nearer to Dublin than the Barrack of Chapel-Izod shall be looked upon as the Quarters of the Regiment.

If Lodgings for Officers cannot be got in the Town of Chapel-Izod, any place farther from Dublin where Lodgings can be got provided the shortest way from Dublin to it be thro' Chapel-Izod, and that it does not exceed a Mile from the Barrack it shall be deemed Quarters, except for the Field Officers who must reside in the House appointed for them.

All Officers quartered at Maynooth shall after the said 30th of this month reside in the Town and if there should not be room for all the said Officers in the House hired for their Barrack, the Quarter Master is to report it to the Board and they will allow him

Lodging Money for the time he resides there according to his Rank.

No Officer quartered at Maynooth who does not reside in the said Town shall be deemed at Quarters but shall be returned Absent.

These Orders must be entered and remain as Standing Orders.

ARTILLERY PRACTICE IN THE PARK.

9th July.—Advertisement.

The Royal Irish Regiment of Artillery begin the long Gun and Mortar Practice in the Phœnix Park on Monday next the 11th. To prevent accident this is to give Notice, that during the Time that said Practice continues each day, a Flag will be erected on the top of the Butt in said Park, near the Magazine.—(*Dublin Gazette.*)

PAY OF ADDITIONAL OFFICERS AND NON-COMMISSIONED OFFICERS.

19th July.—Board of Ordnance.

Ordered that the Agent be acquainted that the Bridge Master* and Surgeon's Mate* take Pay from the date of their Warrants, Quarter Master Armstrong* from the 1st August, 1762, the Day he commenced Duty, and that Captain Gray be paid up to said Time :

* The Master-General's Warrants to these Officers are dated 1st May, 1763. Their names do not appear in the Annual Army Lists.

and that the Serjeant and Drum Majors commence from 1st May last.

Horse and Cow Killed during Artillery Practice.

12th August.—Board of Ordnance.

Received a Petition from Margaret Smith, praying to be allowed Six pounds Sterling for her Cow that was killed in the Phœnix Park, 21st July last by a shot from the Practice of the Royal Irish Regiment of Artillery.

9th September.—Margaret Smith attended on the Board with proper Evidences and proved her cow which was lately killed by a shot at the Practice of the Royal Irish Regiment of Artillery was worth six pounds.

Ordered that she be paid the same, viz.:—Two pounds by the Quarter Master, being the amount of what the cow sold for after she was killed, and the remaining Four pounds out of Contingencies.

22nd November.—Lord Ranelagh waited on the Board to acquaint them that a Horse belonging to him had been killed by a shot at a great distance from the Butt which he valued at Thirty Guineas and praying the Board will grant him a Compensation for said Horse.

Ordered that Lord Ranelagh's Application be referred to the Master General.

Chapel-Izod Parish Church.

13th September.—Board of Ordnance.

Received a Memorial from the Revd. Peter Sterne, Minister of Chapel-Izod Parish, praying the Board will erect or cause to be erected in the Church, a Gallery or Return or such other Improvement as may be thought fittest for the reception of the Men of the Royal Irish Regiment of Artillery, for whom at present there is not sufficient room.

Ordered that said Memorial be referred to the Master General.

Company Pay Lists.

8th November.—Board of Ordnance.

Ordered that after the 30th Instant, the several Companies belonging to the Royal Irish Regiment of Artillery be paid by Pay Lists given by the Board, that every Man sign his name agreeable to his Rank in the Company, which Pay Lists are to be returned Monthly to the Agent and Quarterly to the Surveyor General's Office, by him sent as Vouchers to his Accounts, and that all Men belonging to the Regiment who desert, die, or otherwise make Vacancies be borne on the Muster Roll and Pay List for sixty-one Days and no more for which the Captain of each Company is to sign, and whenever it happens they are not filled up at the expiration of the sixty-one Days, then the pay of such Vacant Men to be stop't by the Agent, to go to defray other Contingencies of the Regiment, and that the Commanding Officer and Agent of the Regiment be acquainted therewith.

Orders to Officers in Writing.

11th November.—Board of Ordnance.

The Surveyor-General presented to the Board by desire of the Master General, the undermentioned Copy of a Letter from Lord Ligonier to Sir Jeffery Amherst, which His Lordship desired should be kept in the Office for a precedent.

Copy of a Letter from Lord Ligonier to Sir Jeffery Amherst, the 22nd January, 1762.

Dear Amherst,

I have forgot in my former Letter to mention it to you that the Copy of Captain York's Tryal has been sent over to me by which it appears that that Officer has been Tried at a General Court Martial for disobedience of Verbal Orders, where his Instructions from the Master-General or the Board require such Orders to be in writing.

His Majesty therefore commanded me to tell you that where the Instructions of an Artillery Officer or an Engineer require them to receive Orders contrary to their Instructions from any Commander-in-Chief those Orders must be given in writing by the said Commanders, and it is His Majesty's pleasure that you give such Orders to all Officers and Governors under your Command; it is also His Majesty's pleasure that in case Captain York should be cashiered by the said Court Martial for the Disobedience of such Verbal Orders that he be immediately restored to his post, and I do hereby send you these His Majesty's Orders accordingly.

I am, Dear Amherst, etc.,

(Signed) Ligonier.

Guns Wanting for Salute Battery.

18th November.—Board of Ordnance.

Read at the Board a Memorial to His Excellency the Lord Lieutenant, representing that there are wanting for the Salute Battery in the Phœnix Park, twenty-two Iron 9 Pounders with Iron Carriages, the

Guns formerly used for said service having been long since condemned as Unserviceable, and acquainting His Excellency that notwithstanding there are two very good Iron Founderies in the County of Wexford, the Proprietors of neither of them will undertake to cast the Guns, the Board are therefore under the disagreeable necessity of acquainting His Excellency that the Guns must be cast in England but that the Iron Carriages and other Appurtenances may be provided in Ireland, and have therefore annexed an Estimate of the Expense of Providing the said Guns and Carriages amounting to £882 4s. 0d., and humbly pray His Excellency will be pleased to issue such Orders to contract for the same as His Excellency shall think proper.

BARRACKS AT CHAPEL-IZOD AND MAYNOOTH.

29th November.—Board of Ordnance.

Received a Warrant from His Excellency the Lord Lieutenant on the Vice Treasurer of this Kingdom for £1,387 10s. 9½d., to defray the Expense of fitting up the House at Chapel-Izod (commonly called the King's House) for a Barrack for the Reception of part of the Royal Irish Regiment of Artillery, also two Houses at Maynooth for the reception of One Company, and for providing Beds and other necessaries for the use of the said Barrack.

THE FORTS AND FORTIFICATIONS.

The Forts and Fortifications in Ireland were not under the Direction of the Master General and Principal Officers of the Ordnance till the year 1763, when by His Majesty's new Establishment of the Ordnance dated 31st December, 1762, they were put into their care and charge.

An Account rendered by the Master General and Board in November, 1763, shows the following numbers of serviceable Mortars and Guns at the places mentioned.

In Dublin,
Mortars	8 inches	3	
	5½ ditto	18	
	4 ditto	30	
			51
Brass Guns	12 Pounders	2	
	6 ditto	28	

In Dublin Park
Saluting Battery . 12 ditto] 5

In Duncannon Fort,
Iron Guns	24 Pounders	10
	18 ditto	15

In Cork Cove,
Iron Guns . 24 Pounders 8

In Charles Fort,
Iron Guns . 24 Pounders 11

With 11 Battalions,
Brass Guns . 6 Pounders 22
——— 101

In all 51 Mortars and 101 Guns.

Supply of Stationery.

20th December.—Board of Ordnance.

Received a Letter from the Secretary to the Master General, together with some Paper which was delivered by Mr.———, Stationer, for His Lordship's use who is much surprised to find it so very bad, and desires the Board will send for Mr.——, and not only Reprimand him but assure him that the first time he sends any bad Paper to him he will remove him, and that His Lordship hopes he supplies the Office with good Goods.

The Board sent for Mr.——, the Stationer, and read the Secretary to the Master General's Letter to him and reprimanded him agreeable thereto.

Payments Made in the Treasury.

In the Account of Payments made for Ordnance Services during the year, the following appear:—

To Clothing the Band of Music	£12 8 7
Removing stones from the old walls to the new one built between the Barrack at Chapel-Izod, and Mr. Ebbs's	£22 12 4
To the Principal Storekeeper, for his Extra Expenses to Maynooth and Chapel-Izod, to Muster the Regiment of Artillery	£3 17 1

Establishment.

One Bridge Master, one Surgeon's Mate, one Quarter-Master, one Serjeant Major, and one Drum Major, were added to the Establishment this year, which was increased to 432 of all ranks.

1764

Artificers' Payment for Places.

13th January.—Board of Ordnance.

The several Artificers of the Old Establishment attended on the Board, and made a Report agreeable to their Order of 9th December last, and what Duty they performed formerly, and that they gave the following Sums for their respective Places,

viz. :—

Master Armour	Thomas Trulock	£390
Assistant Armourers	John Shannon	130
	Mathew Collins	140
	Benjamin Lord	140
	James Trulock	
Smith	John Turner	267
Carpenter	John Chambers	270
Harness Maker	John Owtram	220

Ordered.—That the same be referred to the Master General.

Lamps for the Barracks.

31st January.—Board of Ordnance.

The Surveyor General acquainted the Board that he had been at Chapel-Izod to see what Lamps were necessary for lighting the Barrack-yard and Barracks, agreeable to the Request of the Lieut.-Colonel Commandant, and was of Opinion that the following Numbers will be necessary, viz. :—

		No.
Outside	At the Gate	2
	At the Field Officer's Door	1
	At the Centre Door of the Barrack	1
	At the Gate opposite the Entrance	1
	At the present Infirmary Door	1
		6
Inside	On the Five Flights of Stairs	5
	Total	11

Ordered a Warrant to the Master Tinman to provide the above Lamps and that the Clerk of the Works cause the necessary Iron Work to be made for them in the King's Shops; That the Out Side Lamps be lighted so as to burn from Evening to Morning, from 1st September to 30th April, and the Inside Lamps to burn till the Officer goes his Round at Night, during the said Eight months.

The Quarter Master is to demand a proper quantity of Oyl for this Service, for which he is to account to the Board, and the Labourers attending the Quarter Master is to light them.

SPRINGS TO BAYONETS.

7th February.—Board of Ordnance.

The Lieut.-Colonel Commandant of the Royal Irish Artillery represented that said Regiment is now practising a new Method of Exercise ordered by His

Majesty, that many Accidents have happened for Want of Springs to the Bayonets, and humbly Prayed the Board would take the same into Consideration.

Ordered.—That the Master Furbisher do examine the said Arms and report whether they are capable of the Alteration proposed by the Lieut.-Colonel Commandant, and if capable to make an Estimate of the Expense.

17th February.—The Master Furbisher reported that he had examined the Arms of the Royal Irish Regiment of Artillery and finds the Bayonets are capable of having Springs fixed to them, an Estimate of the Expense of which amounting to $4\frac{1}{2}d.$ he laid before the Board.

1st June.—Sums to be paid.

Master Furbisher for 360 Bayonets and
 Springs for the Arms of the Royal
 Irish Regiment of Artillery . . £6 15 1

REGIMENT REVIEWED BY LORD LIEUTENANT.

13th April.—The Royal Irish Regiment of Artillery was reviewed in the Phœnix Park by His Excellency the Earl of Northumberland, and went through their Evolutions and Firing of the Great and Small Arms.—(*Dublin Gazette.*)

BUILDING A NEW BARRACK.

8th May.—Board of Ordnance.

Read at the Board a Memorial to His Excellency acquainting him that some Time since the Board presented a Memorial with an Estimate for building a new Barrack for the Royal Irish Regiment of Artillery at Chapel-Izod, but having received no Answer, they are apprehensive His Excellency may think the Expense thereof too much to grant at One Time, that should His Excellency think the whole sum too much to be granted at Once, they have considered what sum would be necessary to carry the Building on to the first Floor only, which is as much as can conveniently be performed this year, and apprehend about £5,000 will be sufficient for that Service.

HEARTH CHARGES.

22nd May.—Board of Ordnance.

Received from the Quarter Master a Report of Chimneys in the Possession of the Royal Irish Regiment of Artillery at Chapel-Izod, charged by the Hearth Money Collector; and also that the Pump is out of Repair.

Ordered that he do pay for said Hearths and charge the Expense in his Disbursements; And that the Clerk of the Works repair the Pump immediately.

FIRE IN THE LABORATORY.

3rd July.—About six o'Clock in the morning a Fire broke out in the Laboratory in the Lower Castle-yard, which communicating to some barrels of Powder, the whole Building was blown up. The explosion was so great that most of the windows in the neighbourhood were broke and other damage done. The inhabitants in the adjacent houses were so terrified that many of them fled, but happily no life was lost. One of the Mattrosses was dangerously hurt.—(*Dublin Journal.*)

DRUM MAJOR DESERTED.

6th July.—The Dress of the Drum Major can be learned from the following :—

Chapel-Izod, 6th July, 1764.

Deserted from Royal Irish Artillery A—— B——, Drummer, lately reduced from being Drum Major. Was formerly in the —— Regiment of Dragoons, and went off in his Drum Major's uniform, being a suit of scarlet clothes, faced with Blue and Gold Lace.—(*Dublin Journal.*)

ORDERS FOR THE GUNPOWDER MAGAZINE.

17th July.—Board of Ordnance.

Received from the Secretary to the Master-General, a Letter enclosing a Copy of the following Order from His Lordship to the Commanding Officer of the Royal Irish Regiment of Artillery, relative to the Powder Magazine, viz. :—

Orders for the Gunpowder Magazine.

By the Most Honourable the Master General of the Ordnance.

I do hereby direct and require that the following Orders be punctually observed.

1st. That whosoever is authorized by the Principal Storekeeper of His Majesty's Ordnance to issue

Powder from the Magazine do shew an Order from the Board of Ordnance to the Officer of the Guard for any Quantity of Powder to be taken out of the Magazine.

2ndly. That the Officer of the Guard is to order all the Fires to be put out before he suffers the Doors of the Magazine to be opened.

3rdly. That a Sentinel be posted at the Magazine Door before it be opened, with a Bayonet only, who is to prevent any Persons from going into the Magazine with Nails in their Shoes, with Swords and Spurs on, or with Steel Buckles in their Shoes, and he is likewise to oblige the Labourers who are to rummage the Powder to put on the Slippers appointed to be wore upon that Occasion upon their entering into the Magazine.

4thly. That no Person whatsoever be admitted within the Magazine to carry or remove Powder but the Ordnance Labourers.

5thly. That all the Doors of the Magazine are to be locked before the Sentinel be taken off, and before the Fires are suffered to be lighted.

This Order to be a Standing Order and to be put up in the Officers Guard Room at the Magazine in the Phœnix Park.

KILDARE.

15th July, 1764.

EXERCISE GROUND AT CHAPEL-IZOD.

17th August.—Board of Ordnance.

The Major of Artillery reported to the Board that the Exercise Ground behind the Barrack at Chapel-

Izod is almost quite covered with Weeds so that there is not sufficient Room left for the Men to exercise, and prayed the same may be cleared.

Ordered.—That the Office Labourers be sent to dig up the Weeds in the Exercise Ground, and that the Major of Artillery be acquainted the Board expect he will order the Men of the Regiment to Keep the Ground cleaned for the Future.

DETACHMENT AT MAYNOOTH.

4th September.—Board of Ordnance.

The Major of Artillery reported that there will not be Room in the Barrack at Chapel-Izod to lodge the Detachment (now at Maynooth) when ordered from thence to be reviewed, by the Master-General, and therefore prayed the Board would please to order the old Infirmary to be repaired and furnished for the Reception of said Detachment.

Ordered.—That the Clerk of Works do forthwith cause the old Infirmary to be fitted up, and that the Quarter Master do make a Return of what spare Furniture are now in his Care.

AMMUNITION FOR REVIEW.

18th September.—Board of Ordnance.

The Major of Artillery reported to the Board that the Master General has signified to him His Lordship's Intention of reviewing the Regiment of Artillery the first week in October, and therefore prayed that

Orders may be issued for the undermentioned Ammunition to be made up for said Service,

viz. :—

Flannel Cartridges containing 12 Ounces of Powder	1,000
Tubes	1,100

Ordered.—That the Comptroller of the Laboratory do cause the said Ammunition to be prepared.

BARRACKS AT CHAPEL-IZOD.

19th October.—Board of Ordnance.

Ordered that a Letter be sent to the Commanding Officer of the Royal Irish Regiment of Artillery to desire he will acquaint the Board as soon as possible, whether the Barrack at Chapel-Izod, with the addition of the Old Infirmary, will be sufficient to lodge all the Men of the Regiment.

23rd October.—Received a Report from the Major of the Royal Irish Regiment of Artillery, representing that having examined the Barrack at Chapel-Izod, in Obedience to the Board's Order of 19th Instant, he finds that the Great House contains . 96 Beds

The Kitchen and small Rooms adjoining . . .	14
And the Old Infirmary will contain	19
In all .	129 Beds

which will accommodate 258 Men. And as the Married Men of the Regiment who can be depended upon have

Leave to lie in the Town, and the Men of the Old Establishment not being present, he is humbly of opinion there will be sufficient Room to Lodge the remaining Part of the Regiment.

Laboratory at Chapel-Izod.

23rd October.—Board of Ordnance.

The Comptroller of the Laboratory reported to the Board that agreeable to their Order of 19th Instant, he examined the two Turrets in the Garden of the Barrack at Chapel-Izod, and finds they may be made to answer the Purpose of a Laboratory till a new One is built and humbly proposes that the Whole of them may be immediately fitted up and made as convenient as possible for that Service, the Expense of which will amount to about £15.

Barracks at Maynooth.

26th October.—Board of Ordnance.

Read at the Board a Letter to the Marquis of Kildare, to acquaint His Lordship that the Old Infirmary at Chapel-Izod being now fitted for the Reception of the Detachment of the Royal Irish Artillery quartered at Maynooth, the Commanding Officer of said Regiment hath reported there will now be sufficient Room for the whole of the said Detachment. The Board propose therefore delivering up His Lordship's House at Maynooth (which was taken for quartering said Detachment) on 24th June next, the Expiration of the Third Year,

Clothing for Old Establishment.

11th December.—Board of Ordnance.

Ordered that a Letter be written to the Commanding Officer of the Royal Irish Regiment of Artillery to desire he will acquaint the Captains of said Regiment, that the old Men in the several Companies are not to be allowed Clothing for the Future, and that if any of the said old Men disapprove thereof, upon signifying the same to the Master General they may obtain their Discharge ; And also that a Letter be wrote to the Clothier to acquaint him that there will be only 303 Coats and Breeches wanting for Gunners and Mattrosses instead of 340 his Contract, and that there are to be no Worsted Shoulder Knots for Bombardiers.

Establishment.

The Establishment continued this year at 432 of all ranks.

1765

Artificers on Old Establishment.

12th February.—Board of Ordnance.

The Board have received a Petition from the several Artificers belonging to the Old Establishment of the Ordnance, that they have examined the Same, and are of opinion their Case greatly merits Relief, as it appears to the Board the Petitioners did purchase their Places, and that the sums given by some of them amounted to their whole Substance . . . The Board therefore pray His Excellency will . . . and to obtain His Majesty's Letter for granting them Half Pay from 1st of January, 1762, the Time their Employments ceased, and that they may be placed on the List with some others who were reduced upon a former Alteration of the Ordnance Establishment in the year 1756, or in such manner as His Excellency shall think proper.

Regulations for the Gentlemen Cadets.

19th February.—Board of Ordnance.

Ordered a Letter to the Board of Ordnance in England, requesting they will favour the Master General of the Ordnance here with two of the printed copies of the last Rules and Regulations for the Gentlemen Cadets of the Royal British Artillery.

Infirmary at Chapel-Izod.

26th February.—Board of Ordnance.

The Major of the Royal Irish Regiment of Artillery having reported to the Board that the Infirmary at Chapel-Izod was finished and the Sick of said Regiment lodged therein 1st August, 1764, notwithstanding which the Stoppages for the Royal Infirmary in Dublin were still continued from that Time at the usual Rate of £1 10s. 1d. per Month.

Ordered.—That a Letter be drawn up to the Deputy Vice-Treasurer to acquaint him therewith, and to desire he will give Orders that the said Stoppages may cease from 1st August, 1764, the Time the Regimental Infirmary at Chapel-Izod was completed; As it appears to the Board by His Majesty's new Establishment of the Ordnance that it was intended " That all the Salaries and Allowances therein contained under the Heads respectively of Civil Branch, Laboratory, Military Branch (including the Establishment of the Royal Irish Regiment of Artillery and Establishment of Engineers,) and Contingencies, be payable from 1st January, 1762, the whole to be free of all Deductions whatsoever."

Ricochet Firing.

5th March.—Board of Ordnance.

The Secretary to the Master General enclosed to the Board a Letter His Lordship received from the Lieut.-Colonel Commandant of Artillery, representing to His Lordship that to carry on the Practice of the Ricochet Firing with more Exactness it will be neces-

sary to have a small Front of a Fort, or at least a
Parapet or Breast Work, erected to the Right or Left
of the Butt in the Park, by which means the Officers
and Men of the Regiment will have an Opportunity
of perfecting themselves in so useful a Part of the
Artillery Exercise.

Ordered.—That the Commanding Officer of the Royal
Irish Regiment of Artillery be acquainted that what-
ever Works are necessary to be made for perfecting the
Men belonging to said Regiment may be performed by
them when they are at Practice as they are allowed
Intrenching Tools for any Service of this Sort, but that
no such Works are made for exercising the British
Regiment of Artillery.

REGIMENTAL MAGAZINE.

4th June.—Board of Ordnance.

The Commanding Officer of Artillery reported to the
Board that there is greatly wanting at Chapel-Izod,
a small Regimental Magazine, as the Quarter Master at
Present has no other Place to lodge any Ammunition
delivered to him but a Loft over One of the Coal
Holes, which being so near the Barrack, is an improper
Store for Powder; and therefore prayed the Board
would give such Orders therein as shall seem most
proper.

Ordered.—That said Report be referred to the
Surveyor General of the Ordnance to give such Orders
thereupon as he may think proper.

ARTILLERY FIRING AT CHAPEL-IZOD.

28th June.—Board of Ordnance.

The Board being informed there was a Great Firing

by the Regiment of Artillery yesterday at Chapel-Izod.

Ordered.—That the Commanding Officer of said Regiment acquaint the Board what was the Occasion thereof, as the Practice is not yet commenced.

2nd July.—Received a Letter from the Commanding Officer of Artillery in Answer to the Board's Order of 28th June, to acquaint the Board that he was practising the Recruits of said Regiment last Thursday in quick Firing to Use them to Powder, which he was enabled to do with Cartridges that remained in the Quarter-Master's Hands over and above what were used at the late Review.

Ordered.—That the Commanding Officer of the Royal Irish Regiment of Artillery be acquainted that the Recruits are to be exercised with the Great Guns by dumb Firing only, except at the General Annual Exercise. That what Ammunition and Stores remained Surplus after the Review should have been returned into Store and issued in Part of the Demand for the Exercise in the Park, which the Board expected the Quarter-Master would have taken Care of ; And a Letter to the Quarter Master to acquaint him that he is to send an exact Account of the Expenditure of Powder and other Stores to the Board immediately after every Review, certified by the Commanding Officer of Artillery, and that he be directed to return the Surplus into Store otherwise it will be charged against him.

MASTER GENERAL OF THE ORDNANCE RESIGNS.

12th July.—Board of Ordnance.

Received a Letter from the Master General acquainting the Board that His Lordship had obtained His Majesty's Permission to retire from His Service, and that His Lordship had wrote to the Lords Justices to resign his Post of Master General of the Ordnance.

Ordered.—That a Letter of Thanks be immediately drawn up and sent to His Lordship.

20*th July.*—We are well informed that the Most Noble the Marquis of Kildare has resigned all his employments; that in consequence of which, he has wrote a Letter to the Officers of the Royal Irish Regiment of Artillery; returning each of them his thanks for their good behaviour while under his command, and has likewise been pleased to give Twenty Guineas to the private Men of said Corps to drink His Majesty's health.—(*Dublin Journal.*)

OFFICERS' PAY.

26*th July.*—Board of Ordnance.

Enquiry having been made at the Muster Office agreeable to the Board's Order of 21st June, whether it is customary in the Army when a Vacancy happens by the Death of an Officer for the Person succeeding to receive Pay from the Death of His Predecessor or only from the Date of his Commission, an Answer has been received that the Pay during such Vacancy is always a saving to Government.

RIOTS AND DISTURBANCES.

7*th August.*—A number of Soldiers, part of those who compose the Garrison of Dublin, assembled themselves in a riotous manner, and forcibly broke open

His Majesty's Gaol of Newgate and set at liberty all the Prisoners confined therein to the amount of one hundred and upwards. Ten of the most active offenders have been apprehended. Their Excellencies the Lords Justices have issued a Proclamation and diligent search is making after the rest of the Persons concerned in this audacious outrage.—(*Dublin Journal.*)

The King's Displeasure.

His Excellency the Earl of Hertford, Lord Lieutenant of the Kingdom, having laid before the King an Account of the Outrages committed by the Soldiers in Dublin, on the 6th and 7th August last, His Majesty was thereupon pleased to order His Excellency to signify his Pleasure to the Lords Justices, that it be given out in public Orders in every Quarter in Ireland, and the Lords Justices have accordingly directed it to be given out in Orders:

"That His Majesty received with the utmost surprise and displeasure, the accounts of the late behaviour of the Garrison in Dublin, of such dangerous tendency to the peace and safety of Society, and so utterly subversive of all Military discipline: That His Majesty expects and requires from his Army in Ireland, that they do upon all occasions demean themselves quietly and peaceably, and in perfect obedience and submission to the Laws; and that it is His Majesty's fixed resolution to show the highest marks of his displeasure to all Military Persons whatsoever who shall in any Respect act contrary thereto."

His Majesty also commanded that as his third

Regiment of Horse or Carabineers had not been any way concerned in those Riots, the good behaviour of that Regiment be particularly noted in the above mentioned Orders.—(*Dublin Journal.*)

Rioters Punished.

16*th September.*—The riotous Soldiers that were taken up and confined in the Provost-Marshalsea for breaking open Newgate, were whipped severely in Oxmantown Green, in presence of the Army on Dublin Duty and many thousand spectators. When the sentence of the Court Martial was read, some of them requested to be shot on the spot, rather than undergo the severe scourging of 800 Lashes.—(*Dublin Journal.*)

POLITICAL DEMONSTRATION.

On the 4th November, being the Anniversary of the Birth of our great Deliverer, King William III. of Immortal Memory, the Lord Lieutenant received the compliments of the nobility and gentry at the Castle, where a Squadron of Horse was drawn up, and the Royal Flag displayed on Birmingham Tower. About 2 o'Clock His Excellency the Lord Lieutenant, escorted by the Squadron of Horse, went in state from the Castle to the Equestrian Statue of that Monarch in College Green and thence round Stephen's Green. He was attended in Procession by the Right Hon. the Lord Mayor with his proper Regalia; the Primate, Lord Chancellor, Judges, and a numerous Levee of the first Personages, whose Brilliancy of Dress, and elegance of equipages, ornamented with the emblems of the Day (Orange and Blue Ribbons and Cockades) justly demonstrates the sense entertained in this Kingdom of the happy Æra, that contributed to the Glorious Revolution of 1688.

§. Be it remembered, *the Great Guns in the Park and Vollies from the Soldiers in Garrison were fired*, the Signals being given by Rockets from the Castle. This *we have not been able to say before on this Occasion, since a certain Period commenced*. The Bells rang, and the Citizens Joy was expressed as usual, and to close the Day, the occasional Tragedy of Tamerlane, was performed at the Theatre Royal.—(*Freeman's Journal*.)

CLOTHING OF DISCHARGED MEN.

10*th December*.—Board of Ordnance.

The Adjutant of Artillery reported that he had, agreeable to the Board's Orders, purchased the Clothing of the Men lately discharged.

Ordered.—That he be directed to pay said Men One Third of the Amount of their Clothing, and that for the Future he purchase the Clothing of discharged Men on the most reasonable Terms, and that the Charge thereof be put in his Quarterly Bill of disbursements to be allowed out of the Savings of the Regiment, the said Adjutant first acquainting the Board thereof.

ESTABLISHMENT.

The Establishment continued this year at 432 of all ranks.

1766

The Earl of Shannon, Master General.

22nd March.—Board of Ordnance:
The Right Hon. The Earl of Shannon came to the Board, and his Patent being read appointing him Master General of the Ordnance, he took his seat accordingly.

The Regiment Reviewed by Master General.

25th March.—The Right Hon. The Earl of Shannon, Master General of the Ordnance, reviewed at Chapel-Izod the Royal Irish Regiment of Artillery, which made a fine appearance.—(*Dublin Gazette.*)

Guns for the Salute Battery.

25th March.—Board of Ordnance.
Read at the Board, a Memorial to His Excellency the Lord Lieutenant, setting forth that the Board have imported from Great Britain 22 Iron 9 Pounders for the Salute Battery in the Phœnix Park, agreeable to their Estimate laid before His Excellency the Earl of Northumberland 18th November, 1763, then Lord Lieutenant of this Kingdom, that the Board did not in said Estimate include any Charges for Duty at the Custom House on Landing said Guns, apprehending all Guns and Stores imported from Great Britain for His Majesty's Service should be Duty free, that

£53 9s. 1d. was paid for Duty Fees of said Guns which causes an exceeding on the Estimate of that sum, and that therefore the Board pray His Excellency will be pleased to issue such Orders for reimbursing them the said sum of £53 9s. 1d. as he shall think proper, to enable them to discharge the Demands remaining due on this Service.

Artillery at the Review.

29th April.—Board of Ordnance.

Received an Order from His Excellency for ten Field Pieces with a proper number of Officers and Men from the Royal Irish Regiment of Artillery, and a suitable Quantity of Ammunition, etc., to attend the Garrison of Dublin on the Day of the next Review, and on all practising days preceding the same.

Ordered.—Letter to the Commanding Officer of Artillery (enclosing a copy of His Excellency's Order), and desiring he will make the necessary Preparations agreeable thereto.

The Gentlemen Cadets.

29th April.—Board of Ordnance.

Ordered that the Major of Artillery return a Monthly Report of the Behaviour of the Gentlemen Cadets.

3rd June.—Received a Letter from the Commanding Officer of Artillery to acquaint the Board that the Conduct of the Gentlemen Cadets has been for the last month conformable to the Rules of the Academy where they lodge.

Master General's Warrants.

11th June.—Board of Ordnance.
The Warrants of 1763, to the Bridge Master, Surgeon's Mate, and Quarter Master, were renewed this year by the Earl of Shannon.

Allowance of Coals to Officers.

17th June.—Board of Ordnance.
Received a Memorial from the Officers of the Royal Irish Regiment of Artillery setting forth that the Quality of the Coals hitherto supplied has been for the most part very exceptionable, that it is very costly and inconvenient attending weekly to receive the Allowance, and therefore praying the Board would allow them to receive a sum in lieu thereof agreeable to the Price contracted for.

Ordered.—Letter to the Commanding Officer of Artillery to acquaint him and the Rest of the Officers of said Regiment that the Board do not see how they can with any Propriety allow the Officers a Sum in Lieu of their Allowance of Coals for several Reasons; such as the Death or Removal of an Officer, Absence from Quarters, and the like, on which Occasion the Quarter-Master has Orders that the Weekly Proportions should be stop'd.

Reduction of the Establishment.

24th June.—Board of Ordnance.
Received an Order from their Excellencies the Lords Justices enclosing a Copy of His Majesty's Letter, bearing date 15th May, 1766, together with a

Copy of a Scheme therein mentioned for the Reduction of some parts of the expense of the present Establishment of His Majesty's Ordnance in this Kingdom, and directing that the Board will cause the following Reductions to be made on the 30th June, Instant, in His Majesty's Royal Irish Regiment of Artillery,

viz. :—

- 4 Lieutenant Fireworkers
- 8 Serjeants
- 4 Corporals
- 12 Bombardiers
- 36 Gunners
- 136 Mattrosses
- 4 Drummers

and 8 Gentlemen Cadets.

And also that each Sergeant, Corporal, Bombardier, Gunner, Mattross, and Drummer so to be reduced shall upon his Reduction be paid if a Native of this Kingdom fourteen, if a Native of Great Britain twenty-eight Days full Subsistence to carry him home, and likewise three shillings for his Sword, the Amount of which Sums is to be defrayed from the Amount of the Subsistence accrued upon the Vacancies in the said Royal Regiment of Artillery to the said 30th June, Instant.

Detail of the Guards.

27th June.—Board of Ordnance.

Received a Letter from the Commanding Officer of Artillery (with a Detail of the Guards and Men on Duty), representing that by the reduction of the Regiment there are not a sufficient number of Men to mount the usual Guards, and therefore praying the Board will be pleased to represent the same to Government, viz. :—

DETAIL OF THE GUARDS OF THE ROYAL IRISH REGIMENT OF ARTILLERY.

	Sergeants	Corporals	Drummers	Privates
Magazine or Phœnix Guard	1	1	1	20
Chapel-Izod—				
Barrack Guard	1	1	—	12
Infirmary Guard	—	1	—	6
Battery Guard	—	1	—	4
Laboratory	—	—	—	3
Orderly	1	—	—	1
Total	3	4	1	46

Note.—The Establishment of the Regiment is now 200.

The Following to be deducted to shew the Number remaining to do the above Duty.

Serjeants	4
Corporals	8
Bombardiers (Non-Commissioned Officers)	12
Drummers and Fifers	8
Invalids of the old Establishment	35
Sick (seldom so few)	16
Furloughs (always allowed 2 per Company)	8
	91
Remains for Duty	109

Note.—To mount the Guards, and allow the Men but two Nights in Bed, 29 Men are wanting.

Ordered.—Letter to acquaint the said Commanding Officer that the Board are of Opinion that the usual number of Men for mounting the present Guards may be lessened, and to desire he will cause the said Guards to be mounted agreeable to the following numbers which will make a saving of 15 Men, viz. :—

	Sergeants	Corporals	Drummers	Privates
Magazine or Phœnix Guard	1	1	1	16
Chapel-Izod				
Barrack Guard	1	1	—	9
Infirmary Guard		None		
Battery Guard	—	1	—	3
Laboratory	—	—	—	3
Orderly	1	—	—	1
Total	3	3	1	32

REDUCTION OF FIREWORKERS.

27th June.—Board of Ordnance.

Received a Letter from the Commanding Officer of Artillery, with a Return of the Names of the four Lieutenant Fireworkers that are to retire on Half Pay.

> Alexander Burrowes.
> Lucius Barber.
> James Wilson.
> Henry Baylie.

27th June.—Board of Ordnance.

Received a Memorial from Lieutenant Robison of Artillery, setting forth that by the present Reduction four Lieutenant Fireworkers are to be reduced, which brings him to be Junior of that Rank without Pay: That before the said Reduction the junior Lieutenant Fireworker who received no Pay will by the Alteration receive Half Pay, and the Memorialist who was before on Full Pay for some years will be reduced to serve without Pay, and therefore most humbly praying the Master General and Board to recommend him to the Favour of Government that such Provision may be made for him as they shall think proper.

Ordered.—That the Memorial of Lieutenant Robison be sent to the Master General with the Board's opinion that his case is truly singular and merits His Lordship's and the Board's recommendation, and that a Memorial be drawn up to their Excellencies the Lords Justices to acquaint them of the Hardship Lieutenant Robison lies under by the Reduction.

25th July.—Board of Ordnance.

Ordered.—That the Treasurer do pay Lieutenant Robison out of the Contingent Fund of this Office, the Pay of a Lieutenant Fireworker at such Times as he pays the Subsistence of the said Regiment to the Agent, and that he continue the same till further Orders and charge it in his Disbursements.

INFIRMARY AT CHAPEL-IZOD.

27th June.—Board of Ordnance.

Ordered.—That a Letter be wrote to the Master General to acquaint him that as the Reduction of the Regiment of Artillery will be completed the Beginning of next week, the Board are of Opinion that the Regimental Infirmary may be given up as soon as conveniently can be, as they have no Fund for paying so great an Expense, and the Men belonging to the Regiment of Artillery do pay to the Royal Infirmary the same as the other Troops, and have the same right of Admittance.

19th August.—Received a Letter from the Major of Artillery, praying that the additional stoppage of one halfpenny per Week stopped from the Men of said Regiment for the Surgeon may be discontinued.

2nd September.—Ordered, That the additional Stoppage of One Halfpenny per Week, per Man, stopped from the Men of the Royal Irish Regiment of Artillery to provide Medicines, etc., for the late Regimental Infirmary be discontinued.

REDUCTION OF GUNNERS TO MATTROSSES.

1st July.—Board of Ordnance.

The Commanding Officer of Artillery acquainted the Board that he had received the Master General's Orders for reducing the nineteen Gunners of the Old Establishment to Mattrosses.

Ordered.—Letter from the Board to be drawn up to the Master General representing the Hardships the poor Men will suffer by being reduced, and submitting their case to His Lordship's Re-consideration.

11th July.—Received a Letter from the Master General in Answer to the Board's Letter of 1st Instant, to acquaint the Board that he can't see any Injustice done to the Invalid Gunners by reducing them to Mattrosses, as the Pay of a Gunner at the Time they purchased their Appointments was but $8\frac{1}{4}d.$ per Day, and the present Pay of a Mattross is $9\frac{1}{2}d.$, and that as they have enjoyed Sinecures for several Years past they should bear some Proportion of their Fellow Soldiers sufferings.

PETITION FROM A BOMBARDIER.

1st July.—Board of Ordnance.

Received a Petition from Peter Place, late Bombardier of the Royal Irish Regiment of Artillery, setting forth that he was appointed a Mattross by Warrant in the year 1741, and in the year 1760 he was incorporated in the Regiment, since which Time he has always done his Duty as the Rest of the Regiment.

Ordered.—Letter to the Master General requesting His Lordship (in consideration of Peter Place's long service) will be pleased to consent to his being sent to Duncannon Fort in the station of a Mattross to assist in the Stores.

11*th July.*—Received a Letter from the Master General in Answer to the Board's Letter of 1st Instant, to acquaint the Board that Peter Place late Bombardier had forfeited all Pretence to Favour by a Breach of a Standing Order lately given out for the Observance of the Regiment, but if the Board find that he was ignorant of the said Standing Order, His Lordship has no objection to his being sent to Kinsale in the station of a Mattross.

SUBSISTENCE OF REDUCED MEN.

19*th August.*—Board of Ordnance.

Ordered a Letter to the Commanding Officer of Artillery desiring he will cause four Gunners to be kept vacant for subsisting the fifteen reduced Men of said Regiment that were recommended for His Majesty's Bounty, Repairs of Arms, and other incidental Expenses that may occur till they are admitted to Kilmainham, And a Letter to the Adjutant desiring he will subsist said Men at threepence per day each, except Serjeant Simpson who is to receive sixpence.

DISCHARGED MEN RECOMMENDED FOR HIS MAJESTY'S BOUNTY.

26*th August.*—Board of Ordnance.

Read at the Board a Memorial to their Excellencies

the Lords Justices, to acquaint them that the Board have ordered all the Alterations and Reductions to be made in the Ordnance Establishment pursuant to their Excellencies Order of 20th June last, and agreeable to a Scheme thereunto annexed, and that the Reduction of the Royal Irish Regiment of Artillery was completed on the 30th June inclusive: That the Board beg Leave to enclose to their Excellencies a List of the discharged Men recommended for His Majesty's Bounty, and pray their Excellencies will be pleased to issue such Orders for admitting said Men into the Royal Hospital as they shall think proper: And also that the usual Stoppages may be made for the future out of the Revenue at large as heretofore to entitle the Men of said Regiment to Admission into the said Hospital in the same manner as the other Troops in this Kingdom.

[TABLE:

List of Men of the Royal Irish Regiment of Artillery recommended to His Majesty's Royal Bounty, 1st August, 1766.

Rank	Names	Service									Reasons
		Irish Artillery		English Artillery		Other Corps		Total		
		Yrs.	Mths.	Yrs.	Mths.	Yrs.	Mths.	Yrs.	Mths.	
Captain Bettesworth's Company.										
Bombardier	Peter Place	25	—	—	—	—	—	25	—	Service
Gunner	William Smith	9	5	3	—	13	—	25	5	Service
Mattrosses	George Reynolds	10	1	3	—	13	—	34	7	Service
	James O. Fee	2	10	6	—	18	6	2	10	Accident by shutting the Magazine Gate in a stormy day, on Duty
Captain Desbrisay's Company.										
Corporal	Thomas Meredith	10	2	13	2	—	—	23	4	Service, and Accident at quick Firing
Mattross	Thomas M'Elhenny	6	3	—	—	—	—	6	3	Accident, by blowing up of the Laboratory
Gunner	John Sloan	10	1	8	—	8	—	26	1	Service
Mattross	Joseph Adamson	3	3	—	—	17	1	20	3	Service and Accident, having lost a Finger by cleaning Arms when Armourer
Captain Skipton's Company.										
Serjeants	George Richardson	10	1	4	6	12	—	26	7	Service
	Edward Hudson	6	4	—	—	17	—	23	4	Service
Mattross	James Robinson	3	2	—	—	17	1	20	3	Service
Captain Gray's Company.										
Serjeant	Thomas Simpson	10	—	14	—	16	—	40	—	Service, and Accident in lifting a Pontoon
Gunner	Mathew Farrell	8	—	—	—	—	—	8	—	Deaf, by the unexpected Firing of a 12-Pounder
Mattrosses	John Turner	9	3	—	—	19	—	28	3	Service
	William Mackay	3	2	—	—	7	—	10	2	Rupture, occasioned by severe working, when the Coal Hole was a Fire

Ordered, That said List be referred to the Master General.

Sedan Chair for the Sick.

28th October.—Board of Ordnance.

Received a Letter from the Commanding Officer of the Artillery Regiment praying the Board will be pleased to allow a plain Sedan Chair for carrying the Sick of said Regiment to the Royal Infirmary as is the Custom in Dublin Barracks in which the Sick Men are carried by their Comrades.

31st October.—Ordered, That a Sedan Chair be provided for carrying the Sick.

Establishment.

The Strength of the Regiment after the Reduction completed on the 30th June, was as follows:—

Officers.	*Non-Commissioned Officers and Men.*
1 Colonel in Chief, Master General of the Ordnance.	1 Serjeant Major.
1 Colonel *en Seconde*, Lieut.-General of the Ordnance.	4 Serjeants.
1 Lieut.-Colonel Commandant.	8 Corporals.
1 Major.	12 Bombardiers.
1 Quarter Master.	36 Gunners.
1 Adjutant.	132 Mattrosses.
1 Bridge Master.	1 Drum and Fife Major.
1 Chaplain.	4 Drummers.
1 Surgeon.	4 Fifers.
1 Surgeon's Mate.	
4 Captains.	
4 First Lieutenants.	
4 Second Lieutenants.	
4 Lieutenant Fireworkers.	
26 Total.	**202 Total.**

1767

ALLOWANCE FOR COALS.

13th February.—Board of Ordnance.

Received a Letter from Lieutenant Brady of Artillery, representing that there is One Ton and Five Barrels of Coals due to him by the Storekeeper at Charlesfort since the year 1762, and praying the Board will take the same into consideration.

Ordered.—That he be acquainted it is so long since, the Board cannot have Retrospect to it as he did not make Application before.

ARREARS OF PAY.

20th February.—Board of Ordnance.

Received a Letter from the Agent of the Royal Irish Regiment of Artillery, representing that he is often obliged to advance small sums to different Officers for occasional Services more than their Subsistence, therefore humbly praying that the Board will be pleased to Order that he may receive from the Treasurer of the Ordnance the Balance due to the Regiment of Artillery every three months as is the custom of the British Artillery.

Ordered.—Letter to the Treasurer desiring he will pay the Arrears of the Artillery Regiment every three Months to the Agent.

Band Instruments.

20th March.—Board of Ordnance.

Received a Letter from the Lieut. Colonel Commandant of Artillery, representing that in Obedience to the Master General's Orders, two Clarionets are added to the Band of Musick, and as there is now a Demand of four Guineas, two for Entrance and two for Twelve Teachings, he therefore humbly prayed the Board would be pleased to issue such Orders for Payment thereof as they should think proper.

Ordered.—That the Adjutant pay the Expense attending this Service and charge the same in his Quarterly Bill of Disbursements.

Pistols Supplied.

31st March.—Board of Ordnance.

Received a Letter from the Commanding Officer of Artillery, seting forth that there have been frequent Robberies committed on the High Roads in the garrison of Chapel-Izod, and Robbers apprehended which Service frequently demand the Military Aid, but finding by experience that the Regimental Arms are too cumbersome and alarming for Excursions of this nature, he therefore humbly prays the Board will be pleased to Order Six Case of Pistols to be sent for the use of the Royal Irish Regiment of Artillery to be delivered to the Adjutant on his indenting for the same.

Ordered.—That the Master Furbisher deliver to the Adjutant of Artillery, Six Case of Pistols.

ALTERATION OF THE REGIMENTAL UNIFORM.

7th September,
    Drogheda.   Jn. Ponsonby.

We send You herewith a Copy of a Letter dated the 27th August last, which we have received from His Excellency the Lord Lieutenant, signifying His Majesty's Pleasure, that for the future the Regimental Clothing of the Officers of the Royal Irish Regiment of Artillery be a blue Coat Lapell'd and Cuffed with red, Laced with a very narrow Gold Edging with Button Holes of the same, that being the Regimental Frock, and that the Waistcoats and Breeches be of Buff Coloured Cloth without Lace. And pursuant thereto, We do hereby direct and require You to take care that due Obedience be paid to His Majesty's pleasure accordingly.

Given at His Majesty's Castle of Dublin,
    the 7th day of September, 1767.

                               THOS. WAITE.

To the Master General and Principal
    Officers of His Majesty's Ordnance.

Alterations in Uniform.

15th September.—Board of Ordnance.
Received an Order from their Excellencies the Lords Justices, enclosing a Copy of His Majesty's Letter for altering the Regimentals of the Officers of the Royal Irish Regiment of Artillery.

Received a Letter from the Commanding Officer of the Royal Irish Regiment of Artillery to acquaint the Board that the Master General has approved of an alteration to be made in the Accoutrements of the Regiment, and therefore request the Board will be pleased to direct such number of the old Accoutrements in His Majesty's Stores may be delivered to Mr. Battier as he may want to complete said Alterations: And also to cause a small gold Loop to be put on the Right Shoulder of the Serjeants and Corporals, and new Straps upon the Right Shoulder of the Rank and File.

Ordered.—That the proper Orders be issued accordingly.

ESTABLISHMENT.

A State of the Establishment of the Regiment in the year 1767 (presented to the House of Commons of Ireland, 6th November, 1767) gives the total of all ranks at 228, the same as in 1766.

1768

MATTROSS TRIED BY GENERAL COURT MARTIAL.

DUBLIN CASTLE, 1*st January*, 1768.

My Lord and Gentlemen,

A General Court Martial having pursuant to a Warrant signed by my Lord Lieutenant assembled at the Castle of Dublin upon an appeal from the Determination of a Regimental Court Martial held at Chapel-Izod by the Officers of the Royal Irish Regiment of Artillery upon certain Articles of Complaint signed by David Blakeney a Mattross in said Regiment and exhibited before the said Court Martial, and the said General Court Martial having laid before His Excellency their proceedings and Sentence, whereby the said David Blakeney is adjudged to receive five hundred Lashes at the Head of the Garrison of Dublin; and His Excellency having so far confirmed and approved thereof as that the said David Blakeney do receive two hundred Lashes at the Head of the Garrison of Dublin instead of the number adjudged to him by the said Sentence, And having directed the Commander in Chief of His Majesty's Forces in this Kingdom to cause the same to be carried into execution accordingly.

I am Commanded by my Lord Lieutenant to acquaint you therewith, and His Excellency desires you will Order the Royal Irish Regiment of Artillery to attend on such Day as the Commander in Chief shall appoint for that purpose.

I am, etc.,

FREDERICK CAMPBELL.

Board of Ordnance.

When the Prisoner stripped for flogging at the Royal Barracks, Dublin, on the 4th January, he stabbed himself in three different places with a knife. The man was immediately sent to the Infirmary, and when he recovered of his wounds the sentence was carried into effect.

Naturally the case made a noise in the world, and Doctor Lucas, one of the representatives of Dublin City, who regarded the soldier as the victim of military discipline, tried to institute a parliamentary inquiry into the affair. The Doctor's efforts in Parliament proving unsuccessful, he published the Pamphlet alluded to in the Introductory Chapter. From this Pamphlet we quote here a summary of the grievances complained of by the Mattross with respect to stoppages for Clothing, withholding of Pay, etc., as the particulars given afford glimpses of the internal life of the Irish Artillery in the twelfth year of its existence as a Regiment.

I. That though by the Marquess of *Kildare's* recruiting advertisement, under which he listed, the subsistence of a Matross was fixed at five shillings and six-pence half-penny the week, this Complainant never received more than five shillings and six-pence a week.

II. That upon his entering the regiment, instead of the full cloathing appointed by his Majesty, this Complainant got but an old, bad coat, and in some time after, a new waist-coat and breeches, for which breeches, he was forced to pay six shillings and six-pence, by two shillings a week, stopped out of his subsistence.

III. That though his Majesty, of his royal bounty, has ordered that each soldier, with his annual cloathing, should receive, as what is called Half-mounting, one shirt, one pair of stockings, one pair of shoes, and cloath for gaytres, roller or neck-cloath, in lieu of which, ten shillings in money is ordinarily allowed by the Board, under the denomination of half-mounting money; this Complainant received no half-mounting, nor value for it, until he was a year in the regiment, though furnished with the shabby cloathing first mentioned, and afterwards with full cloathing, and then he received but five shillings, which is but half the allowance.

IV. That of an annual allowance, called utensil-money, he received none, though he was near three years in the service, until he was confined by the Regimental Court Martial, and then, by way of hush-money, he was paid for one year. Of this more hereafter.

V. That in the year 1765, he was charged one pound three shillings and nine-pence; and in the year 1766, thirteen shillings and six-pence, for two pair of leathern breeches, and for the payment of these sums, he was laid under stoppages of two shillings a week, out of his subsistence.

VI. That though there is a certain deduction made out of every soldier's pay for the hospital and infirmary, this Complainant was laid under the additional stoppage of one halfpenny per week, out of his subsistence from *May* 1765 to *July* 1766, which was said to be for the use of the infirmary.

VII. That the stoppage of one half-penny per month was made out of his subsistence, which was said to be for the cleaning the Necessary Office. This, I find, was afterwards given up.

VIII. That while he had one plane and one laced hat in use, and a new laced hat in the stores, he was forced to pay for a fourth, a very small, coarse Felt, two shillings, and for feritting to tye it, two-pence.

IX. That though the cloathing is ascertained by his Majesty's order, and deductions, more than sufficient, made for it out of the established pay, the Complainant and other private men, were put under stoppages, out of their subsistence, for a buff-colored, supernumerary waist-coat, when the King's order for cloathing required the old coat to be made into a waist-coat, and the making paid for by the board. But this article, the General Court Martial, in their sentence, declare to be a grievance, as will hereafter appear; while the Complainant, for the sole crime of complaining, according to law, is ordered to receive five hundred lashes of a Cat-of-nine-Tails, how agreeable to law, let the just and dispassionate judge.

X. That while he had a suit of cloaths in wearing, and a new coat, due in *August*, by the King's order, in the stores, which had been but a day or two worn, he was put under stoppages, out of his subsistence, for the payment of one pound and nine-pence, for a frock, regardless of his Majesty's cloathing order, and that which expressly forbids all stoppages, not warranted by his sign manual.

XI. That the cloathing, which became due in *August*, was not permitted to be worn above two days, when they were taken from the men, and locked up in the stores, where they have been ever since kept from the Complainant, and the rest of the men.

XII. That a deduction of one farthing a week, out of his subsistence, has been often made, for the carriage of his pay to *Chappel-Izod*. The deduction of a farthing a month out of each private man's pay, for this purpose, was confessed by the adjutant on the floor of the House of Commons.

XIII. That there are twenty-five men of the regiment, mustered as soldiers, who never do any part of the duty of soldiers; that one of these mustered men, namely, *John Robinson*, never did any part of the duty of a soldier, or even ever appeared in regimentals, being but a boy, in no sort qualified to be inlisted, or for service; that another of these mustered men, namely, *William Connell*, never did any part of a soldier's duty, or even ever appeared at muster, in three years; and that many of them wear liveries and act as servants, not as soldiers.

APPLICATIONS TO THE MASTER GENERAL.

5th February.—Board of Ordnance.

Ordered.—That Letters be wrote to acquaint all Officers holding employment under the Master General and Board of Ordnance, that no Application is to be made to the Master General on any matters relative to the Ordnance but immediately to himself or thro' the Board, and that any Officer under the Board who shall apply to his Friends to intercede with the Master General for any Indulgencies, His Lordship is determined to displace immediately and appoint Another Officer in his stead.

SECURITY FOR GOOD BEHAVIOUR.

26th February.—Board of Ordnance.

Ordered.—Letter to the Clerk of Works to desire he will acquaint the Office Labourers that every One of them must give One hundred pounds Security for their Good Behaviour otherwise they will be dismissed.

DEATH OF AN OFFICER.

22nd March.—Board of Ordnance.

Received a Letter from Commanding Officer of Artillery to acquaint the Board that Lieutenant—— died and that he was indebted to the Regiment about £—— by his having the payment of Captain —— Company : That in similar cases it has been the Custom of the Army to make up such Regimental Demands by the Successors to each Rank contributing proportionably towards it, which as there will probably be five gentlemen concerned in the Succession each share will be very light : That Lieutenant—— would have been put under Stoppages on that Account but from the Prospect he had of disposing of his Commission.

Ordered.—Letter to the Master General enclosing a Copy of the Above to His Lordship with the Names of the Officers who are in succession.

FIELD DAYS AND REVIEWS.

7th May.—To judge from the columns of the Metropolitan Press, there were many exciting incidents on occasions of Field Days and Reviews in the Phœnix Park.

The following sample taken *verbatim* from this year's newspapers is given here, as probably interesting to the reader :—

In a few days the Regiments on Dublin Duty will be reviewed in his Majesty's Deer Park, Phœnix, by His Excellency the Lord Lieutenant : when it is not doubted, but vast crowds of people will go thither, which will give our nobility and gentry a fair opportunity of breaking their limbs, being squeezed to death by walking, riding, or in carriages, between the Inns and Arran Quays. It may also find employment for all or most of the Surgeons in Dublin, as luckily for them, there are few or no walls or battlements between the Barracks and Chapel-Izod to hinder spirited riders and horsemen, postillions and coachmen, from driving and leaping their cattle down the hills, and over those delightful precipices.—(*Dublin Journal.*)

21st May.—There never was known such a concourse of people, as at the Phœnix-Park to see the Review. Numbers of people were run over by carriages. A man was thrown from his horse, and a woman at the Park-gate was almost crushed to death.—(*Public Gazetteer.*)

DESERTERS PARDONED.

27th May.—Board of Ordnance.

Received an Account from Adjutant Robison of the Royal Irish Regiment of Artillery, of Subsistence by him paid to supernumerary Men returned from

Desertion under the King's Proclamation for pardoning Deserters to 31st December, 1767.

3rd June.—Ordered that following sums be paid :—

Adjutant Robison for Subsistence paid by him to Supernumerary Men returned from Desertion . . £23 15 0

OFFICERS TO RESIDE AT CHAPEL-IZOD.

29th November.—Board of Ordnance.

Ordered.—Letter to the Commanding Officer of Artillery to acquaint him that the Board are sorry to find their Orders bearing Date 6th June, 1763, have not been obeyed, as few, if any, of the Officers reside at Chapel-Izod notwithstanding a constant Demand is made for their Allowance of Lodging ; and that a Copy of said Order be enclosed to the Commanding Officer desiring he will have the same punctually observed for the future, otherwise the Board will not allow of any Demand for Lodgings, nor can they pay the present Demand except to such Officers as have resided with the Regiment ; And also a Letter to the Quarter Master desiring that the Allowance of Coals and Candles may not be issued to any Officers that are Absent.

ESTABLISHMENT.

The Establishment continued this year at 228 of all ranks.

1769

Pay of Lieutenant Fireworker.

31st January.—Board of Ordnance.

Received a Memorial from Lieutenant Fireworker Barber of the Royal Irish Regiment of Artillery, setting forth that he is the Junior Officer of the Regiment and at present without Pay, and therefore humbly prays the Master General and Board will take his Case into consideration.

Ordered.—That the Pay of a Lieutenant Fireworker be allowed him for the present to commence from the Date of his Commission.

Regimental Clothing.

31st January.—Board of Ordnance.

Received a Letter from the Commanding Officer of the Royal Irish Regiment of Artillery, representing that it is impossible to fit the Clothing of the Regiment except each Man's Measure be taken, that almost the whole of the present Clothing want Alteration, and that the new Hats cannot be worn unless they are cut down and new cocked.

Guns at the Salute Battery.

11th April.—Board of Ordnance.

Received a Report from Lieutenant Robison that

the Guns at the Salute Battery are in very great want of Oyling.

Ordered.—That the Clerk of Works cause said Guns to be oyled immediately.

THE REGIMENT REVIEWED.

12*th May.*—The Regiment was reviewed in the Phœnix Park, by His Excellency the Lord Lieutenant.—(*Dublin Gazette.*)

ARTILLERY PRACTICE.

19*th May.*—Board of Ordnance.

Received a Letter from the Commanding Officer of the Royal Irish Regiment of Artillery reporting to the Board that it is two years since said Regiment was out at Practice, and therefore requesting they will be pleased to issue Orders for carrying it on for two months from 1st June next.

30*th May.*—Ordered, That the Ordnance and Stores be prepared and issued for the Practice of the Royal Irish Regiment of Artillery on Tuesday, 6th June, next.

Received a Report from the Quarter Master of Artillery, that thirty five Horses and two Low-back Cars will be wanting on Tuesday next to take the Ordnance and Stores from the Castle-yard to the Practice ground in the Phœnix Park.

Ordered.—That the Master Carman provide 35 Horses and 2 Low-back Cars, with a sufficient number of Drivers against Tuesday next for the said service.

The Regimental Band.

4th August.—Board of Ordnance.

Received a Letter from the Commanding Officer of Artillery, praying the Board will be pleased to Order four of the Band of Musick to be taught different Instruments, that the Band may be at all Times compleat, the Expense of which he computes will be about 25 or 80 Guineas.

Lodging Money to Captain Desbrisay.

1st December.—Received a Memorial from Captain Thomas Desbrisay of the Royal Irish Regiment of Artillery, representing that he has been some Time Absent with Leave soliciting the Commission of Lieutenant Governor of St. John's Island, to which His Majesty was pleased to appoint him, and praying the Master General and Board will be pleased to grant him his usual allowance of Lodging Money during his Absence.

Ordered.—That he be allowed Lodging Money from 80th June, 1768.

Establishment.

The Establishment continued this year at 228 of all ranks.

1770

MATTROSS PLACED ON PENSION LIST.

8th May.—Board of Ordnance.

Received a Petition from Thomas M'Elhenny, late Mattross in the Royal Irish Regiment of Artillery, setting forth that he lost the use of his Arm at the Time the Laboratory was blown up, and praying the Board will be pleased to take his deplorable Case into Consideration, and as he is not able to work, to place him on the sixpence Pension List.

Ordered.—That in consideration of the Commanding Officer's recommending the Petitioner as a real Object, an addition of three pence per day be allowed him; And that the Commanding Officer of said Regiment be acquainted it must not remain as a precedent for the Future, there being no Fund to pay Pensions.

APPOINTMENT OF MASTER GENERAL.

25th June.—The Earl of Drogheda was appointed Master General of the Ordnance, in succession to the Earl of Shannon.

LABORATORY TENT FOR CHURCH SERVICE.

3rd July.—Board of Ordnance.

Received a Letter from the Commanding Officer of Artillery, representing that the Church at Chapel-Izod being shut up for some Time to be repaired, and as the Men have no Opportunity of hearing Divine Service, he begs the Board will be pleased to allow the Laboratory Tent to be pitched every Sunday until the said Church is repaired.

Ordered.—That the Laboratory Tent be delivered for said Service.

ALTERATIONS TO REGIMENTAL CLOTHING.

20th July.—Board of Ordnance.
Received an Order from His Excellency the Lord Lieutenant, for altering the Clothing of the Non-Commissioned Officers and Private Men of the Royal Irish Regiment of Artillery, who are to have for the future Buff Waistcoats and Breeches, and Blue Linings to their Coats.

THE REGIMENT REVIEWED.

30th July.—The Royal Irish Regiment of Artillery was reviewed in His Majesty's Park Phœnix, by Major General Lord Drogheda, when they went through their Evolutions and Firings to the entire satisfaction of His Lordship, the General Officers present, and a great number of spectators.—(*Dublin Gazette.*)

PLAN OF NEW BARRACKS.

14th August.—Board of Ordnance.
The Surveyor General laid before the Board a Plan and Estimate for a new Barrack for the Royal Irish Regiment of Artillery, proposed to be built in the Phœnix Park.

4th September.—Board of Ordnance.

Ordered.—That a Memorial be drawn up to His Excellency the Lord Lieutenant, with a Plan of Six Acres of Land in His Majesty's Phœnix Park, on which the Artillery Barrack is proposed to be built, situated close to the Road leading from Dublin to Chapel-Izod, the Park Wall being the Boundary to the South. The centre of the said Six Acres is in a direct Line with the centre of the new building lately erected for Soldiers' Children. That this situation hath always been thought a healthy One, the Regiment of Artillery have been encamped thereon and found it extremely dry. That the Board are therefore of Opinion it will be the most convenient Part of the Phœnix Park to build the said new Barrack * and other conveniences upon.

GROUND BELONGING TO CROWN AT CHAPEL-IZOD.

31st August.—Board of Ordnance.

Received a Letter from Secretary Sir Geo. Macartney signifying His Excellency the Lord Lieutenant's Desire to be informed whether there be at Chapel-Izod any Ground belonging to the Crown other than that at present occupied by the Artillery Regiment.

Ordered.—That a Letter be drawn up acquainting him that the Board do not know of any Ground at Chapel-Izod belonging to the Crown besides that which at Present appertains to the Artillery Barrack.

* The subject does not appear to have been pursued any further.

Lodging Money to Married Men.

13th November.—Board of Ordnance.

Ordered a Warrant to the Quarter Master Royal Irish Regiment of Artillery, signifying that it is the Board's desire that Lodging Money, Coals and Candles be allowed to the Married Men of said Artillery Regiment who had Leave to lie out of the Barrack at the Time it was pulled down; notwithstanding any former Orders to the Contrary.

Detached Commands.

5th December.—Board of Ordnance.

Received an Order from His Excellency the Lord Lieutenant for

- 1 Captain
- 2 Subalterns
- 1 Serjeant
- 1 Corporal
- 2 Bombardiers
- 6 Gunners
- 20 Mattrosses
- 1 Fifer
- and 1 Drummer,

with six Light 6 Pounders and a proper quantity of Ammunition and Stores to march to Limerick, the said Detachment to be attended by one Clerk of the Stores, one Wheelwright, and one Smith.

The Captain when at Limerick to receive his orders from the Officer Commanding the Garrison who will be directed to select three Men from each Company, and a Serjeant from each of the two Regiments under his command, who are to be taught the exercise of the Field Guns.

And also

    1 Captain
    3 Subalterns
    1 Serjeant
    2 Corporals
    3 Bombardiers
    9 Gunners
    33 Mattrosses
    1 Fifer
  and 1 Drummer,

with six Light 6 Pounders to march to Cork—the two Regiments at Cork to furnish same as at Limerick.

The Captain of Artillery ordered to Cork is to detach 1 Subaltern, 1 Corporal, 1 Bombardier, 3 Gunners and 13 Mattrosses to the Cove of Cork to receive Orders from the Officer Commanding there.

1 Subaltern, 1 Corporal, 1 Bombardier, 3 Gunners, and 13 Mattrosses to march to Duncannon Fort, and to receive further Orders from the Officer Commanding there.

The Lieut.-Colonel Commandant of Artillery directed to issue the necessary Orders for the Detachments to march on 6th December to their respective Quarters.

NUMBER OF MEN WANTED TO ATTEND THE GUNS.

29th December.—Board of Ordnance.

Read at the Board a Letter from Sir Geo.

Macartney signifying His Excellency the Lord Lieutenant's Desire to be acquainted, whether besides the Detachments which are gone to Limerick and Cork, there are a sufficient number of Men in the Royal Irish Regiment of Artillery to attend and serve the following Pieces of Ordnance, viz.:—

Brass Light	6 Pounders mounted	10
	12 Pounders do.	6
	8 inch Howitzer	1
	4½ inch do.	1
	5½ inch Mortars	6
	4½ inch do.	10

and what number will remain to do duty at Chapel-Izod after furnishing the numbers above mentioned.

Ordered.—A Memorial to be drawn up to His Excellency the Lord Lieutenant representing that there are only 59 effective Men of the Royal Irish Regiment of Artillery now remaining at Chapel-Izod, exclusive of Drums and Fifes, there being still living 31 Invalids of the Old Establishment who were continued for Life in consideration of their having purchased their employments, whose vacancies are filled up as they die. That there will be wanting for the Guns, Howitzers, and Mortars, mentioned in said Letter, 300 Men, so that there will remain wanting 241 Men for attending and serving them only, and there will then be not One Man remaining to do duty at Chapel-Izod. That the Board have, besides the List of the number of Men that will be wanting for the Pieces of Ordnance mentioned in Sir George Macartney's Letter, likewise drawn out a List of the number of Men that will be wanted for the Guns, Howitzers, and Mortars that will remain in Store, and under Orders to be Cast, exclusive of any that may be wanted for duty at Charles Fort, the Magazine Phœnix Park, or for the Duties of Chapel-Izod.

Master General's Warrants.

The Warrants of 1766 to the Bridge Master, Surgeon's Mate, and Quarter Master, were renewed this year by the Earl of Drogheda.

Establishment.

The Establishment continued this year at 228 of all ranks.

1771

AUGMENTATION OF THE ROYAL IRISH ARTILLERY REGIMENT.

29th January.—Board of Ordnance.

To His Excellency, Lord Viscount Townsend,
   Lord Lieutenant General and General Governor of Ireland.

The Memorial of the Earl of Drogheda,

REPRESENTETH,

That Your Excellency having lately ordered that a State should be prepared, and laid before You, of the Annual Expense of Pay for Augmenting the Royal Irish Regiment of Artillery, from its present Numbers, to those of which it consisted previous to the last Reduction, with a View, as Your Memorialist apprehends, to recommend an Augmentation of the said Corps, Your Memorialist thought it incumbent upon him, and accordingly has made the strictest Examination whether an Amendment might not be made to the Establishment which subsisted before the said Reduction.

And it appears to Your Memorialist thereupon that it would be of great Advantage to the Service if the said Regiment should be in a small Degree further Augmented and formed into a Corps of Six Companies of 70 Men each, the exact Number to which the Companies of the Royal Regiment of Artillery in England was lately Augmented. Laying aside as was then done the Rank of Lieutenant Fireworkers, and in lieu of them appointing Second Lieutenants. And Your Memorialist is humbly of Opinion, that the small Additional Expense which would be incurred by this Alteration, would be fully compensated in the Service in many Respects, particularly in admitting of a greater number of Detachments, under the Command of Commission Officers.

Your Memorialist therefore begs Leave to lay herewith before Your Excellency a State of the Annual Pay of the said Regiment as it stood before the Reduction in 1766, and a State of its Annual Pay augmented as now proposed by Your Memorialist to Six Companies, —By which Your Excellency will find that the additional Annual Charge over and above the Establishment of 1766, is only £1,368 15s. 0d., of which £456 5s. 0d. is set down as the Pay of a Colonel Commandant in Case His Majesty upon consideration of the long Services and peculiar Circumstances of the Superior Officers of the said Corps, shall be graciously pleased to promote the Lieutenant Colonel to that Rank, and the other Officers in Succession to him, and have hereunto annexed a Memorial from the Lieutenant Colonel Commandant, Major, and eldest Captain.

And Your Memorialist would particularly recommend in the Formation of any new Establishment, the Appointment of Gentlemen Cadets,* whose Education immediately under the Inspection and Care of the Master General and Board of Ordnance, is not only adapted to the Artillery Service and Corps of Engineers, but must be of Advantage to His Majesty's

---

* The system of appointing Cadets to the Irish Artillery service was abandoned.

General Military Service, when those Gentlemen shall be promoted to other Regiments.

All which is humbly submitted to Your Excellency.

29th January. DROGHEDA.

STATE OF THE ANNUAL PAY OF THE REGIMENT OF ROYAL IRISH ARTILLERY AS IT STOOD BEFORE THE REDUCTION IN 1766, AS ALSO A STATE OF THE PAY OF THE SAID REGIMENT, SUPPOSING IT TO CONSIST OF SIX COMPANIES OF 70 MEN EACH COMPANY.

	Numbers	Annual Pay of the Regiment before the Reduction, 1766			Numbers	Annual Pay of the Regiment Augmented as above		
		£	s.	d.		£	s.	d.
Colonel in Chief	1	—			1	—		
Colonel *en Seconde*	1	—			1	—		
Colonel Commandant	—	—			1	456	5	0
Lieutenant Colonel	1	365	0	0	1	365	0	0
Major	1	273	15	0	1	273	15	0
Captains	4	730	0	0	6	1,095	0	0
First Lieutenants	4	365	0	0	6	547	10	0
Second Lieutenants	4	292	0	0	12	876	0	0
Lieutenant Fireworkers	8	535	6	8	—	—		
Adjutant	1	91	5	0	1	91	5	0
Chaplain	1	121	13	4	1	121	13	4
Surgeon	1	146	0	0	1	146	0	0
Bridge Master	1	91	5	0	1	91	5	0
Quarter Master	1	109	10	0	1	109	10	0
Surgeon's Mate	1	63	17	6	1	63	17	6
Gentlemen Cadets	8	194	13	4	12	292	0	0
Serjeant Major	1	45	12	6	1	45	12	6
Drum and Fife Major	1	24	6	8	1	24	6	8
Serjeants	12	438	0	0	12	438	0	0
Corporals	12	401	10	0	12	401	10	0
Bombardiers	24	730	0	0	18	547	10	0
Gunners	72	1,752	0	0	60	1,460	0	0
Mattrosses	268	4,891	0	0	300	5,475	0	0
Fifers	4	73	0	0	6	109	10	0
Drummers	8	146	0	0	12	219	0	0
		£11,880	15	0		£13,249	10	0
Annual Pay of the Regiment before the Reduction						11,880	15	0
Increase of Expense on the proposed scheme						1,368	15	0

29th January.—

THE MEMORIAL OF LIEUT. COLONEL COMMANDANT DANIEL CHENEVIX, MAJOR JOHN STRATON, AND CAPTAIN RICHARD BETTESWORTH, OF THE ROYAL IRISH REGIMENT OF ARTILLERY.

To the EARL OF DROGHEDA,

Master General of the Ordnance, etc., etc.

REPRESENTING

That Your Memorialist Lieutenant Colonel Chenevix has served His Majesty 26 Years, of which 13 in the said Regiment, nine of them as Lieutenant Colonel Commandant, and purchased all his Commissions except an Ensigncy.

That Your Memorialist Major Straton has served His Majesty in the British and Irish Artillery 29 years, of which as Major, which Commission he purchased above Nine years.

That Your Memorialist Captain Richard Bettesworth has served His Majesty near 26 years, of which 11 years as Captain in the said Regiment, and above Nine the eldest of that Rank.

That altho' the Artillery duty requires more constant Attendance and Experience in general than His Majesty's other Military Service, there is less Opportunity for Promotion in it, than in His Majesty's Regiments either of Cavalry or Infantry; and Preferment in the Royal Regiment of Artillery in England, from its first Formation, has by His Majesty's Gracious and invariable Rule, been confined in Succession within the Corps, in exclusion even of Brevets of Superior Rank, upon the addition of a Fourth Battalion.

That from the Orders lately issued to Your Lordships and the Board of Ordnance, Your Memorialists conceive that an Augmentation is intended to be made to the Regiment of Artillery, and in Case any Alteration shall be made therein, Your Memorialists Pray that Your Lordship will represent them and their Services in such a Manner to His Excellency the Lord Lieutenant as will induce His Excellency to recommend them for the following Promotion, similar to the British Establishment :—

For Lieutenant Colonel Daniel Chenevix to be Colonel Commandant, Major John Straton to be Lieutenant Colonel, and Captain Richard Bettesworth to be Major in the said Regiment.

All which is humbly submitted to Your Lordship,

DANIEL CHENEVIX.
JOHN STRATON.
RICHARD BETTESWORTH.

MUSTER OF INVALID PENSIONERS.

9th April.—Board of Ordnance.

As there cannot be a Muster of the Invalid Pensioners of the Royal Irish Regiment of Artillery, on account of many of them having requested and obtained Leave to live in the Country, and some of them in England; And the Board having taken the same into consideration think it highly requisite that all the said Invalids should send to this Office a Certificate of their being alive as is customary in like Cases.

Ordered.—That Letters be wrote to said Invalids to desire they will every half year send to this Office a

Certificate of their being alive signed by the Minister and Church Wardens of the respective Parishes where they reside, otherwise their Allowances will be stopped.

ALLOWANCE FOR A REGIMENTAL OFFICE.

16th April.—Board of Ordnance.

Received a Memorial from the Adjutant of Artillery, praying the Board will be pleased to grant him some Allowance for a Regimental Office, as the Room in the Barrack where the Regimental business was transacted is pulled down.

Ordered.—That £5 per Annum be allowed for a Regimental Office till an Artillery Barrack is built.

MATTROSSES TRANSPORTED FOR LIFE.

27th June.—Two Mattrosses belonging to the Royal Irish Regiment of Artillery who were tried at the Commission of Oyer and Terminer, and found Guilty of robbery on the highway, between Dublin and Chapel-Izod, received sentence to be executed.—(*Dublin Gazette.*)

13th July.—The two Mattrosses who received sentence to be executed this day, have received His Majesty's pardon on condition of Transportation for Life.—(*Freeman's Journal.*)

GRASS OF THE FORTIFICATIONS.

23rd July.—Board of Ordnance.

Received a Letter from the Commanding Officer of the Royal Irish Regiment of Artillery, acquainting the Board of a Dispute subsisting between the Commanding Officer of the Garrison of Charlesfort, and Lieutenant Atkinson Commanding Officer of the Artillery Detachment, each claiming an indisputable Right to the Grass round the Works of the Fortifications at that Place.

Ordered.—That a Letter be wrote to the Storekeeper at Charlesfort, to desire he will immediately acquaint Major C—— and Lieutenant Atkinson, that by His Majesty's Express Instructions the Fortifications of this Kingdom are under the cognizance of the Master General and Board of Ordnance only ; and that the said Storekeeper do mow and clean the Glacis as usual, and take particular Care that no Cattle on any Pretence whatever be suffered to Graze on any Part of the Works.

FIELD GUN EXERCISE.

7th September.—Board of Ordnance.

Received a Letter from Secretary Waite signifying His Excellency the Lord Lieutenant's Desire that ten Field Pieces attended by a proper Detachment of the Royal Irish Regiment of Artillery be sent to the Magazine in the Phœnix Park in order to instruct the Garrison of Dublin in the Exercise of the Field Guns.

Ordered.—That ten Field Pieces be immediately prepared and sent to the Magazine in the Phœnix Park ; And that Orders be given to the Commanding Officer of the Artillery Regiment at Chapel-Izod for a Detachment to attend said Guns.

Admittance to Storehouses.

27th September.—Board of Ordnance.

Ordered.—That no Person whatever be suffered Admittance into the Carriage Yard, Principal Storehouse, Armory, Upper Storehouse and Carriage sheds within the Castle of Dublin, or Powder Magazine in the Phœnix Park; or any other of His Majesty's Ordnance Storehouses or Magazines in the Kingdom of Ireland, unless such Persons be accompanied by the Master General or One of the Board of Ordnance, or by the Master Furbisher, Clerk of the Works or Clerks to the Principal Officers, or the Storekeepers at the Several Stores and Magazines; And that a Copy of these Orders be fixed up at the different Ordnance, Storehouses and Magazines throughout the Kingdom of Ireland; And a Copy sent to the Commanding Officer of the Royal Irish Regiment of Artillery to be entered in the Orderly Books of said Regiment.

Muster of Detachments.

15th October.—Board of Ordnance.

Ordered.—That Letters be wrote to the Storekeepers at Duncannon, Charlesfort, and Cove of Cork, desiring they will muster the Artillery Detachment at those Places regularly on the First Monday in every Month, and transmit the Muster Rolls immediately to this Office.

Establishment.

The Establishment continued this year at 228 of all ranks.

1772

Butt in the Phœnix Park.

8th May.—Board of Ordnance.

Received a Letter from the Commanding Officer of the Artillery, representing that as the season is approaching for practising the Regiment at long Gun and Mortar, he begs leave to inform the Board that some Alteration will be necessary to be made either in the Butt or Batteries, as a Chapel for the Hibernian School has been lately built in the Rear of the Butt in the Range of the Batteries.

3rd July.—Received a Letter from the Commanding Officer of the Artillery, to acquaint the Board that all the Men off Duty were sent to work to scarp the Ground before the Butt agreeable to Major Vallancey's Report, and that it now appears that there is a great Deal more Earth to be removed than was at first imagined, and that he is of Opinion that One small Battery for two Guns at 300 yards Range will be sufficient for the Practice this year, and will be made at a much smaller Expense.

Ordered.—That the Commanding Officer of the Artillery be acquainted that the Board approves, and desire he will set the Men immediately to work and report when the same shall be completed, and that the Quarter Master do attend and keep an Account of the Men employed.

Hired House for Barracks.

23rd June.—Board of Ordnance.

Received Proposals from Mr. Philip Byrne for setting his House at Chapel-Izod with the Garden behind it and the Out Offices for the Accommodation of the Royal Irish Regiment of Artillery at £70 per Annum, for five years certain at the Board's Pleasure, nevertheless to keep it for Nine Years. Should the Board cut down any of the Trees on the Premises for their Use, Mr. Byrne will expect Payment for them at a fair Valuation.

Resolved.—That as it appears to the Board the said House will be sufficient to lodge all the Non-Commissioned Officers and Men of said Regiment, and much more eligible than their being lodged in different Places as at Present, and less expense, Mr. Byrne's Proposal be accepted of.

29th September.—Board of Ordnance.

Mr. Philip Byrne attended and perfected a Lease to the Board of his House at Chapel-Izod, known by the name of the *King's Arms,* for a temporary Barrack for the Royal Irish Regiment of Artillery.

Ordered.—That Notice thereof be sent to the Commanding Officer of the Artillery Regiment, and a Letter to desire he will issue the proper Orders for the Non-Commissioned Officers and Privates to go into the said Barracks on Saturday* next.

The Regiment Reviewed.

7th August.—Received a Letter from the Com-

* 2nd October, 1772.

manding Officer of the Artillery requesting the Board will Order

> 1200 Twelve ounce Cartridges
> 1350 Tubes
> 24 Dozen Portfires
> 3 Skeins of Slow Match
> and 44 Pound Cartridges

to be delivered to the Quarter Master at Chapel-Izod preparative to the intended Review by His Excellency the Lord Lieutenant.

Ordered.—That said Ammunition be prepared and delivered on Tuesday next.

24th September.—The Royal Irish Regiment of Artillery, commanded by the Right Hon. the Earl of Drogheda, were reviewed in the Phœnix Park by His Excellency the Lord Lieutenant, and went through their Evolutions and Firings to the entire satisfaction of His Excellency, a great number of General Officers and a vast concourse of spectators.—(*Freeman's Journal.*)

ESTABLISHMENT.

The Establishment continued this year at 228 of all ranks.

1773

Cost of Regimental Clothing.

30th April.—Board of Ordnance.

Read at the Board a Letter to the Master General, representing that the Clothing of the Non-Commissioned Officers, Musick and Drummers exceed the Stoppages made from their Pay in the sum of £53 5s. 7d. per Annum, by which means the Clothing Fund is greatly in Debt, and submitting it to His Lordship whether the Clothing of these Men should not be reduced so as to come within the Amount of the Stoppages.

7th May.—Board of Ordnance.

Ordered.—That a Letter be wrote to the Commanding Officer of the Artillery Regiment, to acquaint him, that as the Expense of the Clothing of the Non-Commissioned Officers, Musick and Drummers belonging to the said Regiment at present exceed the amount of their Stoppages in the sum of £53 5s. 7d. per Annum, the Master General and Board have thought it expedient to reduce the Expense of the Clothing of the Serjeants, Corporals, Drum Majors and Drummers, and therefore desire he will as soon as possible get pattern Clothing made (agreeable to a Scheme proposed) calculated upon the most Saving Principle and lay the same before the Master General for his Approbation.

29th July.—Board of Ordnance.

Received from the Commanding Officer of the Artillery Regiment, a Scheme for reducing the Expense of Clothing the said Regiment; And the Clothier being called in he agreed to supply the said Clothing at £64 14*s.* 0*d.* less than the Expense of last year's Clothing, by which there will be a saving of the Stoppages of £21 3*s.* 3*d.* per Annum.

Ordered.—That Contracts be prepared for the Clothier to supply the said Clothing against 1st November next.

New Accoutrements.

29th July.—Board of Ordnance.

The Master General having signified his Desire that a new Set of Buff Accoutrements should be provided for the Artillery Regiment against the Review.

Ordered.—A Warrant to supply the same.

The Regiment Reviewed.

11th August.—His Excellency the Lord Lieutenant reviewed the Royal Irish Artillery Regiment in the Phœnix Park, when they practised with Long Gun, Mortar and Howitzers, to the entire satisfaction of His Excellency, several General Officers, and a vast concourse of spectators.

Cess on Old Barrack.

7th December.—Board of Ordnance.

A Collector for the Barony of Castleknock came to

the Board to demand £1 11*s.* 6*d.* for a Cess applotted on the old Barrack at Chapel-Izod.

Ordered.—That he be informed the said old Barrack and Land belonging thereto were granted by His Majesty for the Royal Irish Regiment of Artillery. That it is still under the Care of the Board of Ordnance, and therefore cannot be subject to any Taxes.

PAYMENTS MADE IN THE TREASURY.

Paid Lord Palmerston, for Rent of a Piece of Ground, near His Majesty's House at Chapel-Izod, formerly used as a Melon Garden, eight years to 29th September, 1772—£28 15*s.* 9*d.*

ESTABLISHMENT.

The Establishment continued this year at 228 of all ranks.

1774

Ordnance, etc., for a Review.

8th July.—Board of Ordnance.

The Secretary to the Board reported that he had received at the Office yesterday An Order from the Lord Lieutenant signifying His Excellency's Desire "That sixteen Light 6 Pounders, two 3 Pounders, and Seven Pontoon Boats with the Royal Irish Regiment of Artillery, and a sufficient Quantity of Ammunition be ordered to attend on such Days as the Commander in Chief shall appoint." And that he had upon Receipt of said Order enclosed a Copy thereof to the Commanding Officer of the Royal Irish Regiment of Artillery.

12th July.—Received a Report from the Quarter Master of the Artillery Regiment, that thirteen Sets of Harness are wanting (in addition to those already delivered) for the Review Day; And eighty-four Horses to be in Readiness for that Service.

Ordered.—That 13 Sets of Harness be delivered accordingly, and that the Contractor for Horses have Notice to provide 84 Horses and 37 Drivers for the Review.

"Record" Review and Sham Fight.

12th-14th July.—A three-days' Review of the Regiments in Dublin by the Lord Lieutenant took place, and as it was a record Military inspection and sham fight in Ireland's capital, the following account of the disposition of the Troops on that occasion may be found interesting :—

Last Thursday, His Excellency the Lord Lieutenant, reviewed in His Majesty's Park the Phœnix, the following Regiments, viz. :—

3rd Regiment of Horse or Carbineers,
Royal Regiment of Artillery,
24th, 35th, 40th, 49th, 53rd, and 57th Regiments of Foot,

who all went through their different Firings and Exercise to the entire satisfaction of His Excellency and all the Principal Officers.

Friday, the same Regiments were again reviewed. The Men were in the Field at $\frac{1}{2}$ after 3 in the morning; they divided into two Bodies, each of whom had a small Train of Artillery, Wagons, etc., and drew up on each side of the Liffey, in order to dispute the Passage. On the arrival of Lord Harcourt, which was at 5 o'Clock in the morning, the Batteries of each little Army (which extended from below Island Bridge to Chapel-Izod) began to play, and the Soldiery kept a continued Firing. One Army attempted to force a Passage both at Island and Chapel-Izod Bridges, and were repulsed at both Places. A Party of the repulsed then filed off, crossed Lucan Bridge without Opposition, possessed themselves of the Heights near Knockmaroon-hill, and threw a floating Bridge over the River of Pontoons or Tin Boats, which they defended from their Eminences while their Foot, Cannon, Baggage Wagons and Horse crossed it, who then drove the opposite Army into the Phœnix Park, where they formed on the Side of a deep Valley; here a smart Cannonading and Firing ensued, but they were again obliged to retreat, and were pursued to the Fifteen Acres, where they rallied, were broke and pursued by the Horse, who fell into an Ambuscade of Light Infantry, that fired so smartly on them, as to oblige them to retreat and give up the Pursuit. It lasted almost eleven hours; the variety of water, wood, hill, and dale, on the scene of Action, affording a Display of every possible situation an Army could fall into, which, added to so novel and noble Exhibition, could not fail of giving infinite satisfaction to the spectators. General Elliot, who conducted it, gave a grand cold Collation in the Wood to His Excellency the Lord Lieutenant and the Officers. There were five Tables laid out in a most elegant manner, surrounded with festoons of flowers and garlands, and a fine Band of Music. In short the Day concluded, and joy appeared in the countenance of the numerous spectators, being so highly entertained by a Sight that never was seen before in the Kingdom.

And Saturday, the Royal Regiment of Artillery only was reviewed; after which the Officers belonging thereto gave His Excellency Lord Harcourt, General Elliot and other Officers, an elegant Entertainment at Candy's in Church Street.—(*Dublin Journal.*)

GUNPOWDER FOR SALUTES.

6th September.—Board of Ordnance.
Received a Report from the Adjutant of the Artil-

lery, that 710 Pounds of Powder will be wanting to prepare Cartridges at the Salute Battery for the following Days,

viz. :—

	lbs.
22nd September—Their Majesties' Coronation	142
23rd October—Irish Rebellion	142
25th ,, The King's Accession	142
4th November King William's Birthday	142
5th ,, Gun Powder Plot	142
	710

Ordered.—That a Warrant be drawn up for the Storekeeper to deliver the Same.

PROOF HOUSE IN DUBLIN CASTLE.

8th November.—Board of Ordnance.

As frequent complaints have been made to the Board of Ordnance of the very inconvenient Situation of the Proof House in the Lower Castle-yard being so near to the Inhabitants of Ship Street, Stephen Street, and George's Lane; And His Excellency the Lord Lieutenant having been spoke to thereupon, He was pleased to signify His Approbation to the Surveyor General of the Ordnance that the said Proof House should be removed to the Phœnix Park behind the Salute Battery.

Ordered.—That the Clerk of the Works have Notice to cause the said Proof House to be removed as soon as the Weather will permit.

The Rank of Fireworkers Abolished.

DUBLIN CASTLE, 14*th December*, 1774.

His Majesty hath been pleased to grant the Rank of Second Lieutenant to the following Gentlemen who were Lieutenant Fireworkers in the Royal Irish Regiment of Artillery, and Commissions are come over accordingly,

viz: :—

John Robison, Gent.
William Smith, Gent.
William Wright, Gent.
John D. Arabin, Gent.

—(*Dublin Gazette.*)

Establishment.

The Establishment continued this year at 228 of all ranks.

1775

Proof House in Dublin Castle.

28th February.—Board of Ordnance.

Ordered.—That the Commanding Officer of the Artillery be acquainted that the Board intend immediately to remove the Proof House (for proving Small Arms) from the Lower Castle-yard to the Back of the Salute Battery in the Park, agreeably to His Excellency the Lord Lieutenant's Permission, And that therefore they desire he will issue Orders to the Persons who may from Time to Time command the Guard at the said Battery to be very attentive in preventing any of the Materials that may be sent thither for the Building, from being stolen.

Pontoon Boats.

2nd June.—Board of Ordnance.

Read a Memorial to His Excellency setting forth that in the year 1760, there were provided for the Use of the Army in this Kingdom ten Pontoon Boats with their Carriages and Apparatus. That as these Boats were the first that were made in Ireland, and the Persons who made them quite Strangers to that Sort of Business, they were not completed in that permanent Manner they ought to be, but by some Repairs and Alterations since made to them they are now in Condition to be made Use of whenever the Service may require; But as the number of ten

Pontoon Boats would be very insufficient for crossing most of the Rivers in this Country, should any be required, the Board beg Leave to represent the Number they have in Store, and submit it to His Excellency whether it will be necessary to provide any further Number.

VOLUNTEERS TO SERVE IN AMERICA.

16th August.—Fourteen Private Men of the Regiment of Blue Horse on Dublin duty, and forty-seven Men of the Royal Irish Regiment of Artillery, went to the Castle and offered themselves as Volunteers, to serve in the Royal American Army under General Gage.—(*Dublin Gazette.*)

RECRUITING IN CORK.

16th August.—In connexion with recruiting, it is interesting to compare the Official Advertisements on the subject, noted in previous pages, with the artifices adopted at this time to attract Recruits in the South of Ireland.

On the 16th August, Major Boyle Roche,* Representative in Parliament for Tralee (who is raising a Body of Men for his Majesty's Service), began recruiting in Cork, and met with great success, which is not surprising, if we consider his connexions, and the uncommon support he has received from the Noblemen and Gentlemen of the Province. His method of enlisting was as uncommon, as it was pleasing to those who viewed the Procession, which was as follows :—

* Celebrated as a perpetrator of " bulls."

Major Roche, bearing a large Purse of Gold,
Captain Cowley,
A great number of likely Recruits,

An elegant Band of Music, consisting of French Horns,
Hautboys, Clarionets, and Bassoons, playing
"God Save the King."

A large Brewer's Dray with five Barrels of Beer, the
Horse richly caparisoned and ornamented
with Ribbons,
Two Draymen with Cockades, to serve the Beer,

The Recruiting Serjeant,
Drums and Fifes,
Another Division of Recruits,
The Recruiting Soldiers,
A Prodigious concourse of Spectators.

Speeches were then made by Major Roche to the Populace.

. . . . . .

—(*Dublin Journal.*)

Lodging Allowance to Officers.

29th September.—Board of Ordnance.
Ordered.—That the Commanding Officer of the Royal Irish Regiment of Artillery be acquainted that no Officer absent from Quarters is to be allowed Lodging Money, Coals and Candles, after the 1st January, 1776.

Establishment.

The Establishment continued this year at 228 of all ranks.

1776

Discharged Men for Garrison Duty.

20th February.—Board of Ordnance.

Received an Order from His Excellency the Lord Lieutenant, directing the Board to order the several discharged Men of the Artillery Regiment to be examined by the Surgeon of said Regiment, and that such of them as upon examination shall appear to be fit for Garrison Duty be acquainted that they may be incorporated into the Company of Invalids which are to be formed in this Kingdom, but that if they shall decline that Service, they are no longer to receive any Provision from the Board of Ordnance.

24th February.—

Royal Irish Regiment of Artillery.

Whereas His Excellency the Lord Lieutenant has signified to the Board of Ordnance, that such Men who now receive their Pensions, or Men discharged and not provided for, who may be entitled to Pensions, on account of their service in said Regiment, as shall appear to be fit for Garrison duty, should be incorporated into the Companies of Invalids which are to be formed in this Kingdom, and that any of them who shall decline that Service are no longer to receive or be entitled to any provision whatsoever. This is therefore to require and command all such Men as above specified, to appear before the Officers appointed to examine them, on Thursday, the 14th of March, at Chapel-Izod.

Signed by Order of the Commanding Officer,

LUCIUS BARBER,
Adjutant.

Chapel-Izod,
24th February, 1776. —(*Dublin Gazette.*)

DEATH OF LIEUT.-COLONEL CHENEVIX.

15th March.—Board of Ordnance.

Received a Letter from Lieut. Colonel Straton, Major of the Royal Irish Artillery Regiment, to acquaint the Board that Lieut. Colonel Chenevix[*] died this morning.

PROMOTION OF MAJOR STRATON.

5th April.—

Promotions in Royal Irish Regt. of Artillery.

Major J. Straton [†] to be Lieut. Colonel, *vice* Chenevix, deceased.—(*Dublin Gazette.*)

"DUBLIN GAZETTE" NEWS.

27th March.—Dublin Castle.

Whereas His Majesty hath been pleased to signify His Royal Pleasure that for the future the *Dublin Gazette* shall as nearly as possible be put on the same footing with the *London Gazette,* and that it shall contain no other articles of news than such as are author-

---

[*] For services of Colonel Chenevix, see Memorial of the Senior Officers in Events of the year 1771, previous pages.
[†] Major Straton was the Officer of the British Artillery who organised the first Company of the Royal Irish Artillery, in 1756.

ised by His Majesty's Government of this Kingdom: or duly authenticated: . . . .

By His Excellency's Command,

W. ROSEINGRAVE.

INVALIDS UNFIT FOR GARRISON DUTY.

3rd May.—Board of Ordnance.

Received from the Adjutant of the Artillery Regiment, a List of eleven Invalids who attended, and were upon examination found quite unfit for Service.*

Ordered.—That they be continued upon the Pension List.

COALS FOR GUARD HOUSES.

31st May.—Board of Ordnance.

Read a Representation from the Subaltern Officers of the Artillery Regiment that the Guard Houses at the Magazine and Salute Battery having no allowance of Coals for the Summer Months, the Officers who mount those Guards are very uncomfortably situated as they have no means of Dressing Dinner and are obliged to send a considerable Distance every night to Light Candles, and therefore pray the Board will be pleased to take the same into Consideration.

Ordered.—That the Quarter Master of the Artillery Regiment deliver Half Allowance of Coals for the Magazine and Battery Guards from 1st April to 30th September in every year, to commence 1st June next.

SUPPLY OF GUNPOWDER.

4th June.—Board of Ordnance.

Received a Letter from Mrs. Susanna Chenevix,

* See official notification, 24th February, 1776, in previous pages.

Executrix to Lieut. Colonel Chenevix, in Answer to the Board's Letter of 30th May, acquainting them that Mr. Arabin has most humanely at his own Expense for the Benefit of the Minor undertaken the Conducting the Gunpowder Manufactory, and will give the Board every Information in his Power.

Ordered.—Letter to Mr. Arabin requesting he will inform the Board (as soon as possible) whether he intends to Contract with them for supplying Gun Powder for his Majesty's Service as the late Lieut. Colonel Chenevix did, and in what Time he would make a delivery.

11th June.—Received a Letter from Henry Arabin, Esqre. . . . to acquaint the Board that he will engage to deliver one hundred Barrels of Powder before the last day of July, and afterwards one hundred Barrels Monthly for the space of One Year at the same Price the late Lieut. Colonel Chenevix received.

Ordered.—The Board accept his Proposal to deliver one hundred Barrels of Powder at a Time, for which he shall be paid on Delivery at the Rate of £6 6s. 6d. per Barrel, the price which was paid to the late Lieut. Colonel Chenevix.

ARTILLERY PRACTICE.

21st June.—Notice.

The Royal Irish Regiment of Artillery will commence Long Gun, Mortar, and Howitzer Practice in the Phœnix Park, on Monday the 24th Instant, and during the Hours of Practice each day, a Flag will be erected on the Butt.—(*Dublin Gazette.*)

Pay to a Lieutenant out of Contingencies.

26th July.—Board of Ordnance.

Received a Memorial from the Commanding Officer of the Artillery, representing that by the Death of the late Lieut. Colonel Chenevix, Mr. John Hill was appointed from Half Pay Cadet, to be a Second Lieutenant, that he is unfortunately without any Pay and must continue so during the Life of Lieut. Colonel Rutter, who retired fourteen years ago on his Pay, unless the Honb. Board is pleased to consider his situation as was done in three Instances before, from the Master General's and the Board's great Humanity.

And the Master General having signified his Approbation that Pay should be allowed to Lieutenant Hill out of the Contingencies from the Date of his Commission.

Ordered.—That the Treasurer of the Ordnance pay Lieutenant Hill of the Royal Irish Regiment of Artillery 3*s.* 8*d.* per Day, the same to commence from the 15th March the Date of his Commission, and to be charged to Account of Contingencies 'till further Orders.

The Regiment Reviewed.

30th July.—The Right Hon. the Earl of Drogheda, Master General of the Ordnance, reviewed the Royal Irish Regiment of Artillery in the Phœnix Park, when the Regiment performed a variety of evolutions and firings with cannon and small arms, together with Howitzer and Mortar practice, and went through the whole entirely to His Lordship's satisfaction; after which the Corps had the honour of being entertained by His Lordship at Chapel-Izod.

PROOF HOUSE AT SALUTE BATTERY.

12th November.—Board of Ordnance.
Ordered.—That an Advertisement be inserted in

> *The Gazette,*
> *Dublin Journal,*
> *Freeman's Journal,* and
> *Saunders's News Letter,*

setting forth that the Principal Officers of His Majesty's Ordnance give this publick Notice, that they have ordered a Flag to be hoisted at the Proof House at the Salute Battery in the Phœnix Park, whenever any small Arms are to be proved there, which Signal they hope will be a sufficient Caution to all Persons not to ride too near the said Proof House at such Times and be the Means of preventing any Accident that might happen by Horses starting.

DETACHMENT TO CORK.

29th November.—Board of Ordnance.
Received a Letter from Secretary Waite, signifying His Excellency the Lord Lieutenant's Desire that a Detachment of the Royal Irish Regiment of Artillery, consisting of a Subaltern Officer and twenty Men do march to the Cove of Cork, and remain quartered there until further Orders.

The Shortage of Duty Men at Head Quarters.

17th December.—Board of Ordnance.

Received a Letter from the Commanding Officer of the Artillery representing that the late Command to the Cove of Cork, the Recruiting Service, and non-effective Gunners have so reduced the Duty Men of the Regiment, that the private Men seldom have more than One night out of three in Bed, and praying the Board will take the same into Consideration.

Ordered.—That Officer Commanding be acquainted that the four gunners vacancies may be immediately filled up, and the Board desire he will lay before them a State of the Regiment.

Allowance to Invalids.

20th December.—Board of Ordnance.

Received an Order from Lord Lieutenant, signifying His Excellency's Approbation that the Board allow Six-pence per Day to such of the Invalids of the Artillery Regiment as are or may be hereafter entitled to Bounty and unfit for any service, and Three-pence per Day to such Others as may appear by their Length of Servitude entitled to His Majesty's Bounty, and to charge the Same in the Annual Account of the Incidental Expenses of the Regiment, taking Care that the Charge of the said Bounty to Invalids shall never exceed the Sum of £200 per Annum, but be as much under it as possible.

Establishment.

The Establishment continued this year at 228 of all ranks.

1777

Draft for North America.

The first employment of the Royal Irish Artillery on Foreign Service was in the American War.

25th February.—Board of Ordnance.

Received an Order from His Excellency the Lord Lieutenant signifying His Majesty's pleasure that Seventy Drafts of the Irish Artillery should be incorporated into the British, and for the immediate march of the said seventy Drafts to Cork, where they are to be received by an Officer sent from Great Britain, and where they are to embark for North America.

3rd March.—A Draft of seventy Mattrosses, from the Royal Irish Regiment of Artillery, young, able, active fellows, marched off the parade of the Barrack at Chapel-Izod for Cork, there to embark on His Majesty's Service for America. They all went off in high spirits, and expressed the warmest ardour to face the Enemies of their King and Country. So laudable an emulation prevailed through the whole Corps, that many more than the number wanting gallantly offered themselves Volunteers on the occasion.—(*Dublin Journal.*)

Levy Money and Clothing for Recruits.

25th March.—Board of Ordnance.

Received a Letter from the Commanding Officer of the Artillery acquainting the Board that he had made Application to the Principal Officers of the Ordnance in England for an Allowance for Levy Money and for Clothing for Recruits to be raised in Lieu of the seventy Drafts, and that he had obtained five Guineas Levy Money for each Draft, and Six Months' Clothing Stoppage for a Mattross.

Ordered.—Letter to Commanding Officer to acquaint him that the Board are much surprised he made any Application in England relative to Levy Money and Clothing for Recruits to be raised in Lieu of the seventy Drafts, these matters being a particular Part of the Official Duty of the Master General and Board, and that as soon as the Drafts are embarked they propose laying before the Lord Lieutenant an Estimate of the Expense of the Ordinary and Extraordinary Clothing for seventy Men.

Draft for North America.

8th April.—Board of Ordnance.

Ordered.—Letter to Captain Jones of the British Artillery, Commanding the seventy Drafts of the Irish Artillery at Cork, requesting he will please to inform the Board what Time the said Drafts commence upon English Pay.

15th April.—Received a Letter from Captain Jones of the Royal British Artillery, dated at Cork the 11th April, acquainting the Board that the Drafts of the Irish Artillery would probably embark the next Day, and that they were to be paid their Subsistence on the Irish Establishment to the Day of their Embarkation.

25th April.—Received a letter from the Commanding Officer of the Artillery, to acquaint the Board that the seventy Drafts from the Regiment embarked on board the *Royal George* for foreign Service on Saturday, the 12th Instant, and that there will be wanting seventy Suits of Clothes for the Recruits to succeed them.

RECRUITING FOR THE REGIMENT.

18*th April.*—The following Official Notification appeared in the *Dublin Gazette*.

Chapel-Izod, 18th April, 1777.

Whereas the few vacancies in the Royal Irish Regiment of Artillery are ordered to be filled up immediately. This is to give Notice, that if any Man not under the size of 5 feet 9 inches nor above 6 feet, nor under 18 Years of Age, or exceeding 25, being strong and well made, and are willing to serve in said Regiment, they may repair to Lieutenant Barber at Chapel-Izod, or to the Ordnance Office in the Lower Castle Yard.

.   .   .   .   .   .

CANNON FOR REVIEW DAYS.

16*th May.*—Board of Ordnance.

Received a Letter from the Right Hon. Secretary Heron signifying His Excellency the Lord Lieutenant's Desire that One Piece of Cannon with a proper Detachment of the Artillery Regiment do join the Regiments of the Garrison of Dublin in the Phœnix Park on their practising and Review Days.

Ordered.—That a Copy of said Letter be sent to the Commanding Officer of the Artillery Regiment.

Ordnance and Stores at Pigeon House.

1st August.—Received a Letter from Secretary Heron signifying His Excellency the Lord Lieutenant's Desire that the Ordnance and Stores with the Party of Artillery be forthwith removed from the Pigeon House.

Ordered.—That a Copy of said Letter be sent to the Commanding Officer of the Artillery Regiment.

Supply of New Arms.

8th August.—Board of Ordnance.

Received a Letter from the Commanding Officer of the Artillery Regiment representing that the Arms of the said Regiment are become unserviceable, and praying the Board will be pleased to Order a new Set of Arms for the Regiment now mostly Recruits, to enable him to shew them with Advantage to His Excellency the Lord Lieutenant.

Ordered.—That a Letter be wrote to Officer Commanding, to acquaint him that the Board are much surprised at his Application for new Arms, as it is not quite five years since a new Set was delivered them, and that the Board have no Fund at this Time to provide any Arms for the Artillery Service.

Ordnance and Stores at Light House.

15th August.—Received a Letter from Secretary Heron signifying His Excellency the Lord Lieutenant's Desire that the Ordnance, Stores, etc., at the Light House be forthwith removed.

Ordered.—That the Commanding Officer of the Artillery Regiment be acquainted therewith.

ORDERS AT FIELD AND REVIEW DAYS.

15th August.—Board of Ordnance.

Received a Letter from the Right Hon. Secretary Heron signifying His Excellency the Lord Lieutenant's Desire that the Royal Irish Regiment of Artillery do obey whatever Orders they may receive from the Commander-in-Chief during the practising of the General Field and Review Days.

Ordered.—That a Copy of said Letter be sent to the Commanding Officer of the Artillery Regiment.

MAGAZINE AND SALUTE BATTERY GUARDS.

26th August.—Received a Letter from the Commanding Officer of the Artillery Regiment to acquaint the Board that said Regiment is now complete and ready to take the Magazine and Salute Battery Guards as soon as the Reviews of the Garrison of Dublin is over.

Read a Letter to Secretary Heron to acquaint him thereof, and to request he will move His Excellency the Lord Lieutenant to issue such Orders for the Artillery Regiment to take the said Guards as he may think proper.

OFFICERS ON GUARD.

26th September.—Board of Ordnance.

Received a Letter from the Subaltern Officers of the Royal Irish Regiment of Artillery who lately had the Duty at the Light House, etc., setting forth the extraordinary Expense they were unavoidably at being obliged to pay a very extravagant Price for their Provisions, and therefore praying the Board will be pleased to take the same into Consideration; And the Surveyor General being of Opinion that as this was a very extraordinary Service attended with considerable Expense to the Officers, they may be allowed a Day's Pay extra on the Days they mounted Guard, but not to be brought as a Precedent in Future.

Ordered.—That the Officers who mounted the Guards at the Light House and Pigeon House be allowed a Day's Pay extra.

RETURN OF RECRUITS RAISED.

17th December.—Board of Ordnance.

Return of Recruits raised in the Royal Irish Regiment of Artillery, to replace Men Discharged, Deserted, Dead, and Drafted, from the 29th September, 1774, to the 29th September, 1777, Inclusive.

From 29 September, '74, to 28 September, '75	30
29 September, '75, to 28 September, '76	41
29 September, '76, to 29 September, '77 Inclusive	104
Total	175

N.B.—Seventy of the above Number were recruited to fill up the Vacancies of those Incorporated in the British Artillery serving in America in the Spring of 1777.

RICHARD BETTESWORTH, *Major*,
Royal Irish Artillery.

GALLANT BEHAVIOUR OF DRAFT SENT TO AMERICA.

23rd December.—The conduct in the Field of the Irish Artillerymen sent to America was highly meritorious and honourable, as is shewn by the following extract of a Letter from the Master General of the British Ordnance to the Officer Commanding the Royal Irish Regiment of Artillery :—

23rd *December*, 1777.
SIR,

By Lieutenant Slack, who this evening arrived from Quebec, and who has related to me many transactions of the late unfortunate campaign in that part of America, I am informed, that none among our gallant troops behaved more nobly than the drafts from the Irish Artillery, who being now exchanged, are to return. I am sorry they have suffered so much, but it is the lot of brave men who, so situated, prefer a glorious discharge of their duty to an unavailing desertion of it. Be assured, Sir, I have a sincere and grateful pleasure in doing this justice to part of that Corps, whose zeal for His Majesty's service, and ambition to distinguish themselves, I have never doubted, would be equal to any whatever.

TOWNSEND.
—(*Freeman's Journal.*)

General Phillips's Report.

As the Men of the Royal Irish Artillery did duty with the British Artillery during the War, and formed part of the force under Major General Phillips, we give the following extract from the report made by him to Lords Townsend and Amherst, dated Albany, 22nd October, 1777 :—

" I have to report to you, my Lords, that the Corps of Artillery which I commanded has acted during the

Campaign with the greatest spirit, and has received the entire approbation of General Burgoyne, and the applause of the Army. In the action of the 19th September the Artillery was of infinite use; and a brigade commanded by Captain Jones, with Lieutenants Hadden and Reid, was particularly engaged, and maintained their post to the last, although in doing of it every man, except five, was either killed or wounded. Captain Jones was killed.

"In the affair of October 7th, Major Williams kept a Battery in action, until the Artillery horses were all destroyed, and his men either killed or wounded; being unable to get off their guns, he was surrounded and taken, with two Officers, Lieutenants York and Howorth, the latter wounded. Captain Blomefield, my Major of Brigade, was also wounded on the 7th Instant, at Major Williams' battery. I cannot sufficiently commend the activity, zeal, and spirit of the Officers. The same gallant spirit remained to the last day when the Convention was signed. I had the honour to deliver a message to the Lieutenant-General from the Corps of Artillery, that they were as ready as ever to undergo any hardships, or to undertake any difficulties, for the King's service. Under this description, allow me to recommend the Corps to Your Lordship's protection, and humbly request that you will represent their conduct to His Majesty."—(*Freeman's Journal.*)

ESTABLISHMENT.

The Establishment continued this year at 228 of all ranks.

1778

Volunteers for North America.

6th January.—A few days ago, one hundred and fifty Men of the Royal Irish Regiment of Artillery waited upon the Lord Lieutenant at the Castle, to request His Excellency would obtain His Majesty's permission for their being sent to America to serve during the present War. They were graciously received, and a promise given that their request should be immediately laid before His Majesty.

—(*Freeman's Journal.*)

Detachments to Charlesfort and Duncannon Fort.

10th March.—Board of Ordnance.

His Excellency the Lord Lieutenant having signified to the Surveyor General of the Ordnance his Desire that a Detachment of the Royal Irish Regiment of Artillery, consisting of one Subaltern Officer, one Serjeant, one Bombardier, one Drummer, one Fifer, and twenty private Men do march this day to Charlesfort; and also a like Detachment to Duncannon fort.

Ordered.—Letter to the Commanding Officer of the Artillery Regiment to acquaint him thereof, and to desire he will give the necessary Orders for the said

Detachments to march this Day to Charlesfort and Duncannon fort.

13th March.—Received a Letter from the Commanding Officer of the Artillery Regiment representing that there are many Recruits in the Parties sent to Duncannon fort, Charlesfort, and Cove of Cork, and that he is of opinion it would be requisite that the Serjeant Major, and a Drill Serjeant should be sent round to those Garrisons to instruct the Men in the exercise and firing of the Garrison Guns.

Ordered.—That the said Commanding Officer be acquainted the Board desire he will send the Serjeant Major and a Drill Serjeant to the said Garrisons immediately.

17th March.—Ordered, That ten Guineas be paid to the Serjeant Major and Drill Serjeant who are ordered to proceed to Duncannon fort, Charlesfort, and Cove of Cork, on Account of their travelling charges.

A RETURN OF THE REGIMENT.

13th March.—Board of Ordnance.

MY LORDS AND GENTLEMEN,

The Detachments of Artillery that have lately marched to the several Garrisons have left the Regiment so weak and insufficient for any material Service that I find it indispensable to represent our Situation to the Honble. Board.

The Return I have the honor to enclose will show that, including Officers and Staff, we have now present and fit for duty but 108 Men, from which deduct the Officers and Staff, the Non-Commissioned Officers, Fifers, and Drummers, there will remain but 74 Private Men, most of whom are Recruits; and if our Barrack Guard, the men working at the Laboratory, the Sick, Absent, etc., are deducted, there will be hardly Men enough left to Man four Light six Pounders.

As Our Numbers so reduced appear to me very inadequate to the Duty that may be required of the Regiment; I hope the Honble. Board may think it proper to represent our Weakness to Government.

I have, etc.,

J. STRATON, Lieut.-Colonel.

Commanding Royal Irish Artillery.

Chapel-Izod,
 18th March, 1778.

[TABLE.

RETURN OF THE ROYAL IRISH REGIMENT OF ARTILLERY, CHAPEL-IZOD, 13th March, 1778.

	Commissioned Officers							Staff Officers						Non-Commissioned Officers						Rank and File			Total
	Colonel in Chief	Colonel en Seconde	Lt. Col. Commandant	Majors	Captains	First Lieutenants	Second Lieutenants	Chaplain	Adjutant	Quarter Master	Bridge Master	Surgeon	Surgeon's Mate	Serjeant-Major	Drum Major	Serjeants	Corporals	Drummers	Fifers	Bombardiers	Gunners	Mattrosses	
Present and fit for Duty			1	1	3	3	2	1	1	1		1	1	1	1	3	7	1	2	5	31	43	108
Sick {Infirmary																				1		2	3
Sick {Quarters																				2		3	5
Absent {By Leave							1																1
Absent {Without Leave	1	1				1	3				1									1	2	3	13
In Garrisons																			2			3	3
Invalids							3									1	1	3		4	3	57	74
Vacant																						18	18
Total	1	1	1	1	4	4	8	1	1	1	1	1	1	1	1	4	8	4	4	12	36	132	228

J. STRATON, Lieut.-Colonel Commandant,
Royal Irish Regiment of Artillery.

13*th March.*—Board of Ordnance.

Received a Letter from the Commanding Officer of the Royal Irish Regiment of Artillery, enclosing a State of the Regiment, in which he sets forth that there are only 108 Men at Chapel-Izod, of which, after deducting the Officers and Staff, Non-Commissioned Officers, Fifers, and Drummers, there remain no more than 74 Privates, and therefore hopes the Board will be pleased to present the weak state of the Regiment to Government.

Ordered.—That a Memorial be drawn up to His Excellency the Lord Lieutenant enclosing the Commanding Officer's Report, and submitting the same to His Excellency's Consideration.

AUGMENTATION TO THE REGIMENT.

3*rd April.*—Board of Ordnance.

Received a Letter from the Right Hon. Secretary Heron to acquaint the Board that it being intended that an Augmentation shall be made to the Royal Irish Regiment of Artillery, and that the Same in Case His Majesty shall approve thereof shall extend to Six Companies, to consist in the whole of 500 Men exclusive of Commissioned Officers and Staff Officers, and that His Excellency desires the Board will immediately prepare a List of the said proposed Regiment with the Expense attending the completing the Same.

Read at the Board a Memorial to His Excellency the Lord Lieutenant enclosing a List of the said proposed Regiment of Artillery, and the Annual Expense of Pay for the Same, with an Estimate of the Expense of Arms, Accoutrements, Clothing, and Levy Money that will be wanting to complete the Augmentation.

ANNUAL EXPENSE OF THE ARTILLERY REGIMENT.

3rd April.—ESTIMATE OF THE EXPENSE OF A REGIMENT OF SIX COMPANIES OF ROYAL IRISH ARTILLERY (83 MEN TO EACH COMPANY) PROPOSED TO BE RAISED IN LIEU OF THE PRESENT REGIMENT OF FOUR COMPANIES OF 50 MEN EACH.

		Full Pay per Diem for each			Full Pay per Diem for the whole			Full Pay per annum for the whole		
		£	s.	d.	£	s.	d.	£	s.	d.
1	Colonel in Chief Master General of the Ordnance				Without Pay					
1	Colonel *en Secondé* Lieut. General of the Ordnance									
1	Lieut. Colonel Commandant	1	0	0	1	0	0	365	0	0
1	Major	0	15	0	0	15	0	273	15	0
6	Captains	0	10	0	3	0	0	1,095	0	0
1	Captain Lieutenant	0	6	0	0	6	0	109	10	0
5	First Lieutenants	0	5	0	1	5	0	456	5	0
12	Second Lieutenants	0	4	0	2	8	0	876	0	0
1	Chaplain	0	6	8	0	6	8	121	13	4
1	Adjutant	0	5	0	0	5	0	91	5	0
1	Quarter Master	0	6	0	0	6	0	109	10	0
1	Bridge Master	0	5	0	0	5	0	91	5	0
1	Surgeon	0	8	0	0	8	0	146	0	0
1	Surgeon's Mate	0	3	6	60	3	6	63	17	6
1	Serjeant Major	0	2	6	0	2	6	45	12	6
12	Serjeants	0	2	0	1	4	0	438	0	0
12	Corporals	0	1	10	1	2	0	401	10	0
18	Bombardiers	0	1	8	1	10	0	547	10	0
48	Gunners	0	1	4	3	4	0	1,168	0	0
390	Mattrosses	0	1	0	19	10	0	7,117	10	0
1	Drum Major	0	1	4	0	1	4	24	6	8
12	Drummers	0	1	0	0	12	0	219	0	0
6	Fifers	0	1	0	0	6	0	109	10	0
					38	0	0	13,870	0	0
	Full Pay of the Present Regiment							7,196	11	8
	Annual Expense of Pay for the Augmentation							£6,673	8	4

The Cannon at Salute Battery.

7th April.—The Cannon lately taken from the Salute Battery in the Phœnix Park, where they had remained thirty years, formerly belonged to the Dublin Privateer. They are 9 Pounders, and esteemed even at this day, the finest Iron Ordnance in the British Dominions.—(*Dublin Journal.*)

Barrack Accommodation.

24th April.—Board of Ordnance.
Ordered.—Letter to the Commanding Officer of the Royal Irish Regiment of Artillery to desire he will inform the Board how many Men the Barrack at Chapel-Izod will accommodate, and whether any and what number can be lodged in the Old Barrack.

5th May.—Received a Return from the Quarter Master of the Artillery by which it appears that when the Regiment is completed there will be Lodgings wanted for 327 Men.

Detachments to Cork and Clonmel.

27th April.—Board of Ordnance.
Received a Letter from Secretary Heron, signifying His Excellency the Lord Lieutenant's Desire that

>two Howitzers,
>two 8 Pounders, and
>two short 6 Pounders

with a Detachment of the Royal Irish Regiment of Artillery, be in Readiness to join the Troops near Cork.

That two Howitzers, ten Field Pieces, and some Pontoons with a Detachment of the same Regiment be in Readiness to join the Troops near Clonmel, and that a large quantity of Ammunition for Small Arms be made up and carried with the Artillery.

Ordered.—That the Commanding Officer of the Artillery be acquainted with the proposed March of these two Detachments and the Number of Guns and Howitzers that are to go with each Command, and that he be desired to make a Return to the Board of the Number of Men he intends to send on each Command that the necessary Camp Equipage may be got ready.

Augmentation to the Regiment.

5th May.—Board of Ordnance.

Received a Letter from Secretary Heron, acquainting the Board that His Excellency having transmitted to Lord Weymouth the Plan for Augmenting the Royal Irish Regiment of Artillery which they had laid before him, His Majesty had been pleased to approve thereof.

The Commissions of the Officers added and promoted by the Augmentation, bore date the 21st April, 1778.

From that date the Senior First Lieutenant of the Regiment bore the rank of Captain Lieutenant.

A Captaincy was conferred upon a Lieutenant from 12th Dragoons, and two Subalterns from the Corps of Engineers of Ireland were made First Lieutenants.

Recruits Enlisted.

12th May.—Board of Ordnance.

No. 1.—Return of Recruits enlisted for the Royal Irish Regiment of Artillery, commencing 1st April, 1778.

	Present	Not Joined	Total
At Chapelizod	172	—	172
Derry	—	28	28
Antrim	—	11	11
Strabane	—	8	8
Down Patrick	—	7	7
Newry	—	5	5
Lisburn	—	3	3
Cork	—	2	2
Total	172	64	236

No. 2.—Received Bounty Money

from Government for	88 Recruits
Captain Handcock has furnished for	none
Lieutenant Shewbridge ditto	none
Lieutenant Nash ditto	none
Mr. Robert Straton	30
Richard Bettesworth	30
St. George Robison	30
Nenon Armstrong	30
—— Moore	30
	238

Remains Levy Money due
for . . . 60
———
Total Augmentation 298

J. STRATON, Lieut.-Colonel
  Comdg. R. Irish Artillery Regt.

NON-COMMISSIONED OFFICERS TO WOOLWICH.

12th May.—Board of Ordnance.

Received a Letter from the Commanding Officer of the Artillery Regiment, requesting Leave to send two Non-Commissioned Officers to Woolwich, to learn some useful Improvements in the Artillery Exercise.

Ordered.—That he be acquainted that the Board have no Objection and that they will allow Double Pay to the Non-Commissioned Officers who shall be sent upon that Duty.

DETACHMENTS TO CLONMEL AND KINSALE.

29th May.—Board of Ordnance.

Received a Letter from Secretary Heron to acquaint the Board,

That 1 Captain, 50 Artillerymen, and a Proportion of Subalterns and Non-Commissioned Officers will be ordered to Kinsale.

That a Field Officer, Lieut.-Colonel Straton of the Artillery Regiment, will be ordered to the Camp at Clonmel with Directions to superintend the Detachments at Kinsale, Charlesfort, Cove, and Duncannon fort.

That as the Artillery Men in Camp will require much Practice, a sufficient Allowance of Stores for that Purpose is to be made.

7th July.—Board of Ordnance.

Received a Letter from the Commanding Officer of the Artillery representing that it will be necessary that a Detachment of 1 Subaltern, 1 Serjeant, 1 Corporal, 2 Bombardiers, and 26 Privates do march on the 9th Instant, with the two 6 Pounders to Clonmel.

And 1 Captain, 3 Subalterns, 1 Serjeant, 1 Corporal, 4 Bombardiers, 1 Drummer and 66 Privates to march on the 16th Instant to Clonmel on their way to Kinsale.

And also that 1 Captain, 3 Subalterns, 1 Serjeant, 1 Corporal, 4 Bombardiers, 1 Drummer and 74 Privates to march on the 17th Instant to Clonmel Camp.

Ordered.—That the said Detachments be prepared to march on the Days specified in Commanding Officer's Letter.

THE REGIMENT REVIEWED.

15th June.—The Royal Irish Regiment of Artillery, Commanded by Lieut. General Charles Earl of Drogheda, were all drawn up in the Castle-yard, by the desire of His Excellency the Lord Lieutenant for his inspection. They are reckoned to be the finest Corps in this Kingdom, and now consists of 500 Men. They were before only 800.*—(*Dublin Journal.*)

HALBERTS FOR SERJEANTS AND CORPORALS.

17th July.—Board of Ordnance.

Received a Letter from the Commanding Officer

* Should be 200.—AUTHOR.

of the Artillery Regiment requesting the Board will be pleased to Order 24 Halberts for the Serjeants and Corporals in Lieu of Carbines, and also 25 Sashes for their Use.

Ordered.—That said Particulars be provided.

AUGMENTATION TO THE REGIMENT.

4th August.—Board of Ordnance.

Received an Order from His Excellency the Lord Lieutenant (with a copy of His Majesty's Letter bearing Date the 2nd of July last), for discontinuing upon the Ordnance Establishment from the 1st April, 1778, inclusive, the present established Numbers of the Royal Irish Regiment of Artillery together with their Pay amounting to the Annual Sum of £7,196, 11s. 8d., and for placing upon the said Establishment in Lieu thereof, from the same Day inclusive, the said Regiment augmented to 500 Men amounting to £13,870, 0s. 0d.

7th August.—Ordered a Letter to the Commanding Officer of Artillery enclosing a List of the new Establishment of the said Regiment on the 1st April last inclusive, pursuant to His Majesty's Letter of 2nd July—Also to acquaint him that His Majesty has been pleased to grant Levy Money at £2, 8s. 3½d. per Man for the Augmented Numbers amounting to £719, 10s. 11d.

DETACHMENT TO BELFAST.

31st August.—Board of Ordnance.

Received a Letter from Sir Richard Heron, signifying His Excellency the Lord Lieutenant's Desire that two Light 6 Pounders with a proper quantity of Ammunition be sent forthwith to Belfast to be disposed of in such manner as Colonel Luttrell should think proper, and that a Detachment of the Royal Irish Regiment of Artillery under the Command of an experienced Officer do march with the said Light 6 Pounders and put themselves under the command of the said Colonel Luttrell.

FLOATING BATTERIES FOR DUBLIN HARBOUR.

11*th September*.—Board of Ordnance.

Received a Letter . . . enclosing a Letter from John Boddington, Esqre., Secretary to the Board of Ordnance in England, giving an Account that two strong Vessels had by His Majesty's Command been purchased and fitted out to serve as floating Batteries for the Defence of this Harbour, . . .

Read a Memorial to His Excellency, setting forth that the Board have been on Board the said Vessels, and beg leave to represent that the *Britannia* has 18 12-Pounders and twelve Seamen exclusive of Officers, the *Hibernia* 16 9-Pounders with eleven Seamen. That they are humbly of Opinion the Number of Men on board the said Vessels is insufficient for Manning the Guns in Case of Actual Service, and submit it to His Excellency's consideration whether a proper Number of the Military should not be stationed on board each Vessel for Manning the Guns in case of actual Service.

18*th September*.—Board of Ordnance.

Read a Memorial to His Excellency representing that

as the said Vessels can be considered only as a fixed Battery, and require no other Naval attendance than what may be done by the number of Seamen contracted for in England, the Board are of Opinion, that the undermentioned Number of the Military will be sufficient at Present for the Harbour Duty, to be under the Direction of the Non-Commissioned Officer of Artillery, viz. :—

For the *Britannia*,
    1 Non-Commissioned Officer
and 9 private Men of the Artillery
    1 Non-Commissioned Officer
and 18 private Men from the Garrison of Dublin.

29 Total.

For the *Hibernia*,
    1 Non-Commissioned Officer
and 8 private Men of the Artillery
    1 Non-Commissioned Officer
and 16 private Men from the Garrison of Dublin.

26 Total.

And that the Board are further of Opinion that Bedding and Utensils should be provided and sent on board by the Commissaries of the Barracks; and in Regard to subsisting the Men, they cannot suggest a more eligible Mode than their being Victualled by the Masters of each Ship.

6th October.—Board of Ordnance.
Received a Letter . . . that the Lord Lieu-

tenant has directed the Commander-in-Chief to give
Orders for the Parties from the Garrison of Dublin
to hold themselves in readiness to embark on board
the *Britannia* and *Hibernia* Guard Ships, and that
the said Parties are to be commanded by the Non-
Commissioned Officer of the Artillery Regiment : the
Detachment of Artillery to embark at the same Time
with the Parties from the Garrison of Dublin.

That His Excellency also desires that sixpence per
day, extraordinary Pay for each Man, during the
Time of his being employed on that Duty, may be
issued to the Non-Commissioned Officer of Artillery :
And that His Excellency has directed the Commissaries of the Barracks to cause Bedding and Utensils
to be provided for the Use of the said Parties and
Detachments.

6th November.—Board of Ordnance.

Received a Letter . . . the Lord Lieutenant's
Desire that the Artillery Detachments do embark on
board the *Britannia* and *Hibernia* Guard Ships at
12 o'Clock on Saturday next (7th) and that Boats be
provided for conveying the said Parties from the
Pigeon House to the said Vessels accordingly.

Ordered.—That Letter be written to the Commanding Officer of the Artillery to desire he will order the
Detachments to march to the Pigeon House to-morrow
morning.

13th November.—Board of Ordnance.

Received a Letter . . . the Lord Lieutenant's
Desire the Board contract with the Masters of the
Britannia and *Hibernia* for Victualling the Troops on
board the said Vessels at the Rate of Tenpence a Day

for each Man, and that the Extra Allowance of Sixpence a Day be discontinued. And the Masters of the said Vessels having agreed to Victual the Men at Tenpence per Day for each Man.

Ordered.—Warrant to Mr. George Jenkins, Master of the *Britannia*, to Victual 29 Men; and a Warrant to Mr. John Newins, Master of the *Hibernia*, to Victual 26 Men.

LEVY MONEY OF RECRUITS.

29th September.—Board of Ordnance.

Received a Letter from Sir R. Heron signifying His Excellency the Lord Lieutenant's Desire, that in stating the Account of Levy money for the late Augmentation of the Royal Irish Regiment of Artillery, Care be taken that no Charge is made for the Levy Money of 150 Recruits which were to be raised by the five Second Lieutenants who were appointed on the said Augmentation, it being upon the Terms of raising thirty Men each, that those Gentlemen were to receive their Commissions.

Ordered.—That a Copy of said Letter be sent to the Commanding Officer of the Artillery.

ORDNANCE CAST IN IRELAND.

8th October.—A great number of brass Mortars and Howitzers have lately been cast and bored at our Arsenal. They are of the new construction, and extremely beautiful. These, with the cannon landed from England about three weeks ago, have furnished us with a Train of Ordnance sufficient for any emergency.—(*Freeman's Journal*.)

DETACHMENTS AT CHARLESFORT AND CLOGHEEN.

8th December.—Board of Ordnance.

Received a Letter from the Commanding Officer of the Artillery, representing that as the Detachment of the Artillery from the Camp near Kinsale are quartered at Charlesfort, it appears to him unnecessary to keep any longer in that Fort the Subaltern's Detachment that was ordered there in February last. That he is therefore of opinion that it tend much to the Good of the Regiment if the Detachments of Artillery at Charlesfort and Clogheen were each reduced to the strength of a Company, and to consist for the Future of 1 Captain, 1 First Lieutenant, 2 Second Lieutenants, 2 Serjeants, 2 Corporals, 2 Drummers, 1 Fifer, 3 Bombardiers, and 73 private Men, and all over that Number to be ordered to join the Regiment at Chapel-Izod.

11th December.—Received a Letter signifying His Excellency the Lord Lieutenant's Approbation that the Detachment of Artillery at Charlesfort and Clogheen should be reduced to the strength of a Company at each Place agreeable to the Board's Memorial of the 4th Instant.

ESTABLISHMENT.

Two Companies being added this year, the total of all ranks stood at 584.

1779

Floating Batteries for Dublin Harbour.

19th January.—Board of Ordnance.

Received a Memorial from the Superintendents of the Guard Ships in the Harbour of Dublin, setting forth that at the Time they agreed to Victual the Detachments at the small Allowance of ten pence per Day, and give each Man two Pounds of beef they could provide that Article for twopence per pound.

That the Price of Beef is now risen to threepence halfpenny by which they are losers and therefore submit their case to the Board's consideration.

Ordered.—That the said Superintendents be acquainted that when beef is twopence per Pound the Men are to have two pounds each, and when threepence and upwards they are to have One pound and a Half.

21st May.—Board of Ordnance.

Ordered.—Letter to the Commanding Officer of the Artillery to desire he will Order a proper Officer to Command the Detachments on Board the Floating Batteries in Dublin Harbour.

Detachments to Carrickfergus, etc.

21st May.—Board of Ordnance.

Ordered.—That a Letter be wrote to the Commanding Officer of the Artillery to desire he will order proper Detachments to march to-morrow morning with the undermentioned Guns to Carrickfergus, etc., viz. :—

    4 Light 6 Pounders to Carrickfergus,
    2   ditto -   Galway.

That he will also prepare proper Detachments to march as soon as possible from Clogheen with the undermentioned brass Guns and their Stores from that Place to Waterford, Youghal, and Limerick, viz. :—

    4 Light 6 Pounders to Waterford,
    2   ditto   Youghal,
    2   ditto   Limerick.

That the Officers appointed to those several Commands should be perfectly informed of their Duty and must wait on the Commanding Officers of the Troops at the places of their Destination and follow such Orders as they shall receive from Time to Time.

That in removing the Men from the Detachment now at Clogheen, a sufficient number with an Officer be left there to guard the Artillery and Stores that will remain when those mentioned above are sent away.

THE MAGAZINE GUARD.

12th June.—Board of Ordnance.

MY LORD AND GENTLEMEN,

Having laid before my Lord Lieutenant your letter dated the 9th instant, enclosing a letter to you from the Commanding Officer of the Artillery, representing that there are only two Subaltern Officers at Head Quarters, and they being both sick it is not possible to mount an Officer's Guard at the Magazine in the Phœnix Park, I have His Excellency's Command to signify to you His Desire that the said Guard be mounted under the Direction of a Careful Non-Commissioned Officer of the Artillery Regiment until there shall be a sufficient Number of Subaltern Officers fit for duty.

I have, etc.,

J. HAMILTON.

The Board of Ordnance.

AUGMENTATION TO THE REGIMENT.

8th July.—Board of Ordnance.

MY LORD AND GENTLEMEN,

His Excellency My Lord Lieutenant proposing to recommend it to His Majesty, That an Augmentation of Thirteen Mattrosses be made to each Company of the Royal Irish Regiment of Artillery, His Excellency desires you will immediately prepare a List of the said Regiment including the said proposed Augmentation with the Expense attending the completing the same, and the Annual Expense that will attend the Augmentation.

I have, etc.,

J. HAMILTON.

The Board of Ordnance.

Detachment to Limerick.

6th September.—Board of Ordnance.

My Lord and Gentlemen,

His Excellency My Lord Lieutenant desires you will forthwith send ten Brass Medium 12 Pounders and two $5\frac{1}{2}$ inch Howitzers with a proper Quantity of Ammunition to Limerick to be mounted on Temporary Batteries to be formed on the River Shannon for the purpose of Securing the East India Ships now lying in the said River, from any Attempt that may be made by the Enemy, and that an Officer of the Royal Irish Regiment of Artillery, with as many Men as can be spared, do proceed with the said Guns to Limerick: And upon your acquainting me when they shall be in readiness, an Escort of Fifty Men from the Garrison of Dublin will be ordered to attend them.

I have, etc.,

R. Heron.

The Board of Ordnance.

Condition of the Salute Battery.

12th November.—A Report of the state and condition of the Salute Battery, furnished to the House of Commons, contains the following:—

The Salute Battery in the Phœnix Park is in good condition. There has not been any money laid out upon the said Battery from the 1st November, 1769, to the

1st November, 1779, except very small repairs to the roof and windows of the Guard House.

The Proof House for small arms has been lately removed from the Lower Castle-yard and rebuilt within the walls of this Place, but the expense thereof is not brought to the account of the Salute Battery.

ESTABLISHMENT.

A State of the Ordnance Establishment from 31st March to 1st October, 1779.

An Augmentation is ordered to be made to the Artillery Regiment of Seventy-eight Mattrosses, which when placed on the Establishment of the Ordnance, will make an increase thereto of £1,423 10s. 0d. per Annum, to commence from the 16th August last.—(*Journals of the Commons, 1st November,* 1779.)

The Establishment on the 1st April, 1778, was 84 Officers and 500 Non-Commissioned Officers and Men, and the addition of 78 Mattrosses this year raised the total of the Establishment to 612 of all ranks.

1780

Floating Batteries in Dublin Harbour.

21st November.—Received a Letter . . . the Lord Lieutenant's Desire that the Board should report what Accommodations are provided for the Detachments on board the Guard Ships, and whether anything and what remains further to be done to make their Situation as convenient as the Service will permit, and also whether the Harbour of Dublin derives real Security from these Guard Ships, and whether they should not be otherwise modelled and constructed and in what Manner and at what Expense.

Read a Memorial to His Excellency representing that the Accommodations which were provided for the Detachments consist of Hammocks with the necessary Bedding which were all that was reported to the Board as necessary for the Detachments, and they are furnished with Provisions by the Superintendent of the Ships at ten-pence per Diem, that the Bedding and Victualling for those Detachments are the whole belonging to the said Ships for which the Board have ordered any Payment to be made;

That the Board do not know of anything further in their Department that can be done, the said Ships having been sent from England and being the Property of the British Ordnance by whom they are paid, the Board have not considered them as any Part of the Irish Ordnance.

That the Board having consulted Lieut. Colonel Vallancey, he is of Opinion that the Fear of Opposition has prevented many Privateers from attempting to cut out Ships at Poolbeg, but that a King's Cutter stationed in the Bay or Harbour of Dublin would be of much greater Use and not more Expensive than the Guard Ships.

Lieut.-Colonel Straton Promoted.

In November, Lieut. Colonel Straton was promoted to the rank of Colonel in the Army.

Establishment.

The Establishment continued this year at 612 of all ranks.

1781

Detachment to Cork.

3rd April.—Board of Ordnance.

Ordered.—That six Medium 12 Pounders be sent to Cork immediately with One Subaltern, two Non-Commissioned Officers, and thirty Men of the Royal Irish Regiment of Artillery.

6th April.—His Excellency also desires that the Detachment of Artillery at Clogheen, except one Serjeant and twelve Men be ordered to march without Loss of Time to Cork, and put themselves under the command of General Mocher.

Company of Invalids.

27th April.—Board of Ordnance.

Received a Letter . . . enclosing a Copy of a Letter from the Earl of Hillsborough (in Answer to the Master General's Memorial relative to the Difference between the Establishment of the Royal Regiment of Artillery in Great Britain and that in Ireland), and signifying His Excellency's Desire that a Report be made to him whether any and what Part of the Artillery Service in this Kingdom can be performed by Invalids, and if any Part can that an Establishment be laid before him of One or more Companies of Invalids, to be added to the Royal Irish Regiment of Artillery as a Provision for Officers worn Out in the Service.

Ordered.—That a Copy of said Letter be sent to the Commanding Officer of the Artillery Regiment, with Directions to report to the Board thereupon.

GUNPOWDER FOR PRACTICE.

12th June.—Board of Ordnance.

Received a Letter . . . the Lord Lieutenant's Orders that the Board report to him what Allowances of Powder are made to the Artillery Regiment for their Practice, etc., and whether any Saving can be made on this Article.

26th June.—Read a Memorial to the Lord Lieutenant, . . . and the Board beg Leave to represent that they never issued any Orders to deliver Powder for the Practice of the Artillery Detachments at any of the Out Garrisons, and that when the Practice with Field Guns has been at any Time carried on in Dublin, the Commanding Officer of the Regiment always certifies the Quantity of Powder that will be wanted and is always accountable to the Board for what is issued, and any Redundancy is constantly returned into Store, but there is no stated Allowance of Powder made to the Artillery Regiment for Practice or any other Service whatever.

THE BOARD OF ORDNANCE EFFICIENT AND CORRECT.

10th July.—Board of Ordnance.

Mr. Keen laid before the Board, the following Letter which he received from General Cunninghame :—

SIR,

I was favoured with your Letter of the 26th June

when I was in the Country, enclosing one from Lieut. Colonel Vallancey endeavouring to explain away the Charge he seemed to have brought, and which I am sure he did not intend against the Board of Ordnance.

I have sent it to Mr. Eden for the Information of the Lord Lieutenant, and have thought it but Justice to the Board of Ordnance on this Occasion to declare that of all the publick Boards that ever came within my knowledge, the Board of Ordnance in Ireland is the most efficient, the most correct and the most zealous for the King's Service.

I am, etc.,

ROBERT CUNNINGHAME.

QUALIFICATIONS OF ARTILLERY OFFICERS.

14th August.—Board of Ordnance.

Received an Order from the Lord Lieutenant for the Board to report to him what Course of Education and what Qualifications are most particularly adapted to render an Officer Useful in the Artillery Service, in Order that if the same should be approved, proper attention may be paid thereto as well in the Recommendation of Gentlemen for Second Lieutenants as in their Course of Discipline, Instructions and Service, after having received their Commissions.

DETACHMENT TO CASTLEBAR.

21st September.—Board of Ordnance.

Received an Order from the Lord Lieutenant for a

Detachment of the Royal Irish Regiment of Artillery, with two 5½ inch Howitzers, two 6 Pounders, and fifty Rounds of Ammunition, to march forthwith to Castlebar, there to be under the Command of the Officer Commanding His Majesty's Forces at that Place who is ordered to be aiding and assisting to the Sheriff of the County of Mayo with the Forces under his Command in the Execution of a Writ lately issued from the Court of Chancery for liberating the Person of George Fitz Gerald, Esquire, who has been illegally detained by his Son.

IMPROVEMENT IN THE METHOD OF FIRING.

28th September.—Board of Ordnance.

Received a Letter . . . the Lord Lieutenant's Consent that Captain Pratt's Improvement in the Method of Firing the Battery Guns with Shot be adopted.

Ordered.—That Notice thereof be immediately sent to the Commanding Officer of Artillery at Chapel-Izod.

ESTABLISHMENT.

The Establishment continued this year at 612 of all ranks.

1782

Proportion of Ammunition.

11th January.—Board of Ordnance.

Received a Letter . . . enclosing a Copy of a Letter from Lord Hillsborough to the Lord Lieutenant, mentioning that the Field Trains in England have 300 Rounds of fixed Shot ready, and that the Irish Field Trains should have the same Proportion. That every private Soldier has 60 Rounds ready with Powder and Ball, and Paper for 60 Rounds more, and a Million of Cartridges are kept ready made in the Tower, besides a Proportion in the Out Ports.

Augmentation to the Regiment.

31st May.—Board of Ordnance.

Received an Order from the Lord Lieutenant for placing upon the Ordnance Establishment from the 1st of April last an Addition of

> 1 Serjeant,
> 1 Corporal,
> and 3 Bombardiers

to each Company of the Royal Irish Regiment of Artillery.

A further addition of one Second Lieutenant to each of the six Companies from the 13th April, raised the total of the Establishment to 648 of all ranks.

Floating Batteries in Dublin Harbour.

21st June.—Board of Ordnance.

Received a Letter . . . the Lord Lieutenant's Desire that the Board issue the necessary Orders to the Superintendent of the *Britannia* Guard Ship to put her Guns and Ordnance Stores on Shore, and lodge them in His Majesty's Magazine, in Dublin, in order that the said Ship may be made a Receptacle for such Men as Captain McBride may direct to be sent on board, and to continue in this State until further Orders.

Ordered.—That the necessary directions be immediately sent to the Superintendent of the *Britannia*;

And a Letter to the Commanding Officer of the Artillery to desire he will immediately withdraw the Artillery Detachment.

Detachments in Cork Harbour.

17th December.—Board of Ordnance.

Received from the Barrack Master of Cork, an Account of Coals and Candles and sundry Bedding and Utensils supplied for the Artillery Detachments in the Harbour of Cork from the 1st June, 1781, to the 1st June, 1782, with several Barrack Masters Charges therein for taking care of the Bedding, etc.

Ordered.—Letter to acquaint Mr. Lawe that there is no Barrack Master allowed for the Artillery Regiment; That the Ordnance Storekeepers at the several Places where Artillery Detachments are quartered act as Barrack Masters for which particular Service they never receive any Allowance or Gratuity whatever, as it has always been considered as a Part of the Duty of the Ordnance Storekeeper.

The Board therefore desire he will please to deliver into the charge of Mr. Cope, (Ordnance Storekeeper at Cove) all the Beds, Bedding, and Utensils belonging to the Artillery Detachments in Cork Harbour, taking Mr. Cope's Receipt for the same, which he must transmit to the Board as a Voucher to his Account.

1783

1st March.—RETURN* OF THE ROYAL IRISH REGIMENT OF ARTILLERY, COMMANDED BY THE EARL OF DROGHEDA, MASTER GENERAL OF THE ORDNANCE, FOR THE MONTH OF FEBRUARY, 1783.

		Present and Fit for Duty	On Command	Aide-de-Camp to the Lord Lieutenant	Under Arrest at Cove of Cork	In Bedlam	Sick Present	Sick Absent	Absent by Leave	Invalids	Total Effective
Commissioned Officers	Colonel in Chief	—	—	—	—	—	—	—	1	—	1
	Colonel en Seconde	—	—	—	—	—	—	—	1	—	1
	Lieut. Colonel Commandant	1	—	—	—	—	—	—	—	—	1
	Major	1	—	—	—	—	—	—	—	—	1
	Captains	2	3	1	—	—	—	—	—	—	6
	Captain Lieutenants	—	1	—	—	—	—	—	—	—	1
	First Lieutenants	—	5	—	—	—	—	—	—	—	5
	Second Lieutenants	10	5	—	1	—	—	1	1	—	18
Staff Officers	Chaplain	1	—	—	—	—	—	—	—	—	1
	Adjutant	1	—	—	—	—	—	—	—	—	1
	Quarter Master	1	—	—	—	—	—	—	—	—	1
	Bridge Master	—	1	—	—	—	—	—	—	—	1
	Surgeon	1	—	—	—	—	—	—	—	—	1
	Surgeon's Mate	1	—	—	—	—	—	—	—	—	1
Non-Commissioned Officers	Serjeant Major	1	—	—	—	—	—	—	—	—	1
	Serjeants	8	10	—	—	—	—	—	—	—	18
	Corporals	7	11	—	—	—	—	—	—	—	18
	Drum Major	1	—	—	—	—	—	—	—	—	1
	Drummers	7	5	—	—	—	—	—	—	—	12
	Fifers	4	2	—	—	—	—	—	—	—	6
Rank and File	Bombardiers	3	33	—	—	—	—	—	—	—	36
	Gunners	21	25	—	—	—	—	1	1	—	48
	Mattrosses	88	331	—	—	1	7	—	4	14	445
Total		159	432	1	1	1	7	2	8	14	625
Non-Effectives, 6 Mattrosses, Wanting to complete, 17 Mattrosses		—	—	—	—	—	—	—	—	—	23
Total of the Establishment		159	432	1	1	1	7	2	8	14	618

* Return in Record Office, Dublin.

1st March.—Detachments included in the Return.

Places Detached to	Captains	Captain Lieutenants	First Lieutenants	Second Lieutenants	Serjeants	Corporals	Drummers	Fifers	Bombardiers	Gunners	Mattrosses	Total
Cove of Cork	1	–	–	1	1	–	–	–	1	1	5	10
Spike Island	–	–	1	–	1	1	1	–	2	1	31	38
Ramhead	–	–	1	–	1	1	–	–	3	3	30	39
Carlisle Fort	1	–	–	1	1	2	1	1	6	5	57	75
Roche's Tower	–	–	1	–	–	1	–	–	2	–	31	35
Cork	–	–	1	1	2	1	1	–	5	2	30	43
Charles Fort	–	1	–	1	2	1	1	–	5	8	48	67
Clogheen	–	–	–	–	1	–	–	–	1	2	10	14
Duncannon Fort	1	–	1	–	–	1	1	1	3	–	25	33
Passage Waterford	–	–	–	1	–	1	–	–	1	–	24	27
Tarbert Fort	–	–	–	1	1	–	–	–	1	–	19	22
Attached to the 4th Regiment	–	–	–	–	–	–	–	–	2	2	5	9
Attached to the 32nd ,,	–	–	–	–	–	1	–	–	1	–	8	10
Attached to the 49th ,,	–	–	–	–	–	1	–	–	–	1	8	10
Total	3	1	5	6	10	11	5	2	33	25	331	432

Batteries in Cork Harbour, etc.

7th March.—Board of Ordnance.

A State of the several Batteries in Cork Harbour and the Southern Ports of this Kingdom, specifying the Number of Guns, Howitzers and Mortars mounted on each Battery, with the Detachment of Artillery stationed at each, viz. :—

Batteries in Cork Harbour, etc.		No.	Detachments
Spike Island — Iron Guns — 24 Pounders		18	1 Subaltern Officer
Brass Mortars — 8 inches		1	2 Non-Com. Officers
There is a Barrack for the Detachment of Artillery.			35 Men.
Roche's Tower.—Iron Guns — 24 Pounders		12	1 Subaltern Officer
			2 Non-Com. Officers
A Barrack for the Detachment of Artillery.			33 Men
Ramhead — Iron Guns — 24 Pounders		8	
18 do.		5	
12 do.		6	1 Subaltern Officer
Brass Howitzers — 8 inches		1	2 Non Com. Officers
5½ do.		4	36 Men
A Barrack for the Detachment of Artillery			
Carlisle Fort — Iron Guns — 24 Pounders		20	
12 do.		10	1 Captain
6 do.		30	1 Subaltern Officer
Brass Mortars — 8 inches		2	3 Non-Com. Officers
5½ do.		12	70 Men
A Barrack for the Detachment of Artillery.			
Cove of Cork.—No Guns at this Place			1 Captain
			1 Subaltern Officer
The Artillery Detachment is lodged in the Infantry Barracks.			1 Non-Com. Officer
			7 Men
Duncannon Fort.—Iron Guns — 24 Pounders		10	1 Captain
18 do.		10	1 Subaltern Officer
			1 Non-Com. Officer
There is a small Artillery Barrack for 24 Men, but not any apartments for an Officer.			30 Men
Passage — Iron Guns — 24 Pounders		5	1 Subaltern Officer
12 do.		3	1 Non-Com. Officer
A Barrack for the Detachment of Artillery.			25 Men
Charles Fort — Iron Guns — 24 Pounders		11	1 Captain
			1 Subaltern Officer
There is a small Artillery Barrack for 32 Men, but no apartments for an Officer.			3 Non-Com. Officers
			62 Men
Island of Tarbert.—Iron Guns — 24 Pounders		8	1 Subaltern Officer
A Barrack for the Artillery Detachment.			21 Men

R. WARD.   J. KEEN.

THE KNIGHTS OF ST. PATRICK.

14th March.—Board of Ordnance.

The Lord Lieutenant desires you will issue the necessary Orders for a Captain, 3 Subalterns, and 100 Privates of the Royal Irish Regiment of Artillery to put themselves under the command of the Commanding Officer of the Garrison of Dublin on Monday next, the 17th Instant, at such hour as the Commanding Officer of the Garrison shall appoint, to assist the Regiments on Dublin Duty in lining the Streets on account of the Installation of the Knights of St. Patrick.*

THE INVALID COMPANY.

28th March.—Board of Ordnance.

TO THE RIGHT HON. EARL OF DROGHEDA,
    Master General of the Ordnance and Colonel in
        Chief of the Royal Irish Regt. of Artillery.

The Memorial of Colonel Straton,
    Lieut Colonel Commandant of the Royal Irish
        Artillery,

Humbly Representeth,

That there are at present twenty-seven Invalids who are worn out or disabled in the Regiment and now paid a bounty of sixpence and threepence per Day by the Ordnance.

That when the Reduction takes place there will be likewise twenty-seven more who from length of Service or by hurts received in the Service will be entitled to bounty.

Your Memorialist humbly apprehends the best mode of providing for the above Invalids of the Royal Irish Regiment of Artillery will be to form them into

---

* The Order of St. Patrick was instituted in February this year by King George III.

a Company as in the annexed Scheme by which Your Lordship will see that the Pay of the several Ranks is much inferior to the pay of the same Rank of Invalids in the British Artillery.

Your Memorialist humbly apprehends an Invalid Company formed on so economical a Plan may be of great utility to His Majesty's Service, as it will be a Provision for four Officers either worn out or disabled in the Service, and as at present our Invalids are of no sort of use by not being formed into a Company, but by this Scheme those who are most able may be detached to the Garrisons or Batteries, and others employed in the Laboratory.

Your Memorialist therefore hopes your Lordship will see the necessity of the above Scheme, and that you will be pleased to recommend it to His Excellency the Lord Lieutenant.

J. STRATON, Lt. Col : R.I.R. of Artillery
(Colonel Brevet).

Chapel-Izod,
    28th March, 1788.

10th April.—Board of Ordnance.

MY LORD,

  .   .   .   .   .   .

I lost no time in laying Your Excellency's said Letter and the Papers above-mentioned before the King, and I have received His Majesty's Command to acquaint you that he entirely agrees with Your Excellency in the Utility, Justice and Humanity of the Measure, and that He very much prefers this mode of Provision for Captain Robison and other worn out Officers of the Irish Artillery to any other that has been before recommended. Your Excellency will therefore cause the arrangement immediately to take place in the manner you have proposed.

I have, etc.,

NORTH.

His Excellency
    The Lord Lieutenant of Ireland.

DETACHMENT TO CARLOW.

4th April.—Board of Ordnance.

The Lord Lieutenant desires you will issue the necessary Orders for two 6-Pounders with a proper quantity of Ammunition and a suitable Detachment of the Royal Irish Regiment of Artillery to march forthwith to Carlow, the Officer Commanding the Detachment to obey such Orders as he shall receive from General Luttrell, Commanding at Kilkenny.

THE INVALID COMPANY.

1st July.—Board of Ordnance.

. . . have received Your Excellency's Warrant bearing Date the 23rd past for placing upon the Ordnance Establishment in this Kingdom from the 1st April last, an Invalid Company to be added to the Royal Irish Regiment of Artillery, and have issued the necessary Orders for carrying Your Excellency's commands into immediate Execution.

The Invalid Company consisted of :—

    1 Captain (David Robison)
    1 First Lieutenant (Nenon Armstrong)
    1 Second Lieutenant (William Grey)
    1 Serjeant
    2 Corporals
    1 Drummer
    3 Bombardiers
    4 Gunners
  39 Mattrosses
  ——
  53   Total

The Commissions of the Officers appointed to the Company bore date the 26th May, 1783.

This addition raised the total of the Establishment to 701 of all ranks.

REDUCTION OF THE REGIMENT.

Whitehall, 16th *September*, 1783.

MY LORD,

I have had the Honor to lay before the King Your Excellency's Letter of the 7th of last month enclosing a Memorial of the Earl of Drogheda, Master-General of His Majesty's Ordnance in Ireland, and a Scheme annexed for the Reduction of the Royal Regiment of Artillery in that Kingdom, and I am commanded to acquaint Your Excellency that His Majesty is pleased to approve of the Mode of Reduction therein recommended, and that in consideration of the Merit and faithful Services of Colonel Straton, Commandant of that Regiment, His Majesty has been pleased to consent that his Pay shall be augmented to Forty Shillings per Diem agreeably to the Recommendation of the Master General.

Your Excellency will therefore take immediate Measures for carrying into Execution His Majesty's Gracious Intentions with regard to the Reduction of the said Regiment, and I have the Honor herewith to transmit to Your Excellency the final Reply from the Chairman and Deputy Chairman of the East India Company respecting such Men as may be discharged in consequence of that arrangement.

I am, etc.,

NORTH.

His Excellency,
    The Lord Lieutenant of Ireland.

233

3rd October.—AN ESTABLISHMENT FOR THE ROYAL IRISH REGIMENT OF ARTILLERY, AS IT NOW STANDS, AFTER THE REDUCTION, 1ST OCTOBER, 1783.

	Full Pay per Diem for each		Full Pay per Diem for the whole			Full Pay per Annum for the whole		
	s.	d.	£	s.	d.	£	s.	d.
1 Colonel in Chief	—		—			—		
1 Colonel *en Seconde*	—		—			—		
1 Colonel Commandant	40	0	2	0	0	730	0	0
1 Lieutenant Colonel	20	0	1	0	0	365	0	0
1 Major	15	0	0	15	0	273	15	0
6 Captains	10	0	3	0	0	1,095	0	0
6 Captain Lieutenants	6	0	1	16	0	657	0	0
6 First Lieutenants	5	0	1	10	0	547	10	0
6 Second Lieutenants	4	0	1	4	0	438	0	0
1 Chaplain	6	8	0	6	8	121	13	4
1 Adjutant	5	0	0	5	0	91	5	0
1 Quarter Master	6	0	0	6	0	109	10	0
1 Bridge Master	5	0	0	5	0	91	5	0
1 Surgeon	8	0	0	8	0	146	0	0
1 Surgeon's Mate	3	6	0	3	6	63	17	6
1 Serjeant Major	2	6	0	2	6	45	12	6
6 Serjeants	2	0	0	12	0	219	0	0
12 Corporals	1	10	1	2	0	401	10	0
18 Bombardiers	1	8	1	10	0	547	10	0
248 Gunners	1	0	12	8	0	4,526	0	0
1 Drum Major	1	4	0	1	4	24	6	8
6 Drummers	1	0	0	6	0	109	10	0
6 Fifers	1	0	0	6	0	109	10	0
			29	7	0	10,712	15	0
Invalid Company.								
1 Captain	10	0	0	10	0	182	10	0
1 First Lieutenant	5	0	0	5	0	91	5	0
1 Second Lieutenant	4	0	0	4	0	73	0	0
1 Serjeant	1	10	0	1	10	33	9	2
2 Corporals	1	8	0	3	4	60	16	8
3 Bombardiers	1	4	0	4	0	73	0	0
4 Gunners	1	0	0	4	0	73	0	0
39 Mattrosses	0	9	1	9	3	533	16	3
1 Drummer	0	9	0	0	9	13	13	9
Total Annual Amount of Full Pay for the Royal Irish Regt. of Artillery as it now stands, including the Invalid Company (net)			32	9	2	11,847	5	10

By this reduction, five Second Lieutenants were placed on Half Pay, and 310 Non-Commissioned Officers and Men discharged the Service.

The total of the Establishment fell from 701 to 386 of all ranks.

Promotions.

Lieut. Colonel and Brevet Colonel J. Straton was promoted to the rank of Colonel Commandant; the Major (R. Bettesworth) was advanced to the Lieutenant-Colonelcy,

and the Senior Captain (W. Brady) to the Majority.

The First Lieutenants bore from this time the rank of Captain Lieutenant, and six of the Second Lieutenants were promoted to the rank of First Lieutenant.

Two hundred Mattrosses were advanced to Gunner's Pay and called Gunners, and the appellation of Mattross was abolished in the Marching Companies.

PETITION FROM THE DISCHARGED MEN.

14th October.—Board of Ordnance.

. . . In Answer to which I have the honour to acquaint the Board that the Non-Commissioned Officers and Private Men have been allowed, ever since the Regiment was formed, Money in Lieu of a part of their Clothing, called Small Mounting. The Non-Commissioned Officers 15*s*. each, the Drummers, Fifers, and Private Men 10*s*. each, which has been regularly paid to them. That since the King's Order for White Waistcoats, the Board have allowed each Non-Commissioned Officer and Private Man 1*s*. 6*d*. Waistcoat Money, which Allowance from that time, has been regularly paid to them, with the Half or

Small Mounting Money, the Non-Commissioned Officers having since the Order for White Waistcoats received Annually 16s. 6d. each, and rest of the Men 11s. 6d. each, being all they were entitled to on that Head.

With regard to Swords for the Non-Commissioned Officers, I am to acquaint the Board that upon the Formation of the Regiment, The Non-Commissioned Officers agreeable to the custom of the Artillery in England, provided Silver Mounted Swords at their own Expense, that after the King's Order for the Army in general to have Swords Mounted of the same Colour of the Regimental Lace,—The Master General ordered the Irish Artillery to conform to the Same, upon which the Non-Commissioned Officers were directed to dispose of their Silver Swords and to provide Yellow Mounted Ones, agreeable to a Pattern approved of which cost them 19s. 6d. each,—That when a Non-Commissioned Officer was reduced, or died, his successor took the Sword, and when put in good Repair, paid the original price for it. The Regiment being very much dispersed during the late War, the Additional Non-Commissioned Officers at the late Augmentations, were not ordered to provide themselves with Swords, consequently those Non-Commissioned Officers who were discharged at the Reduction having been promoted at the Augmentations and *Not* having purchased Swords, can have no claim to any Allowance for Swords.

I have, etc.,

J. STRATON, Lt. Col. Comdt.,
Royal Irish Artillery (Colonel Brevet).

Enlistments in East India Company's Service.

18th November.—By the following Official Notification, the Men lately discharged were encouraged to enlist in the East India Company's Service.

Ordnance Office, Dublin Castle,
18th November, 1783.

Pursuant to the Orders of His Excellency the Lord Lieutenant, the principal Officers of His Majesty's Ordnance, do hereby give Notice to all such Men of those lately discharged from the Royal Irish Regiment of Artillery, as may be desirous of enlisting in the East India Company's Service, to apply to Colonel Straton, at Chapel-Izod, who will immediately enlist them, and from whom they will receive, upon their being attested, One Guinea each Man, to defray his expenses to Woolwich; that upon their arrival there they will be paid the further sum of One Guinea per Man, be entered on pay from the time of their being attested, and entitled to all the other encouragements given to the Men from the English Battalions, viz., Bounty to each Non-Commissioned Officer on embarking for the East Indies, Six pounds Six shillings; and Bounty to each Private Man on embarking, Five pounds Five shillings.—(*Freeman's Journal.*)

1784

Allowance for Stationery.

30th January.—Board of Ordnance.

Ordered.—That the Adjutant of the Artillery Regiment be acquainted that as the Regiment is now reduced, the Allowance for Stationery of Fifteen pounds per Annum must be reduced to Ten pounds as formerly from the 1st of January last.

Burial Expenses.

2nd April.—Board of Ordnance.

Received a Letter from the Commanding Officer of the Artillery Regiment, representing that when any Man dies in the Marching Companies of Artillery, three Crowns are allowed out of the Stock Purse to bury him, but the Captain of the Invalids cannot make that Allowance not being entitled to a Share in the Stock Purse; And therefore praying the Board would please to allow that every Invalid who should die might be borne on the Muster Roll for One Month from the Day of his Decease to defray that Expense.

Ordered.—That the Commanding Officer be acquainted the Board approve of an Invalid being borne on the Muster Rolls for One Month from the

Day of his Decease, and that three Crowns be allowed out of the Pay to bury him.

INSPECTION OF THE REGIMENT.

22nd June.—Board of Ordnance.

The Secretary to the Board laid before them a Letter which he received yesterday from the Master General to acquaint the Board that His Lordship had given Colonel Straton Orders to shew the Artillery Regiment to the Commander in Chief at any Time that he should wish to see it, and to desire that the Commanding Officer of the Regiment be immediately furnished with such Cannon and Ammunition as will be necessary for the Occasion.

Ordered.—That the necessary Orders be immediately sent to the Principal Storekeeper and Comptroller of the Laboratory to issue the Guns and Stores accordingly.

30th June.—The Royal Irish Regiment of Artillery was reviewed by the Commander-in-Chief.

THE INVALID COMPANY.

25th June.—Board of Ordnance.

As by the King's Letter the Invalid Company is intitled " an Invalid Company to be added to the Royal Irish Regiment of Artillery," all Orders from the Board relative to the said Company are to be sent to the Colonel of the Regiment, and from him to the Officer Commanding the Company; the Colonel by this means becomes responsible to the Board for the due Execution of their Orders.

* * * * * *

DROGHEDA.

R. WARD.
J. KEEN.

To the Colonel Commandant
   of the Royal Irish Regiment of Artillery.

Ordnance Office, 25th *June*, 1784.

THE REGIMENT SKIRMISHING.

27th September.—The Regiment of Royal Irish Artillery skirmished from the gate of His Majesty's Park leading into Barrack Street, to the gate leading to Castleknock, with twenty Field Pieces. Nothing could exceed the skill and dexterity with which they performed their different manœuvres, and which did infinite credit not only to Officers that commanded, but to every Private in the Regiment, each distinguishing himself in his respective station.—(*Dublin Journal.*)

REVIEW IN PHŒNIX PARK.

1st October.—The Garrison of Dublin, consisting of the 18th Light Dragoons, the 4th, 6th, 15th, 26th, 48th, and 65th Regiments, with 12 Pieces of Cannon, were reviewed by his Grace the Lord Lieutenant, in his Majesty's Park the Phœnix.

The plan of this military exhibition was not of that

formal useless pageantry, in which troops are accustomed to be reviewed, but composed of those active and brilliant manœuvres in which an Army should be employed, to give the nearest representation of real service.

Without entering into the particulars of the day it will be sufficient to mention, that the troops were equally divided into two bodies, an attacking and retiring Army, and that from nearly the entrance of the Park-gate to the Gulley that terminates Mr. Gardiner's domain, was a continued scene of new positions, skirmishing, and busy evolutions, disputing every pass, and taking every advantage of each other, kept up with an incessant fire from the musquetry and Artillery, and concluding with a pitched battle across the Ravine.

The beauty of the surrounding scenery, the favourable weather, the different movements of the Cavalry and Infantry through the woods and plains, the firing that resounded through the Park, the crowd of spectators, not to mention the splendid equipage and beauty of our vice-queen, formed altogether the most animating and pleasing spectacle we remember to have seen.

The troops on their return home marched by their Graces the Duke and Duchess of Rutland, and paid the usual honours. The Commander-in-Chief deserves the highest praise for employing the troops in this warlike manner, and the inferior Officers partake a share of the applause, in executing his military ideas. The Generals, Field Officers, and Staff, had the honour of partaking of a sumptuous banquet given by his

Grace the Lord Lieutenant on this occasion, at the Castle.—(*Dublin Journal.*)

RECRUITING FOR THE REGIMENT.

11*th October.*

Royal Irish Regiment of Artillery.

There being now a few Vacancies in the Royal Irish Artillery, young Men not exceeding 28 years of Age, who are 5 feet 9 inches high, strong, and well made, and who can produce a Certificate of their being Protestants, and of a good moral Character, signed by a Clergyman or a Justice of the Peace, will be received by applying to the Commanding Officer at Chapel-Izod.

Chapel-Izod, 11*th October*, 1784.

ESTABLISHMENT.

The Establishment continued this year at 886 of all ranks.

1785

The Regiment Reviewed.

27th May.—Board of Ordnance.

Received a Letter from the Commanding Officer of the Artillery Regiment, acquainting the Board that the Master General intends to Review the Regiment on Monday next (30th), and that His Grace the Lord Lieutenant proposes to Review the Regiment on the Wednesday following:

And the Commanding Officer having represented that twelve Light 6 Pounders are wanting for the said Service.

Ordered.—That twelve Light 6 Pounders be immediately sent to Chapel-Izod, and that Ammunition for the Review of the Artillery Regiment be prepared and issued accordingly.

31st May.—To-morrow the Royal Irish Regiment of Artillery is to be reviewed, in the Phœnix Park, by His Grace the Duke of Rutland; a regiment that has always been held in high estimation, ever ready, on actual service, to cope with an assailing foe, and face the most tremendous dangers.—(*Freeman's Journal.*)

2nd June.—Yesterday His Grace the Lord Lieutenant reviewed the Royal Irish Regiment of Artillery at the Phœnix Park; when they went through their manœuvres and firings with the greatest expertness to the satisfaction of His Grace, and many thousand spectators.—(*Freeman's Journal.*)

Memorial from the Captains.

30th August.—Board of Ordnance.

To His Grace the Duke of Rutland,
    Lord Lieutenant, etc., etc., etc.

The Memorial of the Master General and Principal Officers of His Majesty's Ordnance.

Enclosing Colonel Straton's Report in consequence of a Memorial from the Captains of the Irish Artillery praying that they may be put on the same Footing with the Captains of Artillery in Great Britain relative to Contingent Men and other Allowances to enable them to bear sundry Expenses of their Companies.

. . . . . .

Your Memorialists called upon Colonel Straton for his Information on those Heads, and directed him to make a regular Report upon the whole of the matter contained in Secretary Orde's said Letter.

Your Memorialists beg leave to enclose the same to Your Grace, and to represent that the Captains of the Irish Artillery are not allowed any Non-effective Men, but as all necessary Incidental Expenses on account of the Regiment at large are, and have always been paid by Your Memorialists upon proper Demands being given into the Office, Certified by the Commanding Officer, they are humbly of Opinion that the only Extra Expenses which may fall upon the Captains arise by Desertion, Men dying in their Debt and such like Casualties, towards discharging which, Colonel Straton reports he has hitherto appropriated the

Surplus on the Non-Effective Fund, and found it insufficient to the Expenses of the Captains.

Which is, etc.,

DROGHEDA.

R. WARD.
J. KEEN.

CHAPEL-IZOD, 30*th July*, 1785.

MY LORD AND GENTLEMEN,

Agreeable to Your Order of the 19th Instant, I have the Honor to make You my Report on the several particulars in said Order.

Particulars to report on.	*Answers to the Particulars to be reported on.*
1st. In what way and from what Fund the Royal Irish Regiment of Artillery is now Recruited, what sum is allowed the Recruiting Officer, and what Bounty is given to the Recruit.	By an Order of Government bearing Date 31st August, 1757, "Sixty-one Days Subsistence of a Mattross amounting to £2 8s. 8½d., is allowed the Captains for Levy Money for each Recruit, and also when a Vacancy happens

it is to be kept open for Sixty-one Days, in order to make good the above Allowance for Levy Money, agreeable to said Order, which forms a Fund for recruiting the Regiment, and every Officer sent out on the Recruiting Service is allowed the aforesaid Sixty-one Days Subsistence for every Recruit he sends up to the Regiment that is approved of by the Commanding Officer."

The Bounty given by the Recruiting Officer is never inquired into, he gets Recruits on the best terms he can, as the Allowance he receives is so very inadequate to the Expense he is at on this Service.

Particulars to report on.	*Answers to the Particulars to be reported on.*
2.—What becomes of the Subsistence of Vacancies.	The Regiment is always kept as complete as possible by Inlisting Men to fill up the Vacancies as

soon after the 61 Days are elapsed as Recruits can be found. But if it should happen that Recruits cannot be had at the expiration of the 61 Days, the Surplus Subsistence until the Vacancy is filled up is appropriated to the following purposes, viz. :—

Subsistence of Deserters, and all their Expenses from the time of their being apprehended until they join the Regiment.

Subsistence for Recruits who Die or Desert, before they join the Regiment and for those rejected by the Commanding Officer.

Burial of the Dead.

Allowance to a Paymaster there being no fund for that purpose.

Bounty Money to Discharged Men to carry them home.

Subsistence to Discharged Men who are recommended for Invalids until they pass the Board.

Advertising Deserters for some time past.

And should any Balance remain after defraying such like Expenses, it is divided among the Captains, which dividend has been found very inadequate to the various Losses and Expenses that they have been at on account of their Companies.

Particulars to report on. *Answers to the Particulars to be reported on.*

3.—How many Contingent Men are allowed the Captains, and to Answer what Expenses.

No Contingent Men are allowed the Captains.

4.—What Expenses relative to their Companies fall upon the Captains, and what Fund have they to defray them.

All Expenses whatever fall upon the Captains, such as being always in advance to supply their Companies with Necessaries, Men Deserting or Dying in their Debt, the repairs of Arms and Appointments of their Companies, and many other matters, tho' too trifling to enumerate, yet comes heavy upon them, and they have no Funds to defray these Expenses, except the Dividend mentioned in Answer to the 2nd Paragraph.

Particulars to report on. *Answers to the Particulars to be reported on.*

5.—What Allowances are made to the Regiment for Postage, Stationery, and Contingent Expenses, and how paid.

The Adjutant is allowed by the Board of Ordnance £10 a year for Postage of Regimental Letters, and £15 a year for Stationery for the Regimental Office ;

Particulars to report on.	*Answers, etc., continued.*
	the Major is allowed £15 a year, the Adjutant and Quarter Master £10 a year, each to keep Horses to enable them to attend the Board of Ordnance, which Allowances are also paid by the Board.
6.—If any for Contingencies what such Contingencies are.	The Regiment of Artillery receive no Allowance for Contingencies, all necessary Contingent Articles being provided by the Board's Order, and the Persons who supplied them paid on Delivery of such Necessaries upon the Certificate of the Commanding Officer.
7.—What other Allowances are made of whatever nature to the Officers of the Royal Irish Artillery.	The Officers receive the same Allowance for Lodging Money as those belonging to the British Artillery and the same Quantity of Coals and Candles as delivered to

the Army on this Establishment, there are no other Allowances of any nature whatever, except One Shilling a mile to an Officer when ordered on command without a Party, in lieu of a Baggage Car, Billets, Turnpike, etc.; But it is necessary to observe that charges are incident upon Marches, especially with a Field Train, and in Out Garrisons, which the Officer Commanding the Detachment is obliged to pay, and upon transmitting those charges to the Board properly authenticated, he is reimbursed.

8.—And whether there are any and what difference between the Allowances made to them, and those made to the Officers of Artillery in Great Britain.

Allowances to the Officers of the British Artillery.	*Allowances to the Officers of the Irish Artillery.*	*Difference of Allowance.*
The Pay of One Gunner and the Surplus on the Widow's Fund equal to the Pay of another Gunner to each Captain to bear sundry Expenses of their Companies; as Repairs of Arms, Burial of the Dead, and loss by Men's Debts, etc.	No Pay of a Gunner is allowed the Captains to bear the sundry Expenses of their Companies, but the Surplus on the Non-Effective Fund is appropriated as far as it will go towards the said sundry Expenses.	The Pay of One Gunner and the Surplus on the Widow's Fund equal to the Pay of another Gunner in favour of each Captain of the British Artillery. . . . .

I have nothing farther to observe but that the Captain of the Invalids of the Irish Artillery has no

Allowance, whereas the Captains of Invalids of the British Artillery are allowed two Non-Effectives per Company and the other Allowances contained in this Report.

I have, etc.,

J. STRATON, Col. Comdt.,
Royal Irish Artillery.

ESTABLISHMENT.

The Establishment continued this year at 886 of all ranks.

1786

Guard at the Magazine in Phœnix Park.

14th March.—Board of Ordnance.

Ordered a Letter to the Commanding Officer of the Artillery Regiment to acquaint him that the Board are of opinion that the Guard at the Magazine in the Phœnix Park should always consist of an Officer and twenty Men at least, agreeable to the old Standing Order; the Board therefore desire that he will cause strict attention to be paid to this matter, and issue the proper Orders that the said Guard may not be lessened upon any Account whatever without their Approbation.

The Invalid Company.

27th June.—Board of Ordnance.

Received a Letter from the Commanding Officer of the Artillery Regiment, recommending A— B— late of the Royal Irish Regiment of Artillery who was Discharged for Insanity, and C— D— worn out in the Service, for Admission into the Invalid Company.

Ordered.—That they be admitted into the Invalid Company.

26th August.—Received a Letter from the Commanding Officer of the Artillery Regiment, acquainting the Board that there is a vacancy of a Bombardier in the Invalid Company by the death of —— and that he recommends Corporal —— to be appointed Bombardier in the Invalids from 1st September next.

Ordered.—Letter to the Commanding Officer to acquaint him that the Board have no objection to Corporal —— being admitted into the Invalid Company in the Room of Bombardier —— deceased.

ALLOWANCE TO REGIMENTAL PAYMASTER.

5th December.—Board of Ordnance.

Received a Memorial from Lieutenant—— of the Royal Irish Regiment of Artillery, setting forth that he has done the duty of Paymaster to the said Regiment from the 1st July, 1778, which has been attended with a great deal of trouble Labour and Expense to him, the Regiment having been for some years divided, and Detachments frequently ordered to march at the shortest notice.

That the Allowance he received for paying the Regiment and keeping a very troublesome Account, did not upon an Average exceed £25 a year which was paid to him out of the Non-Effective Fund of the Stock Purse and the Stoppages which were formerly paid to the Royal Infirmary: That the Board having been pleased on the 1st October, 1784, to Order that the Stoppages for the Royal Infirmary should be discontinued, and there being now not any Non-Effective Fund allowed (over and above the sixty one days for Recruits) the Memorialist therefore humbly prays the Board to take his case into consideration, and grant him such Allowance for acting as Paymaster to the Artillery Regiment as they may judge most proper.

And the Board having this day taken into consideration Lieutenant—— Memorial, and the great Trouble attending the Duty of Paymaster to the Regiment are pleased to make the following Order, viz. :—

Ordered.—That an Allowance of Five Pounds per Company be paid to Lieutenant—— at the Office until further Orders, the same to be charged in the incidental Account of the Artillery Regiment, etc.

Establishment.

The Establishment continued this year at 386 of all ranks.

1787

DEATH OF THE LORD LIEUTENANT.

26th October.—On Wednesday night (24th) His Grace the Duke of Rutland died at the Lodge in the Phœnix Park. His Grace was the first Lord Lieutenant that died in the Government of this Kingdom, although since the year 1711, thirty-seven Noblemen have filled that important station.—(*Freeman's Journal.*)

FUNERAL PROCESSION OF LATE LORD LIEUTENANT.

14th November.—Board of Ordnance.

MY LORD AND GENTLEMEN,

I enclose to you herewith by Command of Their Excellencies the Lords Justices General Governors of this Kingdom the Order of March for the Royal Irish Regiment of Artillery at the Funeral Procession on Saturday, and Their Excellencies desire you will issue all such Orders as may be proper and necessary for the above Purpose accordingly.

I have, etc.,
C. F. SHERIDAN.

The Board of Ordnance.

Order of March for the Royal Irish Artillery at the Funeral Procession on Friday.

Corporal and Six
Arms reversed.

Adjutant
on Horseback.

Two Field Pieces abreast
drawn by two Horses each.

Two Tumbrils abreast
drawn by Horses.

Detachment of Artillery
Arms reversed.

Flag Howitzer
drawn by two Horses.
The Flag to be Tied at the Top with Crape which must hang down very low—the Flag to be tied in two or three places to the Pole with Crape.

Two Tumbrils abreast
drawn by Horses.

Two Field Pieces abreast
drawn by two Horses each.

Detachment of Artillery
Arms reversed.

Drums and Fifes
Lieut. Colonel—— Major
each on Horseback.

State Ordnance Kettle Drum
drawn by Horses.

Band of Musick Artillery
General Straton
on Horseback.

Engineers.

In the foregoing Order of March, we find the first notice of the Irish Artillery Band and the State Ordnance Kettle Drums, at a General Parade.

With regard to the State Kettle Drums, it may be interesting to the reader to learn that

"In the old pre-regimental days, when the Master-General took the field in time of war, in his official capacity, he was attended by a Chancellor, thirty gentlemen of the Ordnance, thirty harquebussiers on horseback, with eight halberdiers for his guard; two or three interpreters, a minister or preacher, a physician, a master-surgeon, and his attendant, a trumpeter, kettledrums, and chariot with six white horses, two or three engineers, or more if required, and two or three refiners of gunpowder. These kettledrums do not seem to have been used in the field after 1748. They were used by the train of Artillery employed in Ireland in 1689, and the cost of the drums and their carriage on that occasion, was estimated at

£158 9s. 0d. As the reader comes to compare the wages of the drummer and his coachman—4s. and 8s. per diem respectively—with the pay given to other by no means unimportant members of an Artillery train, he will realize what a prominent position these officials were intended to hold. The drummer's suit of clothes cost £50, while a gunner's was valued at £5 6s. 4d. Even the coachman could not be clad under £15—nearly three times the cost of a gunner's clothes." *

Warrant Appointing a Kettle Drummer.

We quote the wording of the Warrant, dated 1756, appointing a Kettle Drummer, taken from the Book of Commissions of Artillery Officers, in the Public Record Office, London.

Charles Duke of Marlborough, Etc.

To C.—— B.——, Kettle Drummer.

Whereas the King's Most Excellent Majesty hath by His Warrant under His Royal Sign Manual bearing Date the Twenty Seventh Day of March, 1756, Authorized and required that a Train of Artillery should be forthwith provided to attend His Majesty's Forces in Great Britain; and that the several Attendants belonging to the said Train should be regulated and Established with their respective Pays per diem, as is mentioned in the List annexed to the said Warrant, and having received a good Testimony and assurance of your Loyalty, Integrity, and Ability,

---

* Duncan's *History of the Royal Regiment of Artillery*.

I do hereby nominate, constitute, and appoint you the said C.—— B.——, to be Kettle Drummer, to attend the said Train commanded by Me. You are therefore carefully and diligently to discharge the duty of a Kettle Drummer in the said service, by doing and performing all manner of Things thereunto belonging; and likewise to observe and follow such Orders and Directions as you shall from time to time receive from Me, the Lieutenant General and Principal Officers of His Majesty's Ordnance, or any other your superior Officer according to the Rules and Discipline of War, in pursuance of the Trust herein reposed in you. And for your Care and Diligence to be taken herein, you are to have and receive the Allowance of Three shillings per diem, to be paid you by the Paymaster of the said Train, the said Allowance to commence the First day of March last, and to continue so long as shall be thought requisite and necessary for His Majesty's Service.

Given at the Office of Ordnance, under my Hand and Seal this Tenth day of June, 1756, in the Twenty-ninth Year of His Majesty's Reign.

MARLBOROUGH.

By Command of His Grace the
    Master General of the Ordnance,

    JACOB BRYANT.

19*th November*.—In reference to the attendance of the Royal Irish Artillery Regiment at the Funeral Procession, a Dublin Newspaper Account states that:—

" The Town Major attended by a Troop of Horse

preceded the processions: The Train of Royal Irish Artillery followed: the melancholy movement of their march, the still features of their countenances, the arms of the musquetry motionless and reversed, excited the most reverential awe in spectators of every description. Their rear was brought up by the regimental band playing a solemn dirge."—(*Freeman's Journal.*)

FUNERAL PROCESSION OF LATE LORD LIEUTENANT.

23rd November.—Board of Ordnance.

Received a Letter from Secretary Sheridan, signifying their Excellencies Approbation of the Conduct of the Officers and Men of the Artillery Regiment during the Funeral Procession of the late Lord Lieutenant, which their Excellencies desire may be communicated to the Regiment.

Ordered.—Letter to General Straton to acquaint him with the Approbation of their Excellencies the Lords Justices.

ESTABLISHMENT.

The Establishment continued this year at 386 of all ranks.

1788

REMOVAL OF REGIMENT FROM IRELAND.

In January it was reported in the columns of the Dublin Press, that the Royal Irish Regiment of Artillery would be removed from Ireland.

We take the following extracts on the subject from the *Dublin Journal* :—

3rd January.—The change in the Ordnance Establishment in England, has reached to this Kingdom, and if we are rightly informed is of a serious and very unexpected a nature, being no less than the unregimenting of the Royal Irish Artillery and blending it with the British, as a fifth or additional Battalion, by which that part of it in Ireland will only be considered as a Detachment, and to be quartered occasionally, as any Marching Regiment in Barracks, etc.

12th January.—If the Royal Regiment of Artillery is ordered out of this Kingdom, as reported, we hear the Corps of Engineers will enlist two Companies of Mattrosses who are to be trained for doing occasional duty in his Majesty's Garrisons in Ireland.

22nd April.—The Regiment of the Royal Irish Artillery is not, we hear, to be incorporated with the British Corps; the measure having been reconsidered and found ineligible. A circumstance that must give real pleasure to the people of this Kingdom, to whom the good conduct, remarkable discipline, and behaviour of the Officers and Privates of that excellent Regiment has long since endeared it.

INCREASED PAY TO GENERAL STRATON.

1st July.—Board of Ordnance.

Received a Letter . . . signifying the Lord Lieutenant's desire that Four shillings a day be paid quarterly to Major General Straton, Colonel Commandant of the Royal Irish Artillery Regiment to make his pay equal to the pay of Colonels Commandant in the British Artillery, in consideration of his long services and very particular merit, the said Additional Pay to commence 1st July, and to be charged in the Account of Incidents for Artillery Regiment, Engineers, etc.

THE GARRISON REVIEWED.

12th July.—Saturday, the Garrison of Dublin, with the Regiments then in Camp, were reviewed by His Excellency the Marquis of Buckingham, at the Fifteen Acres in the Phœnix Park.

After the Review His Excellency had a practice of the Royal Irish Artillery firing at the target.

The Review was concluded much to the satisfaction of the Viceroy.

PAY OF MEN ABSENT.

21st October.—Board of Ordnance.

Ordered.—That the Pay of all Persons not appearing or Doing Duty to be discontinued from the beginning of this Quarter.

ESTABLISHMENT.

The Establishment continued this year at 386 of all ranks.

1789

Insufficient Barrack Accommodation.

19th May.—Board of Ordnance.

Received a Memorial of the Commanding Officer of the Artillery, together with the Report of the Quarter-Master and Surgeon of the Regiment, representing that the Barracks at Chapel-Izod is at present insufficient for the accommodation of Sick Men, and praying for an Additional Barrack.

Ordered.—That Lodging and Accommodation be immediately provided accordingly.

12th June.—Board of Ordnance.

Received an Order from the Lord Lieutenant ordering Lodging Rooms to be hired for such Men of the Royal Irish Regiment of Artillery at Chapel-Izod as the Barrack cannot accommodate, and the expense be charged in the Annual Account of Lodging Money for the Artillery Regiment.

Earl of Carhampton appointed Colonel *en Seconde*.

12th October.—Major General H. L. Earl of Carhampton was appointed Colonel *en Seconde*, in succession to General Hale who retired.—(*Dublin Gazette.*)

Establishment.

The Establishment continued this year at 886 of all ranks.

1790

THE REGIMENT REVIEWED.

23rd June.—Wednesday at eleven o'Clock, His Excellency the Lord Lieutenant reviewed the Royal Regiment of Artillery in the Phœnix Park, when this last remaining Irish Regiment (now the four Regiments of Horse, the Military pride of Ireland, are no more) went thro' the Manual Exercise as a Corps of Infantry, with the utmost precision and dexterity, and after having formed in grand and small divisions, commenced their Artillery practice of the various cannonades, in attack and retreat in front, flank and rear, with the several approved evolutions, particularly that of the square and double potence. After this, His Excellency rode up to the centre of the line, and desired the Colonel Commandant of the Regiment, General Straton, in his name, to convey to the Officers and Privates his entire approbation. He then left the field amidst the discharge of a Royal Salute from the Ordnance.—(*Dublin Journal.*)

ESTABLISHMENT.

The Establishment continued this year at 386 of all ranks.

1791

Changing the Artillery Quarters.*

4th June.—A Removal of the Regiment of Irish Artillery from Chapel-Izod to the Phœnix Park is, we hear, determined on.

The new building in the Park, which has hitherto been a Military Hospital, is to be the Barracks of the Artillery, and an Hospital erected at a greater distance from the Salute Battery, the noise of which, upon rejoicing days, being found hurtful to the patients.

The measure of changing the Artillery quarters is founded in wisdom, a garrison should be as circumscribed as possible ; the more compact the machine is, the more easy it is to manage, and withdrawing the men from a village, removes them from numerous temptations to licentiousness.—(*Dublin Journal.*)

Establishment.

The Establishment continued this year at 386 of all ranks.

---

* The subject does not appear to have been pursued any farther.

1792

GRANT OF BREAD MONEY.

14th January.—To make soldiering more popular and attractive, an additional Allowance of three halfpence per diem was granted this year to the Non-Commissioned Officers and Men, called "Bread Money." The following is a copy of the Regulation on the subject :—

Army Regulations.

ADJUTANT GENERAL'S OFFICE,
January 14*th*, 1792.

His Majesty having been most graciously pleased, by his Royal Warrants, bearing date the 4th of this month, to make allowance of bread to Foot Soldiers in Great Britain, etc., general, which before had been granted to those only who were in Barracks; and likewise to extend this Bounty still farther, so as to afford them, as well in quarters as in Barracks, effectual relief and comfort, provided their full pay, added to their other allowances as specified in the same Warrants, be carefully applied for their benefit and expended on such articles only as are indispensably necessary for their use : His Majesty therefore, strictly enjoins the Commanding Officers of Infantry Corps to take care that the rules and limitations therein prescribed, be inviolably observed, and adhered to : and particularly to see, that complete justice be done to the Soldiers, and that the quality of the different kinds of necessaries, with which they are supplied, be suitable to the prices which are charged for them, conformably to the Lists thereof, inserted in the aforesaid Warrants.

It is his Majesty's further pleasure, That every Captain or Commanding Officer of a Company, in addition to that economy, which it is his immediate duty to exercise, in the provision of necessaries for his men, shall keep a regular account of all such occasional supplies, and of the sums severally paid for them, taking care that they do not exceed the fixed prices, specified in his Majesty's Warrant;—This account is to be settled once in every two months; and the balance, that may be due to any of the men of the Company, is to be paid into their own hands; on which settlement, they will sign the same account, both as a Voucher for their Captain, and an acknowledgment at the same time from themselves, that all their just demands have been satisfied. His Majesty requires the Commanding Officers of Regiments, to take all possible care, that this regulation be strictly and invariably observed in their respective Corps: as they themselves are to be responsible for any neglect, or deviation from it; and they are hereby apprized, that it will make part of his Majesty's future instructions, to his Reviewing Generals, to pay the most scrupulous attention to this important object; not only by carefully inspecting the Regimental Books and those of every distinct Company; but also by personally examining the Soldiers themselves, relative to their respective accounts; and to report to his Majesty, any instances of negligence, or irregularity, concerning them, which they may meet with: as well as any excess in the quantity, or deficiencies in the quality and goodness of the necessaries, furnished for the use of the men, when compared with the prices allowed to be charged for them.

Useless ornaments, and superfluous expense in dress, of every kind, being heavy Drawbacks upon their pay, and not sanctioned, by either regulation or necessity, are no longer to be admitted; so that the soldiers, reaping the full benefit of this his Majesty's most gracious bounty towards them, and having no just cause whatsoever for murmur, or complaint, may be enabled to discharge their duty on all occasions, with alacrity, diligence, and contentment; and be left without any inducement, or excuse, for Desertion, a crime, in itself, of the most heinous nature, and which hereafter will be punished with the utmost and most exemplary severity.

It is his Majesty's further Command, That these Orders, together with the Royal Warrants above specified, shall be communicated to them, in the presence of their respective Officers; and be regularly read to the whole regiment at the same time with the Articles of War, once in every two months; as is directed in the Vth Article of the 23rd Section of the Articles of War; care being also taken that they are entered in the Regimental Book of Standing Orders, to be referred to, as occasion may require.

By his Majesty's Command,

WILLIAM FAWCETT,
Adjutant General.

14th February.—It is a singular circumstance, but it is a fact that since His Majesty's allowance of the advantages lately granted to the Army in England, but one Deserter has appeared upon the Returns to the Quarter Master General. When the regulations proposed by the Chancellor take place *in this Kingdom*, the same good consequences may be expected to follow. The Soldier enjoying comfort will not, in all probability, quit his quarters for the depredations of the highway.—(*Dublin Journal.*)

14th April.—The Soldiery on the Irish Establishment have received for some weeks past, an increase of pay under the grant of Bread-Money, by His Majesty's Order. Their subsistence cannot now be less than three shillings and sixpence per week. Insignificant as the sum of ten-pence halfpenny per week may seem to the affluent, yet to those whose means are one-fourth part augmented by it, the addition is so considerable as to afford not only relief, but comfort.—(*Dublin Journal.*)

THE GARRISON REVIEWED.

26th May.—The 23rd, 38th, 41st, 55th, and 56th Regiments of Infantry, the 4th Regiment of Dragoon Guards, and the 14th Light Dragoons, with the Royal Irish Regiment of Artillery, were reviewed in the Phœnix Park by his Excellency the Lord Lieutenant.

The exercise and appearance of the Military realised the most sanguine expectation, which by the extraordinary number of spectators seemed to be entertained.—(*Dublin Journal.*)

BALL AT CHAPEL-IZOD.

6th June.—Last night a very elegant ball and supper was given at Morris's in Chapel-Izod, to a very brilliant circle of ladies, by the Officers belonging to the Regiment of Light Horse stationed in the Phœnix Park, and the Officers belonging to the Royal Irish Regiment of Artillery quartered at Chapel-Izod.—(*Freeman's Journal.*)

The Regiment Reviewed.

2nd August.—The Royal Irish Regiment of Artillery will be reviewed on the Fifteen Acres in the Phœnix Park, to-morrow, by Lieutenant General James Pattison, one of the Colonels Commandant of the four Battalions of the British Artillery.—(*Freeman's Journal.*)

2nd August.—The Royal Irish Artillery will be reviewed in the Park, by Lieut.-General Pattison, when we have little doubt but the skill and steadiness of that respectable Corps will give them credit. Should they be approved by their Reviewing General, who ranks with the first military characters in Europe, they need no other commendation.—(*Dublin Journal.*)

3rd August.—The Royal Irish Artillery were reviewed by General Pattison, and had the honour to receive his approbation, expressed in terms highly complimentary. Notwithstanding the weather was as unfavourable as frequent and heavy showers of rain could make it, the number of spectators was astonishingly great.—(*Dublin Journal.*)

Establishment.

The Establishment continued this year at 386 of all ranks.

1793

Augmentation to the Regiment.

On the 12th February, an augmentation to the Regiment was ordered, and recruiting on a large scale took place by means of parties scattered over the kingdom. The party furnished with Beating Orders in Dublin was attended by the Regimental Band.

In August the Establishment was raised from six to ten Marching Companies, each Company consisting of 100 of all ranks.

The names of the Officers promoted were notified in the *Dublin Gazette* for December, 1793, their Commissions being dated 7th August, 1793.

It is regretted that no monthly Returns showing the effective strength and distribution of the Regiment for this year are available at the Record Offices.

Artillery Exercise in Phœnix Park.

18th June.—The Royal Irish Regiment of Artillery is exercised daily in the Park; the time of exercise has been changed from six in the morning to 12 at Noon, in consequence of the Countess of Westmoreland's residence at the Lodge.—(*Dublin Journal.*)

Three Companies embark for Foreign Service.

August and November.—Captain Pratt's and Captain Shewbridge's Companies* embarked at Waterford,

---

* It will be noted in following pages that these companies served on the Continent in 1793.

19th August, 1793, and Captain Smith's at Cork, the 16th November, 1793, for the West Indies.—(*MSS. in R. A. Record Office.*)

20th August.—The *Elizabeth* and *Royal Admiral* transports, having on board two Companies of the Royal Irish Artillery, sailed from Passage for Chatham, under convoy of the *Triton* frigate, Captain Murray. —(*Dublin Journal.*)

29th August.—The expedition with which the two Companies of the Royal Irish Artillery were collected, equipped, and embarked for foreign service, does infinite credit to the discipline and the well known ardour of that excellent Corps: for it appears, that the men who composed these Companies, marched from twelve different points to Waterford in as many days; and it is with pleasure we hear that the two Companies ordered to be raised in the room of those embarked, are almost complete in their numbers.— (*Dublin Journal.*)

The services of the Companies on the Continent are mentioned in the Dublin Press in the following terms:—

DUBLIN, *26th September,* 1793.

Private letters were received in town by the last packets from Ostend, which speak in raptures of the intrepid gallantry of the detachment from the Royal Artillery of Ireland lately landed there.

They marched to join the grand army before Dunkirk immediately after their landing, and came into the British lines just at the conclusion of the affair, when the British army were retreating, and just in the interesting moment when a party of British Artillery, appointed to cover the retreat had been for the most part destroyed, and the survivors driven from their guns.

The Irish heroes instantly pushed up with their field-pieces, scattered destruction amongst the French, retook several guns which had fallen into their hands, and effectually covered the retreat of the British forces.

We have the pleasure to assure our readers from indisputable authority, that the story propagated for some days past with much avidity, and received with universal regret, stating that the detachment from the Royal Irish Regiment of Artillery, who lately joined the Duke of York's Army, had been mostly destroyed in action, and that Captain Pratt and other brave Officers had fallen—is so far void of foundation, that letters were yesterday received at General Straton's Artillery Quarters, Chapel-Izod, from Lieutenant Thornton, who is with the Detachment, and dated the 14th Instant, which state, that no part of the Detachment had at that time been in any action whatever, but were all in perfect health and spirits.

General Straton, who is gone for a few days on some business in the north, and had expected letters from some of his Officers, the first opportunity after their arrival at their destination, left instructions with the Officer who commands in his absence, to open any packets which came directed for him from Flanders—and it was by this channel the very agreeable intelligence was communicated yesterday to the remainder of the Regiment who were mourning the reported fate of their gallant brother Officers and brave comrades.—(*Freeman's Journal.*)

Dublin, *5th November*, 1793.

It gives us pleasure to record the gallant behaviour of two Companies of Irish Artillery when the Army retreated on the 8th September. Their orders were to march from Ostend, and proceed with all possible expedition to Furnes. In their route the baggage of the army flying to Ostend, wagons full of wounded and dying men, different detachments of the Army retreating, and every person they addressed giving to them a worse account than they heard before. Many dissuaded them from pursuing their march, and concluded they would never return. They were young men, yet their spirit and good fortune disappointed these conjectures; not an individual shrunk, or showed any symptoms of fear. They arrived time enough to save a valuable depot of ammunition, which, but for their seasonable exertions, would have fallen into the enemy's hands. They received thanks in the handsomest manner from Colonel Congreve of the Artillery, who afterwards reported their conduct to the British Commander-in-Chief.—(*Dublin Journal.*)

8th October.—Yesterday morning a formidable Company of the Royal Irish Regiment of Artillery, commanded by Captain Smith, marched in here (Dublin) from Chapel-Izod, and embarked on board wherries in the river, which are to convey them to Cork, where they are to join the other forces there embarked, and proceed with them to Toulon.

They bring with them ten pieces of Cannon. The men appeared in great spirits, and seemed to be highly pleased with the route they were taking.—(*Freeman's Journal.*)

24th October.—The Company of Royal Irish Artillery now at Cove are to be joined at sea by the two former divisions which went to Ostend, to assist in the siege of Dunkirk, and all to attend the troops destined to the expedition against the French West India Islands.—(*Freeman's Journal.*)

A FLYING SIX POUNDER GUN.

19th September.—A six pounder upon a carriage of a new construction was exhibited in the Castle-yard to the Earl of Drogheda, Master-General of the Ordnance.

The carriage is drawn by two horses, not in the usual way, but side by side, and upon which there is a place for those who work the guns to sit.

The utility of this is, that it can be dispatched with considerably more haste to a place, than one upon the common construction, having besides the advantages of the men being always close to it, whereby it can do immediate execution.

The Gun upon this plan is called a *flying six pounder*, and is generally approved of. Everything that can be thought of for dispatch, utility, and convenience, is adopted in the Ordnance Department, under the direction of the Earls of Drogheda and Carhampton; indeed in every official situation of it, activity, regularity, and attention prevail.—(*Freeman's Journal.*)

1794

Three Companies Embark for Foreign Service.

In this year, three Companies embarked for the Continent, and served in the Campaigns in Flanders and in the Netherlands, under the Duke of York.

Captain Wright and Captain Arabin's Company* embarked at Waterford for the Continent on 16th January, and Captain Buchanan's† the 17th June following, at Dublin, for the same destination. They consisted of 14 Officers, 28 Non-Commissioned Officers, 250 Gunners, and 6 Drummers.—(*MSS. in R. A. Record Office.*)

Recruiting to Continue.

17th April.—Board of Ordnance.

The Lord Lieutenant desires you will issue the necessary Orders to the Royal Irish Regiment of Artillery not to call in their Recruiting Parties but to continue recruiting, as it is intended shortly to augment the said Regiment, such Men as they shall raise above their present Establishment to be borne as Supernumeraries until they shall be provided on the new Establishment.

---

* The Muster Rolls for the Royal Irish Artillery in the Pay of Great Britain, shew these Companies at Portsea in the month of January.
† In the Roll for July this Company is shown at Camp near Oosterham. (Record Office, London).

Draft for Foreign Service.

24th May.—A fresh Draft has been made from the Regiment of Royal Irish Artillery, who are to sail for the Continent as soon as possible.

Every possible exertion has been made for perfecting the discipline of the Regiment.

For the last month the whole have been at morning and evening practice in the Phœnix Park, and are extremely expert both at the long Gun and Mortar.

The Corps have lately been reinforced by a considerable number of fine healthy athletic young fellows from different quarters of the Kingdom, and from the attention indefatigably paid to the instruction and discipline of the Regiment by General Straton and the other Officers, the whole will be fit for service in any field, in the course of a few weeks.—(*Freeman's Journal.*)

A Company for Immediate Foreign Service.

4th June.—Board of Ordnance.

The Lord Lieutenant desires you will issue the necessary Orders that a Company of the Royal Irish Regiment of Artillery of the same Number as those lately embarked, do hold themselves in readiness for Immediate Foreign Service.

13th June.—Board of Ordnance.

The Lord Lieutenant desires you will issue the necessary Orders that the Company of Royal Irish Artillery now under Orders for Foreign Service do embark on Tuesday next on Board Vessels which have been provided to carry them to Park-Gate where they will receive Orders from His Majesty's Secretary at War.

Alderman Carleton, the Agent for the Embarkation Service, has been directed to receive your Orders relative to the time and Place of Embarkation.

18*th June.*—A Detachment of 100 Men (Officers included) from the Regiment of Royal Irish Artillery marched through this City from their Head Quarters at Chapel-Izod, and embarked at Rogerson's Quay for England, in order to join the Army under the command of the Earl of Moira, encamped at Southampton.—(*Freeman's Journal.*)

AUGMENTATION OF TWO COMPANIES.

7*th June.*—Board of Ordnance.

The Lord Lieutenant desires you will issue the necessary Orders for an Augmentation of two Companies to the Royal Irish Regiment of Artillery, the said Companies to consist of the like Numbers as the present Companies of the said Regiment, and this Augmentation to take place from the Day of the embarkation of the Company now under Orders for Foreign Service.

BEATING ORDERS TO GENTLEMEN RAISING MEN FOR COMMISSIONS.

20*th June.*—Board of Ordnance.

To acquaint you that the Lord Lieutenant has

recommended the following Gentlemen to be Second Lieutenants in the Royal Irish Regiment of Artillery (viz.) :—

Seven Names.

And His Excellency desires you will issue Beating Orders to those Gentlemen who are to raise Men for their Commissions, according to the terms lately adopted for that purpose.

ADDITIONAL LIEUT.-COLONEL AND MAJOR.

28th June.—Board of Ordnance.

Enclosing, by Command of the Lord Lieutenant, a Copy of a Letter dated the 25th Instant, which His Excellency has received from His Majesty's Principal Secretary of State, acquainting His Excellency that His Majesty has been graciously Pleased to approve of the arrangement proposed by His Excellency of Adding a Second Lieutenant Colonelcy and a Second Majority to the Royal Irish Regiment of Artillery, in order to assimilate the Officers of that Regiment to those of a Battalion of British Artillery, and that the Commissions for the Officers entitled to Promotion on this Occasion are Ordered to be prepared for the Royal Signature according to His Excellency's Recommendation.

AUGMENTATION OF EIGHT COMPANIES.

30th June.—Board of Ordnance.

The Lord Lieutenant desires you will issue the

necessary Orders for an Augmentation of Eight Companies in addition to the two directed in my Letter of the 7th Instant, to the Royal Irish Regiment of Artillery, the said Companies to consist of the like Numbers as the present Companies of the said Regiment, and this Augmentation to take place from this day exclusive.

His Excellency also desires you will lay before him a Return of the Officers of the Artillery Regiment as they will stand when this Augmentation shall be completed, and I am directed to enclose to you a copy of a Circular Letter and Proposal which His Excellency has directed to be transmitted to the several Regiments of Militia in this Kingdom in order to facilitate this Levy, and you will please to order thirty-eight Beating Orders and Recruiting Instructions for the Artillery to be sent to this Office to be forwarded with the before-mentioned letter.

BEATING ORDERS TO RAISE MEN.

2nd August.—Board of Ordnance.

Enclosing by Command of the Lord Lieutenant a List of Gentlemen to whom by His Excellency's directions you have from time to time issued Beating Orders to Raise Men for the Artillery Regiment, and His Excellency desires you will Report to him the Names of such as have completed their Quota with the Dates when completed that application may be made for their Commissions, and that you will also make the Proper Application for the Levy Money for the Men that have been raised.

Monthly Return of the Royal Irish Regiment of Artillery, for August, 1794.

1st September.	Officers	Non-Com. Officers and Men	Total all Ranks
Total of the 12 Marching Companies	67	1,149	1,216
Invalid Company	3	50	53
Total	70	1,199	1,269

Detachments included in Return.

West Indies	13	285	298
Duke of York's Army	10	190	200
Cork Harbour and Charles Fort	2	113	115
Limerick and Kilkenny	—	8	8
Galway	2	16	18
Castle and Harbour of Dublin	—	27	27
Drogheda, Dundalk, and Belfast	2	67	69
Tarbert	1	22	23
Recruiting	2	49	51
In England	6	95	101
Total	38	872	910

Companies in the West Indies.

The three Companies which had proceeded to the West Indies (1793) were employed on the capture of Martinique, Guadaloupe, and St. Lucia this year, and in the general operations in those Latitudes. Their strength on embarkation was 15 Officers, 30 Non-Commissioned Officers, 252 Gunners, and 6 Drummers.

Of the 15 Officers only 4 ever returned to Europe, the remaining 11 fell victims to the climate, and the casualties of the Non-Commissioned Officers and Men had been so numerous that only 18 Non-Commissioned Officers and 25 Gunners were alive in September, 1795, when the Detachments to complete them with two additional Companies embarked.—(*MSS. in R. A. Record Office*).

SERVICES OF THE COMPANY AT GUADALOUPE.

The following account of the Military operations in which the Company stationed at Guadaloupe was engaged, is taken from the *Freeman's Journal*, dated Dublin, 16th September, 1794:—

Extract of a Letter from Captain Pratt of the Royal Irish Regiment of Artillery, dated Guadaloupe, 6th July, 1794, and brought to Europe by Major Freemantle.

"Captain Pratt, after lamenting the fatalities in his Regiment, occasioned by the Yellow Fever, and more especially the death of his intimate friend, Lieutenant George, states,—That since his arrival in that island he had been engaged in four battles with the enemy, who had landed there in great force about the 5th of June, in three of which they were completely beaten.

"On one of these occasions, he says, he was ordered to the command of a battery of only three Guns, viz.: two 24-Pounders, and an 8-inch Howitzer, opposed to a two decker, a 40 Gun frigate, a small sloop which flanked him, a Gun-boat, and three batteries on shore; all of which, after a conflict of ten hours, from five in the morning till three in the afternoon, he completely silenced, obliging the frigates, sloop, and boat to sheer off, the two decker having 86 men killed and nearly double the number wounded; the frigate, which was a Commodore's ship, had 8 killed and 26 wounded, and a proportionate number at the batteries.

"Nothing could exceed the body of fire poured during the conflict on the small spot from which the gallant Pratt and his three guns braved the attack, and defeated the fire of his assailants.

"Lieutenant Molony was at Captain Pratt's battery during the whole of this affair, and behaved with the most intrepid gallantry, as did all the men; and when the opposing ships and batteries were silenced, the whole of the ammunition remaining with Captain Pratt's battery was, ten rounds for his 24-Pounders, and seven shells for his Howitzer."

AUGMENTATION OF EIGHT COMPANIES.

25th September.—The names of eight Captains and sixteen Captain Lieutenants, promoted to the additional Companies were duly notified in the *Dublin Gazette* of 25th September, their Commissions being dated 1st of July, 1794.

26th September.—Royal Irish Regiment of Artillery. It is the Marquis of Drogheda's Order,

That all Officers who have been notified in the *Dublin Gazette*, as lately appointed to the Royal Irish Artillery, do as soon as possible, join the Regiment at Chapel-Izod; and it is expected that they will not be later than the 4th day of October next, at farthest.

J. STRATON, *Colonel Commandant,*
Major General.
Ordnance Office, Dublin,
26th *September*, 1794.

27th September.—His Excellency the Lord Lieutenant on the late Augmentation of the Artillery, complimented the Colonels of Militia with the recommendation of an Officer in each of their Regiments to be a Lieutenant in the Corps of Artillery.—(*Dublin Journal.*)

ESTABLISHMENT OF THE REGIMENT.

10th October.—Within these twelve months past upwards of 500 Recruits, all picked young fellows, have been enlisted in the Counties of Antrim, Derry, and Fermanagh, for the Regiment of Royal Irish Artillery.—(*Freeman's Journal.*)

October.—In October, 1794, the Establishment was 20 Marching, and 1 Invalid Companies, the strength of the Regiment being 2,069. The detail of this strength is given in the margin of the King's Letter which organised these twenty Companies into two Battalions, the 20th May, 1795.—(*MSS. in R. A. Record Office.*)

BEATING ORDERS TO RAISE MEN.

November.—We take the following from the *Dublin Gazette* :—

WAR OFFICE, DUBLIN CASTLE,

14th November, 1794.

Notice is hereby given to such Gentlemen as are raising Men for Commissions in the Royal Irish Regiment of Artillery, that should their respective Quotas not be completed, and passed at the Head-Quarters of the Regiment, on or before the 1st day of

January, 1795, their Beating Orders will be cancelled and they will not be considered as entitled to Commissions.

By His Excellency the Lord Lieutenant's Command.

GASPER ERCK.

RECRUITS DRAFTED TO GREAT BRITAIN.

22nd December.—Board of Ordnance.

Enclosing by command of the Lord Lieutenant, a Copy of a Letter dated 19th Instant, which His Excellency has received from His Grace the Duke of Portland, His Majesty's Secretary of State, notifying His Majesty's Determination that three hundred Recruits should be Drafted from the Royal Irish Regiment of Artillery and Passed Over to Great Britain in Order to replace on the Artillery Establishment there a similar number of men Advanced in their Discipline who are immediately to be detached on Foreign Service to fill up the Deficiencies in the Six Companies sent from Ireland for that Service, and signifying His Majesty's Commands that this Measure be immediately carried into execution and that the Drafts be passed over to England under the care of a Proper Officer with all Possible Expedition.

And His Excellency desires you will issue the Necessary Orders for carrying His Majesty's Pleasure as before signified into immediate execution accordingly. A Guinea and a half will be allowed for each Draft, and His Excellency desires you will report to him at what Port they can be most conveniently embarked.

E. COOKE.

1795

Drafts Embark for England.

2nd January.—An Order, by yesterday's mail from England, arrived at the War Office, for the immediate embarkation of another Draft of 300 Men from the Royal Irish Artillery. It is said they are to be shipped off for Bristol.—(*Freeman's Journal.*)

14th January.—A fine body of the Royal Irish Artillery marched to the Pigeon House, to embark thence for England, preparatory to their employment in foreign service. (*Freeman's Journal.*)

1st March.—Yesterday passed through this town (Plymouth), from Dublin, last from Bristol, 120 of the Royal Irish Artillery. They are to be quartered in the Dock Barracks.—(*Freeman's Journal.*)

Bounty Money for Recruits Increased.

12th March.—Board of Ordnance.

In consequence of your application I have my Lord Lieutenant's Commands to acquaint you that His Excellency has been pleased to Approve that the Bounty Money for the Artillery Regiment should be raised from five to seven Guineas, and desires you will issue the necessary Orders accordingly.

MILTON.

At this time there was competition for Recruits

between the Army and the Militia, and as "Gentlemen" Volunteers were encouraged to enrol themselves in the Royal Dublin Regiment and receive a Bounty of Ten Guineas, it was worth while to pay a higher price than Five Guineas in order to induce men to enlist for the Artillery Regiment.

The following Address to stimulate recruiting for the Militia, taken from the *Freeman's Journal*, Dublin, for December, 1794, may be interesting to the reader :—

"A correspondent who was present at the Castle gate on Friday last, when Alderman W——, at the head of a recruiting party for the Duke of York's Royal Dublin Regiment, made the following harangue, begs leave through the channel of your excellent paper to communicate it to the public.

(1) "All Gentlemen Volunteers (says the Alderman) who wish to distinguish themselves as loyal subjects, faithful citizens, and patriotic Soldiers, have now an opportunity of being enrolled in this honourable band commanded by His Royal Highness the Duke of York. Such Irish heroes are invited here to the drum-head, where they will be kindly and honourably entertained, enter into pay, and receive an immediate bounty of *Ten New Guineas* each man, besides Arms, Clothing and Accoutrements—such as a gentleman loyal Volunteer is entitled to.

(2) "Volunteers for this royal loyal Regiment will also be entertained by the Lord Mayor, and every Alderman of this City; also by General Crosbie, Colonel Lightburne, and the other Officers of the Corps, and the Committee.

(3) "Now my gallant countrymen don't miss this glorious opportunity of putting yourselves under the command of our magnanimous Prince, who, at the special desire of his royal father, our most gracious Sovereign, takes the command of this gallant Regiment, thus raised by the loyal Corporation of this City; come forward my gallant fellow citizens, you are thus invited to fight for our beloved King, and our excellent Constitution under the command of our Gracious King's own son, the gallant Duke of York: what Irishman can refuse this invitation? You have not a moment to lose, as the regiment will be complete in a very few days; step forward boldly, my lads, and lend a hand to extirpate tyrants, regicides, and enemies to the human race, who usurp the Government of France, who have already enslaved that unhappy Nation, and who would wish to enslave the whole world.

(4) "I myself, my lads, as an Alderman of this City, and residing almost my whole life among you, am not unknown, let me particularly invite you to breakfast with me at my house in Eccles Street every morning of this and the ensuing week, where you shall receive your bounty, and be immediately introduced to the brave General Crosbie, the Colonel Commandant of this loyal regiment under H.R.H. the Duke.

God Save the King.
(Three Cheers.)

(5) "One word more: General Crosbie provides a dinner at two o'Clock this day, in his barrack, Essex Street, where each loyal Volunteer is invited; Moun-

tains of roast beef and plum-pudding, with rivers of Irish porter—Huzza."

Three Companies from the Continent.

12th May.—Board of Ordnance.

The Lord Lieutenant's Commands to signify the Board that His Excellency has received a Letter from His Majesty's Principal Secretary of State, informing His Excellency that the three Companies of the Irish Artillery which have been employed on the Continent will upon their arrival at Portsmouth be ordered to proceed to Ireland, and that in consequence of this supply and of the 300 Artillery Recruits which have lately been sent back from England, it is expected that about the middle of August the Irish Regiment of Artillery will be able not only to supply a sufficient number of seasoned men for completing the Deficiencies in the three Companies serving in the West Indies, but also to spare in case they should be wanted three Additional Companies for the Same service, and His Excellency desires you will issue the necessary Orders for receiving the three Companies expected from Portsmouth, and take all such steps and make all such arrangements as may be requisite for enabling the Royal Irish Regiment of Artillery to send the supplies before mentioned.

J. Pelham.

Three Companies from the Continent.

2nd July.—On Monday (29th June), 300 Men of the

Royal Irish Artillery, under the command of Major Arabin, marched into Cork from Kinsale (where they landed from the Continent), on their route to Chapel-Izod.—(*Freeman's Journal.*)

4th July.—Such of the Royal Irish Artillery Corps as remained on the Continent, are returned once more to their Barracks at Chapel-Izod.—(*Freeman's Journal.*)

THE REGIMENT FORMED INTO TWO BATTALIONS.

20th May.—The existing Establishment was discontinued on the 19th May, 1795, and on the following day, 20th May, the Regiment was formed into two Battalions, by which measure an addition of 13 Field Officers and Staff Officers, and 1 Serjeant Major and 2 Quarter-Master Serjeants arose, raising the Establishment from 2,069 to 2,085, the strength of the two Battalions being 2,032, and of the Invalid Company 53.

The Companies were still 100 Officers, Non-Commissioned Officers, Gunners and Drummers each.

A Brigade Major was now placed on the strength of the Regiment.—(*MSS. in R. A. Record Office.*)

CAMP AT LAUGHLINSTOWN.

20th June.—Board of Ordnance.

A proposal having been laid before His Excellency by Lord Carhampton for erecting temporary Wooden

Huts for 4,500 Men at the Camp near Laughlinstown, His Excellency was pleased to approve of the same ...

J. PELHAM.

3rd July.—A Train of Artillery consisting of 14 Pieces and 200 Men, with Lieut.-Colonel Wright at their head, marched from Chapel-Izod to the encampment at Laughlinstown where they will remain with the other troops.—(*Freeman's Journal.*)

DETACHMENTS EMBARK FOR WEST INDIES.

31st July.—The Detachments of the Regiment returned from the Continent, having joined at Head Quarters in the early part of July, 1795. On the 31st of that month, two Companies were suddenly ordered to Cork to embark for Foreign Service under the command of Lieut.-Colonel Arabin, but on the 1st September they were still in Ireland and stationed at Clonmel, and from thence proceeded to Ardfinnan Camp.—(*MSS. in R. A. Record Office.*)

24th September.—139 Officers, Non-Commissioned Officers and Men of the two Companies embarked at Dublin, and the remainder of the two Companies and the Detachment to complete those already in the West Indies assembled at Cork under the command of Lieut.-Colonel Arabin, who embarked them about the 28th September. The force sent from these two ports with the survivors of the three Companies already in the West Indies, (45 Non-Commissioned Officers and Privates,) raised the Numbers of the

Irish Artillery for the Service of those Colonies to 500 of all Ranks.—(*MSS. in R. A. Record Office.*)

The Records of the Office of Ordnance, England, show that the Detachment which embarked at Dublin, 24th September, arrived at Portsmouth on 5th October, and the Detachment under the command of Lieut.-Colonel Arabin reached the same post nine days later. Both Detachments were quartered in Hilsea Barracks, awaiting the arrival of Transports.

The following are the details of the Bill for the Hire of Wagons, etc., for Lieut.-Colonel Arabin's Detachment on the march.

		£	s.	d.
1.	Pill to Bristol, by water	1	11	0
2.	Guard Room, Bristol	0	10	6
3.	Bristol to Bath	2	12	0
4.	Bath to Devizes	6	0	0
5.	Devizes to Salisbury	6	16	0
6.	Guard Room, Salisbury	0	16	3
7.	Salisbury to Romsey	4	16	0
8.	Guard Room, Romsey	0	8	0
9.	Romsey to Fareham	6	12	0
10.	Guard Room, Fareham	0	7	0
11.	Fareham to Hilsea	1	17	0
		£32	5	9

The Monthly Return of the Regiment for May, 1796, shows that 24 Officers and 480 Non-Commissioned Officers and Men sailed from Portsmouth, 9th December, 1795, for the West Indies.

MONTHLY RETURN OF THE ROYAL IRISH REGIMENT OF ARTILLERY FOR AUGUST, 1795.

1st September.

	Officers	Non-Com. Officers and Men	Total all Ranks
17 Companies in Ireland	117	1,411	1,528
3 Companies on Foreign Service	4	91	95
Vacant for Widow's Fund	—	15	15
Old Establishment	—	5	5
Wanting to complete the 20 Marching Companies	3	881	884
Total	124	1,903	2,027
Invalid Company	3	50	53
Total Establishment	127	1,953	2,080

17 Companies in Ireland.

	Officers	Non-Com. Officers and Men	Total all Ranks
Present and fit for Duty	45	319	364
In Camp and on Command	47	884	931
Sick	5	99	104
Absent by Leave	4	16	20
In the Marshalsea	—	1	1
Not joined	6	—	6
Worn Out and Unfit for Duty	—	17	17
Recruiting	10	67	77
Prisoners of War	—	8	8
Total of 17 Companies	117	1,411	1,528

On Command, included in the Return.

	Officers	Non-Com. Officers and Men	Total
Belfast	3	59	62
Carrickfergus	1	14	15
Charlemont	1	25	26
Drogheda	—	6	6
Dundalk	—	6	6
Charles Fort	—	13	13
Cork	1	15	16
Cork Harbour	9	209	218
Limerick	1	20	21
Athlone	4	57	61
Galway	—	7	7
Kilkenny	—	6	6
Tarbert	1	19	20
Clonmel	1	25	26
Dublin Castle	2	43	45
Dublin Harbour	—	8	8
Ordnance Stores	1	16	17
Laughlinstown Camp	8	98	106
Naul Camp	4	43	47
Clonmel	10	195	205
Total	47	884	931

That went on Foreign Service.
Three Companies to West Indies.

	Officers	Non-Com. Officers and Men	Total
Present	4	58	62
Prisoners of War	—	27	27

Returned home at different periods	.	.	.	1	10	11
Dead	.	.	.	11	190	201
		Total	.	16	285	801

PRESENTATION OF SWORDS TO TWO OFFICERS.

16th October.—At the Quarterly Assembly on the 16th October, the Corporation of Dublin voted two Swords, of the value of five Guineas each, with a complimentary inscription to Captains Armstrong and Moore, of the Royal Irish Regiment of Artillery, for their spirited and successful resistance to a gang of robbers who lately attacked them on the Black-Rock road, three of whom they killed.—(*Dublin Journal.*)

1796

Detachment to Kildare.

29th April.—A Detachment with six Field Guns, marched from the Barracks in the Lower Castle-yard for the Curragh of Kildare, in order to assist the High Sheriff of the County in prostrating the numerous cabins that had been illegally built on the Common.—(*Dublin Journal.*)

Detachment to Cork.

27th May.—A Detachment of 250 Officers and Men, marched from the Barracks in Chapel-Izod for Cork.—(*Dublin Journal.*)

1st September.—Monthly Return of the Royal Irish Regiment of Artillery for August, 1796.

	Officers	Non-Com. Officers and Men	Total all Ranks
15 Companies in Ireland	101	1,801	1,402
5 Companies on Foreign Service	26	471	497
Wanting to Complete	2	131	133
Total	129	1,903	2,032
Invalid Company	3	50	53
Total Establishment	132	1,953	2,085

15 Companies in Ireland.

	Officers	Non-Com. Officers and Men	Total all Ranks
Present and fit for Duty	31	292	323
Sick Present and Absent	6	56	62
Absent by Leave and without Leave	4	11	15
On the different Commands in Ireland	25	535	560
At the different Camps in Ireland	21	257	278
On the March from Belfast	1	21	22
Recruiting	8	64	72
Superintending the Magazine	1	—	1
Aide-de-Camp	1	—	1
At a Military Academy	1	—	1
Not joined	1	—	1
In the Marshalsea	—	1	1
Left Sick on the Continent	—	5	5
Unfit for Service	—	39	39
Prisoners of War	1	—	1
Widow's Fund	—	15	15
Old Establishment	—	5	5
Total of 15 Companies	101	1,301	1,402

On the Different Commands in Ireland.

Where Stationed	Officers	Non-Com. Officers and Men	Total all Ranks
Cork Harbour	11	186	197
Belfast	2	53	55

		Officers	Non-Com. Officers and Men	Total all Ranks
Athlone	.	2	40	42
Charlemount	.	1	27	28
Charles Fort	.	1	29	30
Cork	.	1	28	29
Tarbert	.	1	24	25
Limerick	.	1	25	26
Carrickfergus	.	1	21	22
Galway	.	1	23	24
Drogheda	.	—	7	7
Kilkenny	.	—	7	7
Dundalk	.	—	7	7
Clonmell	.	—	8	8
Duncannon	.	—	5	5
Dublin Castle	.	2	20	22
Do. Ordnance Stores	.	1	17	18
Do. South Wall	.	—	8	8
Total	.	25	535	560

Commands

At the different Camps in Ireland.

Encamped at		Officers	Non-Com. Officers and Men	Total all Ranks
Blaris	.	7	87	94
Ardfinan	.	6	73	79
Laughlinstown	.	5	64	69
Naul	.	3	33	36
Total Camps	.	21	257	278

BRASS CANNON FROM ENGLAND.

6th September.—An entry was made by the Board of Ordnance, Dublin Castle, of thirty-six Pieces of brass Cannon (6 and 12 Pounders,) 2,000 Muskets, and 70 tons of Artillery ammunition from Liverpool.—(*Freeman's Journal.*)

We viewed two Bronze Guns at the Museum of Artillery in the Rotunda, Woolwich, that apparently formed part of the warlike supplies referred to.

The Guns are described in the Official Catalogue as follows:—

"*No.* 73. A brass heavy 12 Pounder from the late Royal Irish Artillery. It bears the Irish harp, with the motto 'Virtutis ad Namurgan premium,' which is nearly the same as that of the 18th Royal Irish Regiment, and refers to the capture of Namur by William III. in 1695. Behind the trunnions are the arms of the Earl of Drogheda, and the motto 'Fortis cadere, cedere non potest,'—The brave may fall but never yield. Maker, F. Kinman,* 1794.

"*No.* 74. A brass 6 Pounder of the late Royal Irish Artillery, bearing the same mottoes, etc., as the preceding. Maker, F. Kinman, 1796."

REVIEW AT LAUGHLINSTOWN.

22nd October.—The Troops encamped at Laughlinstown were reviewed by His Excellency the Earl of Camden, accompanied by the Commander-in-Chief,

---

* Mr. Kinman was Cannon Founder to the Board of Ordnance in England.

General Earl of Carhampton, when they exhibited a number of military evolutions, etc., much to the satisfaction of the noble reviewers, and a great number of spectators. What added much to this grand spectacle was the appearance and manœuvres of ten pieces of flying Artillery, which had been transported for the purpose from the Dublin Castle Arsenal.— (*Freeman's Journal.*)

THE FRENCH FLEET OFF BANTRY BAY.

25th December.—News of the arrival of a French fleet off the coasts of Ireland, having reached Dublin Castle, troops were hurried towards the south.

A number of pieces of flying Artillery, well mounted, with forges for making red hot balls, left the Ordnance Stores in the Castle for Cork and Waterford.

The Squadron anchored in Bantry Bay for a few days without effect.—(*Freeman's Journal.*)

1797

DETACHMENT TO HILLSBORO'.

31st January.—A very formidable park of Artillery, consisting of twenty Pieces of Cannon, amongst which were some of that kind called flying guns, were dispatched from the Ordnance Office to Hillsborough, in the north, escorted by a detachment of Artillery.— (*Freeman's Journal.*)

COMMISSIONS IN IRISH ARTILLERY REGIMENT.

13th April.—The following Advertisement is taken from the Dublin Press:—

Army.

From Two to Three Hundred Pounds will be given to any Lady or Gentleman who can procure a Commission in the Royal Irish Artillery. Letters addressed to A. B. at the Printer's, will be duly attended to. The strictest secrecy will be observed if required.— (*Dublin Journal.*)

INCREASED PAY TO SOLDIERS.

25th May.—A Warrant was issued revising the pay and allowances of the Private Soldier, and an additional two-pence per day was granted to all Soldiers serving at home and abroad.

We quote the General Orders on the subject to

show the disbursement of the Soldier's shilling at the close of the eighteenth century.—(*Dublin Journal.*)

General Orders.

For the Infantry of the Line, the Militia, and Fencible Infantry.

Whereas, over and above the provision made for Clothing, for Chelsea Hospital, for lodgings, and for medical assistance; and likewise over and above the allowance of beer, and other articles provided in Barracks and Quarters; and of bread provided at a reduced rate in Camp, the Private Soldier of Infantry of the Line, serving at home, heretofore received the pay of sixpence per day, which, together with the sum of two-pence farthing per day granted to him by his Majesty's Warrant for establishing and consolidating certain other allowances lately given him, amounts to the sum of eight-pence farthing: his Majesty having been graciously pleased to take the same into consideration, is pleased to direct, that under the following regulations, there shall, from the 25th of this present month of May, be paid to each Private Soldier of Infantry, an addition to the said sum of eight-pence farthing, the further sum of three-pence three farthings, making in the whole the sum of one shilling daily; out of this advance of pay, the Soldier is to pay the extra price of bread and meat now paid by the public, which at present amounts, upon an average, to the daily sum of one-penny three farthings; so that the nett increase in future, to each Soldier, will be two-pence per diem.

With respect to the disbursement of this shilling per day, His Majesty has been pleased to order, that a sum not exceeding Four Shillings per week, shall be applied towards the expense of the Soldier's Mess (including vegetables, etc.) unless he himself shall choose to appropriate a further part of his pay to that purpose.

That a sum not exceeding One Shilling and six-pence a week, shall be retained for necessaries, to be accounted for as usual, monthly :—

That the remainder of his pay, amounting to One Shilling and six-pence per Week, shall be paid to the Soldier, subject to the accustomed deduction, for washing, and articles for cleaning his clothes and appointments :—

And His Majesty, out of his Royal Bounty, is further pleased to order and direct for the benefit of the Soldier,

That in Camp, he shall receive the sum of five-pence farthing per week, being the difference between the allowance and value of bread and beer in quarters or barracks, and the ordinary (increased) supply of bread in Camp.

* * * * *

His Majesty is further pleased to order that the like nett addition of two-pence per diem, shall be made to all his Soldiers serving out of Great Britain.

By Command of Field Marshal H.R.H. the Duke of York.

WILLIAM FAWCETT,
Adjutant General.

Augmentation of Artillery Pay.

A similar increase was made to the pay of the Artillerymen serving in Ireland.

On the 1st June, an Estimate of £8,000 the additional Charge of an Augmentation of the Pay of fifteen Companies of the Royal Irish Regiment of Artillery from the 2nd of June, 1797, to the 1st of April, 1798, was presented to the House of Commons.

Detachment of British Artillery.

Shortly afterwards, on the 15th June, the Non-Commissioned Officers and Men of the Detachment 5th Battalion Royal Regiment of British Artillery, encamped at Laughlinstown, under the command of Major H. Rogers, signed a paper declaring their loyalty to the King, and fidelity to the country.

And further "Although an increase of our pay was never thought of, or even looked for on our parts, we cannot fail taking this opportunity of expressing our most grateful acknowledgments to the best of Sovereigns, and the goodness of Parliament for the further consideration of our comforts, which upon all occasions it will be our pride and ambition to be thought worthy of."—(*Dublin Journal.*)

Draft for the West Indies.

4th June.—A further reinforcement was sent to the West Indies. Captain Crawford with 176 Officers, Non-Commissioned Officers and Men sailed from Cork, first for Gibraltar, and from thence on to the West

Indian Islands, 25th July.—(*MSS. in R. A. Record Office.*)

RECRUITS FROM BELFAST.

11th July.—Colonel Barber arrived in Dublin from Belfast, where he had been on active duty for a considerable time past. He marched at the head of 200 Recruits for the Royal Irish Regiment of Artillery, all of whom had Orange ribbons in their breasts, and were armed with Muskets which had been taken from United Irishmen.—(*Dublin Journal.*)

APPOINTMENTS OF COLONEL IN CHIEF AND COLONEL *en Seconde.*

18th August.—War Office, Dublin Castle.

His Majesty has been pleased to appoint Henry Lawes Earl of Carhampton to be Colonel in Chief of the Royal Irish Regiment of Artillery, and the Commission dated 29th July, 1797, is come over accordingly.—(*Dublin Gazette.*)

2nd September.—War Office, Dublin Castle.

The Hon. Thomas Pakenham to be Colonel *en Seconde* of the Royal Irish Regiment of Artillery, dated 25th April, 1797.—(*Dublin Gazette.*)

COURT-MARTIAL ON AN OFFICER.

19th August.—The General Court Martial sitting at the Barracks, Dublin, finished the proceedings on one of the Officers brought before it for Trial. He was sentenced (for having drawn his sword on an Officer of the same Regiment—the Royal Irish Artillery) to be suspended for one month; but in consequence of the provocation he had received, and his general good conduct, the Court recommended a remission of the sentence, and His Excellency the Lord Lieutenant was pleased to remit it accordingly.—(*Dublin Journal.*)

EXPERIMENT WITH 24 POUNDER GUNS.

22nd September.—The Commander-in-Chief, accompanied by General Eustace and Sir George Shee, was present in the Phœnix Park when an experiment was made of moving 24 Pounders by means of Bullocks, six of which drew with ease these hitherto immoveable pieces of Ordnance.—(*Dublin Journal.*)

FORMING A CORPS OF DRIVERS.

23rd September.—Board of Ordnance.

Earl Carhampton, Master General of the Ordnance, submitted a Plan of forming a Corps of Drivers, and supplying draft Horses for the Artillery, in the event of an enemy landing in Ireland.

The text of the Plan is as follows :—

To turn over to the Board of Ordnance, 150 Horses from the 16 Regiments of Dragoons if there shall appear to be so many fit for draught among the number to be cast.

And from the Men who are without Horses in the Dragoon Regiments I would permit 800 to volunteer to serve during the War as Drivers attached to the

Artillery, every Regiment furnishing a number in proportion to their dismounted, with two Non-Commissioned Officers from each.

Each man to be supplied gratis from the Board of Ordnance with a round Hat, a pair of Shoes, and waggoner's Frock, to have the care of the Horses, to be taught to drive, and occasionally to learn the exercise of the Great Guns.

The Plan met with approval, and in November, the Officers of "A Corps of Artificers and Drivers attached to the Royal Regiment of Artillery in Ireland," were appointed. They consisted of a Captain Commandant, 2 Captains, 3 Lieutenants, and 2 Assistant Surgeons.

A Return dated the 30th December, showing the number of Horses in the service of the Corps of Drivers, is as follows:—

Horses recruited for the Corps	177
Received from 4th Dragoon Guards	6
5th ,,	6
5th Dragoons	4
9th ,,	1
24th ,,	46
Total	240

Present Disposition.

Enniskillen	45
Athlone	64
Castle-yard	77
Man-of-War	47

Chapel-Izod 4
Cast and Sold . . . 8
                                    ———
                            Total 240

CHARLES COMBERS,
Captain, Corps of Drivers.

DETACHMENT TO MUNSTER.

2nd October.—A large Detachment from the different Regiments in garrison, as also of the Artillery at Chapel-Izod, were sent by the southern road in their way to Munster.

At Bantry Bay, and its vicinities there are at present 92 Pieces of formidable Ordnance, and attended by the best disciplined troops in the world.—(*Freeman's Journal.*)

TROOPS FROM LAUGHLINSTOWN CAMP.

3rd October.—The troops encamped at Laughlinstown, marched into Dublin on their way to the westward for a practical lesson of field duty. The troops on marching off formed a grand and striking appearance, being completely equipped as for real action. Each of the Romney Fencible Cavalry having his horse's forage slung by his side; the train of Artillery was appointed in the most perfect style, having in it some pieces of Ordnance of the largest calibre—the twenty-four pounders, each drawn by eight bullocks, were a truly novel spectacle, being rarely used as field pieces.—(*Freeman's Journal.*)

DETACHMENT TO ENNISKILLEN.

13th December.—Two Pieces of Ordnance, 12 Pounders, were despatched from the Ordnance Stores in the Lower Castle-yard, with a Detachment of the Artillery Regiment for Enniskillen, where they are to be stationed.—(*Freeman's Journal.*)

ARRIVAL OF BRITISH ARTILLERY.

26th December.—Several Transports arrived from Liverpool with the Cavalry Corps* which are to form the Flying Artillery for this country.

The men are all well-looking, and the horses of a superior kind.—(*Freeman's Journal.*)

REPOSITORY OF ARTILLERY.

30th December.—As the Castle Arsenal-yard is not sufficiently capacious for the Quantity of National Ordnance, with its appendant Carts and Carriages, a piece of ground contiguous to the Royal Invalid Hospital at Kilmainham, is preparing as a general Park or Repository of Artillery, in the manner of Woolwich Warren in England.—(*Dublin Journal.*)

ESTABLISHMENT.

The Establishment continued this year at 2,085 of all Ranks.

It is regretted that no Monthly Returns showing the distribution of the Regiment for this year, are available at the Record Offices.

---

* The Corps here referred to is the Detachments of the British Royal Horse Artillery sent to Ireland to assist in quelling the Rebellion. (See events for year 1798.)

1798

BRITISH ARTILLERY REVIEWED.

4th January.—His Excellency the Lord Lieutenant, reviewed in the Phœnix Park, the Detachment of Flying Artillery that arrived lately from England. Each piece of Artillery was attended by a party of Horse, and was drove from place to place, upon the Fifteen Acres, with a wonderful celerity, firing in various directions with the greatest skill and agility. Both men and horses are well trained, and they dispatch these guns to a given distance at the rate of ten miles an hour, using which will prevent that great inconvenience that has often occurred to an Army, of waiting a long time for Artillery to come up, to aid their operations.—(*Freeman's Journal.*)

DETACHMENT AT CHATHAM.

January.—A Muster Roll of the Detachment at Chatham, for the month of January, shows the total numbers as follows:

Captain	1
Captain Lieutenant	1
First Lieutenants	4
Second Lieutenants	7
Corporals	4
Bombardiers	8
Gunners	132
Drummers	2
Total all Ranks	159

1*st February.*—MONTHLY RETURN OF THE ROYAL IRISH REGIMENT OF ARTILLERY FOR JANUARY, 1798.

	Officers	Non-Com. Officers and Men	Total all Ranks
14 Companies in Ireland	95	1,335	1,430
6 Companies on Service, viz.:			
5 West Indies, 1 England	32	570	602
Total	127	1,905	2,032
Invalid Company	3	50	53
Total Establishment	130	1,955	2,085

14 *Companies in Ireland.*	Officers	Non-Com. Officers and Men	Total all Ranks
Present and fit for Duty	19	205	224
On the different Commands	56	890	946
At Laughlinstown Camp	2	48	50
Dublin	1	44	45
Magazine Fort	1	14	14
In the Marshalsea	—	1	1
Inspecting Stores	1	—	1
Sick	4	23	27
Absent with and without Leave	3	5	8
Unfit for Service	—	52	52
Vacant for Widow's Fund	—	14	14
Old Establishment	—	3	3
In England	6	—	6
Wanting to complete	3	36	39
Total of 14 Companies	95	1,335	1,430

On the different Commands.

Where Stationed	Officers	Non-Com. Officers and Men	Total all Ranks
Northern District	19	254	273
Southern do.	30	417	447
Western do.	7	115	122
Attached to different Regiments with Battalion Guns	—	95	95
With the British Horse Artillery	—	9	9
Total Commands	56	890	946

	Officers	Non-Com. Officers and Men	Total all Ranks
Militia attached to the Regiment	—	250	250

SUBSCRIPTIONS TO CARRY ON THE WAR.

16th February.—The Officers and Men of the Regiment, subscribed a large sum of money to Mr. Pitt's Loyalty Loan, as will be seen by the following:—

CHAPEL-IZOD, *16th February*, 1798.

The Non-Commissioned Officers and Privates of the Royal Irish Regiment of Artillery now at Head Quarters, having heard that they will be allowed the pleasure of Subscribing at this critical Period, towards the support of their King and Country, take the earliest Opportunity of offering Nine Days' Subsistence, or any further Part of their Pay, which it may be thought necessary to apply to so honourable and precious a Purpose.

  For Self and Brother Soldiers,

    W. WALKER, *Serjeant Major*.

To the Hon. Thomas Pakenham,
 Lieut.-General of his Majesty's
  Ordnance, etc., etc., etc.

ROYAL IRISH ARTILLERY AND ENGINEERS.

17th February.—At a Meeting of the Corps of Royal Irish Artillery and Engineers, at the Ordnance Office, it was unanimously determined, by the Officers of both Corps now at Head Quarters, that they will cheerfully contribute a Month's Pay of each Rank, in support of the noble and generous examples given by the Non-Commissioned Officers and Men whom they have the honour to command.

  THOMAS PAKENHAM, *Lieut.-General*.

Subscriptions.

From the Officers, Non-Commissioned
 Officers and Privates of the Royal
 Irish Artillery, and the Corps of
 Drivers, with the Principal and Inferior
 Officers of the Ordnance Department   £3,816   2   8

    —(*Freeman's Journal.*)

THE ARMY UNDISCIPLINED.

26th February.—At the commencement of the year, the Commander of the Forces found the state of the Army in Ireland so undisciplined and demoralised that he caused the following General Order to be published :—

ADJUTANT GENERAL'S OFFICE,
DUBLIN, 26*th February*, 1798.

GENERAL ORDERS.

The very disgraceful frequency of Courts Martial, and the many complaints of irregularities in the conduct of the Troops in this Kingdom, having too unfortunately proved the Army to be in a state of licentiousness, which must render it formidable to every one but the enemy, the Commander-in-Chief thinks it necessary to demand from all Generals Commanding Districts and Brigades, as well as Commanding Officers of Regiments, that they exert for themselves, and compel from all Officers under their command, the strictest and most unremitting attention to the discipline, good order and conduct of their men, such as may restore the high and distinguished reputation the British troops have been accustomed to enjoy in every part of the world,—It becomes necessary to recur, and most pointedly to attend to the Standing Orders of the Kingdom, which at the same time that they direct military assistance to be given at the requisition of the Civil Magistrate, positively forbid the Troops to act (but in case of attack) without his presence and authority, and the most clear and precise orders are to be given to the Officer Commanding the party for this purpose.

The utmost prudence and precaution are also to be used in granting parties to Revenue Officers, both with respect to the person requiring such assistance, and those employed on the duty.—Whenever a guard is mounted, patrols must be frequently sent out to take up any Soldier who may be found out of his quarters after hours.

A very culpable remissness having also appeared on the part of the Officers, respecting the necessary inspection of barracks, quarters, messes, etc., as well as attendance at roll calls, and other hours, Commanding Officers must enforce the attention of these under his command to those points, and the General Regulations, for all which the strictest responsibility will be expected for themselves.

It is of the utmost importance that the discipline of the Dragoon Regiments should be minutely attended to, for the facilitating of which, the Commander-in-Chief has dispensed with the attendance of Orderly Dragoons on himself, and desires that they may not be employed by any General or Commanding Officer, but on military and indispensable business.

G. HEWITT,
Adjutant General.
Lieut.-General Craig,
Eastern District Barracks,
Dublin.
—(*Freeman's Journal.*)

COMPANIES ON FOREIGN SERVICE.

1st May.—A Monthly Return of the Regiment for April, shows the following:

6 *Companies on Service.*

Embarked at Chatham on 10th April, 1798	10 Officers—	91 N.C. Officers & Men
Left Sick at Chatham		9 do.
Entered into other Regiments		48 do.

Five Companies only on Foreign Service.

15th May.—In the twelve months immediately succeeding the departure of the last force,* six Companies are returned on Foreign Service, but during the latter half-year of the period, one of these Six Foreign Service Companies (Captain Blaquere's) was at Chatham, and in the twelfth month, an Order of the Lieut.-General of the Irish Ordnance, dated 15th May, 1798, regulated that only Five Companies should be accounted for in the British Establishment (Foreign Service), and that Fifteen should remain in Ireland.—(*MSS. in R. A. Record Office*).

1st July.—A Monthly Return of the Regiment for June, shows the following:—

Five Companies only ordered to be accounted on Foreign Service, commencing 1st June, and a 15th Company in Ireland formed out of the Fourteen for Captain Crawford.

Plan to Take Dublin Castle.

23rd May.—It was known that the United Irishmen had laid a plan to take at the same time, the Castle of Dublin, the Artillery at Chapel-Izod, and the Camp at Laughlinstown, but such was the vigilance of Government that the intended movements in the capital were frustrated.

On the 24th the Lord Lieutenant published a Proclamation by which he delegated to the several Military Officers, the power of trying crimes connected

---

See Draft for the West Indies, 25th July, 1797, for Cork.

with Rebellion by Martial Law, which resulted in the publication of the following

Notice.

"Lieut.-General Lake, Commanding His Majesty's Forces in this Kingdom, having received from His Excellency the Lord Lieutenant full powers to put down the Rebellion, and to punish rebels in the most summary manner, according to Martial Law, does hereby give notice to all His Majesty's Subjects, that he is determined to exert the powers entrusted to him in the most vigorous manner, for the immediate suppression of the same: and that all Persons acting in the present Rebellion, or in any wise aiding or assisting therein, will be treated by him as Rebels, and punished accordingly.

And Lieut.-General Lake hereby requires all the Inhabitants of the City of Dublin (the Great Officers of State, Members of the Houses of Parliament, Privy Counsellors, Magistrates, and Military Persons in uniform excepted), to remain within their respective Dwellings from Nine o'Clock at night till Five in the morning under pain of punishment."

By Order of Lieut.-General Lake,

Commanding His Majesty's Forces in this Kingdom,

G. HEWETT,
Adjutant General.

Adjutant General's Office,
Dublin, 24*th May*, 1798.

—(*Freeman's Journal.*)

1*st August.*—MONTHLY RETURN OF THE ROYAL IRISH REGIMENT OF ARTILLERY FOR JULY, 1798.

	Officers	Non-Com. Officers and Men	Total all Ranks
15 Companies in Ireland	104	1,480	1,534
5 Companies on Foreign Service	23	475	498
Total	127	1,905	2,032
Invalid Company	3	50	53
Total Establishment	130	1,955	2,085

15 *Companies in Ireland.*

	Officers	Non-Com. Officers and Men	Total all Ranks
Pigeon House Fort, Present Fit for Duty	17	107	124
Sick Present and Absent	4	20	24
Dublin Castle	4	59	63
Dublin Garrison attached to British Artillery	1	25	26
Dublin Royal Hospital	—	11	11
Magazine Fort	2	43	45
Chapel-Izod	9	94	103
Luttrelstown	1	—	1
With General Needham's Army	1	6	7
Unfit for Service	—	42	42
Widow's Fund	—	15	15
Old Establishment	—	3	3
Commands in Ireland	59	895	954

On Foreign Service and Ordered Home	.	2	—	2
Wanting to complete	.	4	110	114
Total of 15 Companies		104	1,430	1,534

On the different Commands.

Where Stationed	Officers	Non-Com. Officers and Men	Total
Northern District	20	278	298
Southern	32	399	431
Western	7	113	120
Attached to Regiments with Battalion Guns	—	105	105
Total Commands	59	895	954

THE REBELLION IN IRELAND.

In a work of this kind it would obviously be out of place to discuss the origin and causes of the disaffection in Ireland which led up to the Rebellion of 1798, and as regards the Rebellion itself, we confine ourselves to a brief account (taken from *Haydn's Dictionary of Dates*) of the principal events in its suppression.

Kilcullen, 23rd May, 1798.

Here a large body of the insurgent Irish defeated the British forces, commanded by General Dundas.

The General in a subsequent engagement overthrew the rebels near Kilcullen-bridge, when 300 were slain.

Naas, 24th May, 1798.

Here a desperate engagement took place between a body of the King's forces, and the insurgent Irish. The latter were defeated with the loss of 300 killed and many wounded.

Tara, 26th May, 1798.

Near here the royalist troops 400 strong, defeated the insurgent Irish, 500 killed.

Oulart, 27th May, 1798.

Here 5,000 Irish insurgents attacked the King's troops in small numbers. The North Cork Militia, after great feats of bravery, were cut to pieces, five men only escaping.

Gorey, 4th June, 1798.

Near here the King's troops under Colonel Walpole were defeated, and their leader slain, by the Irish rebels.

Ballynahinch, 13th June, 1798.

Here a sanguinary engagement took place between a large body of the insurgent Irish and the British troops, under General Nugent. A large part of the town was destroyed, and the royal army suffered very severely.

Vinegar Hill, near Enniscorthy, 21st June, 1798.

Here the Irish rebels, headed by Father John, a priest, encamped and committed many outrages on the surrounding country. They were gradually surrounded by the British troops, commanded by General

Lake, and, after a fierce struggle, with much slaughter, totally dispersed.

Castlebar, 27th August, 1798.

About 1,100 French troops under General Humbert, landed at Killala, and assisted by Irish insurgents here, compelled the King's troops under General Lake to retreat; but were compelled to surrender at Ballinamuck, 8th September.

[While giving this summary for the sake of convenience, we must dissociate ourselves from many of the writer's views and statements, notably in the account of Oulart and Vinegar Hill. We now resume the general narrative.]

The Irish Artillery in the Field.

The Irish Artillery was actively employed in the Field during the Rebellion, and fought side by side with the British Horse Artillery.

On the 29th May, a Detachment of the Irish Artillery with two Howitzers, were taken by the Irish near Wexford.

On the 4th June, the Irish Artillery left two 6 Pounders and a Howitzer in the hands of the enemy, but the Irish in their flight on the 21st June left the three pieces of Ordnance behind them, as will be seen by the following extract of a Letter from Lieut.-General Lake to Lord Viscount Castlereagh, dated

ENNISCORTHY, 21*st June*, 1798.

MY LORD,

I have the honour to acquaint Your Lordship, for

His Excellency the Lord Lieutenant's information that the Rebel Camp upon Vinegar Hill was attacked this morning at seven o'Clock, and carried in about an hour and a half.

. . . . . .

To the rapid and well-directed fire of the Royal Artillery, and the gallantry of their Officers and Men, for which they have ever been distinguished, I consider myself this day highly indebted; and I am happy in expressing my obligations to Captain Bloomfield, Commanding the Irish Royal Artillery, with the Officers and Men under their command.

I have, etc.,

G. LAKE.

P.S.—Enclosed is a Return of the Ordnance taken on Vinegar Hill, in which are included three taken from us on the 4th of June.

. . . . . .

Cannon Captured by the French.

When the French attacked the King's troops at Castlebar, on the 27th August, and compelled them to retire, six Field Pieces fell into the enemy's hands, but in their retreat at Ballinamuck, on the 8th September, the French were compelled to abandon the Cannon which they had taken in the former actions with His Majesty's forces.

ARTILLERYMAN EXECUTED FOR DISLOYALTY.

6th September.—There is no more hateful duty to Soldiers than the suppression of Civil disturbances.

It destroys the good feelings between the Troops and the Civil population, and estranges long friendships.

In the work of suppressing the Rebellion, the fidelity of native born Irishmen serving in the British Army could hardly have been put to a more crucial test. Those men were required to hang or capture their countrymen and friends and destroy their habitations. In the circumstances it is hardly to be wondered at that there were cases, and not a few, of disloyalty among the King's troops in Ireland, yet we came across only one instance of an Artilleryman who had been tried and found guilty of complicity in the Rebellion.

It was thus chronicled in the *Dublin* newspapers :—

"Thursday, 6th September, 1798, a person named Roberts was executed pursuant to the sentence of a Court Martial, for having engaged in the late ill-omened Rebellion. The above delinquent belonged to the Artillery Regiment, and had obtained a furlough, grounded upon indisposition, but joined the Rebels. He, it appeared on his trial, acted as an Officer of Artillery in most of the recent engagements with the insurgents, particularly at New Ross and Vinegar-hill. Some of his own Regiment, who had been surprised and made prisoners, and were obliged to act for the Rebels, gave evidence against him, who stated that he had the command of the guns they were stationed at, and rode on horseback when giving directions. At one particular period when the poor men who were obliged to work the guns, had levelled them for the Rebels, but not in a manner to do execution, Roberts observed the design, and called out to the pike-men about him to put these men to death, which they would have suffered, were it not for the interference of one Kearns, a superior in command, who said they should not be piked, as it appeared to him they were doing their duty. Roberts had possessed himself of the epaulets worn by the late much-lamented Lord Mountjoy, who fell at the battle of New Ross. One of them he confessed he wore himself, when acting for the Rebels, which he pretended he had been obliged to do, and the other he mentioned he had made a present of, we suppose, to a brother-Officer of the Insurgents. He met a most impartial and indulgent trial; and when cross-examining the evidence, in several instances he confirmed his guilt. We believe there never was a man sentenced to death who died with less pity."

FORMATION OF REGIMENT INTO BRIGADES.

19th September.—An arrangement was made for the formation of the Artillery in Ireland into Brigades—and distinguishing the Brigades as Heavy and Light.

The Establishment of the first to consist of 4 Medium 12-Pounders and 2 $5\frac{1}{2}$-inch Howitzers, and the last of 4 Light 6-Pounder Battalion Guns.

The former to be manned by 48 Non-Commissioned Officers and Men, and the latter by 37 Non-Commissioned Officers and Men of the Regiment, the Guns and their attendant Carriages to be Horsed and Driven by the Driver Corps.—(*MSS. in R. A. Record Office.*)

1799

1st *January.*—Monthly Return of the Royal Irish Regiment of Artillery for December, 1798.

	Officers	Non-Com. Officers and Men	Total
15 Companies in Ireland	105	1,430	1,535
5 Companies in West Indies	22	475	497
Total	127	1,905	2,032
Invalid Company	3	50	53
Total Establishment	130	1,955	2,085

15 *Companies in Ireland.*

	Officers	Non-Com. Officers and Men	Total
Present at Head Quarters, Pigeon House Fort	15	109	124
Brigades and Batteries	71	1,151	1,222
At Luttrelstown	1	—	1
Residing in Dublin	1	—	1
Magazine Fort	2	22	24
Chapel-Izod Laboratory, etc.	7	53	60
In the Provost's	—	2	2
Sick	3	25	28
Absent by Leave	1	—	1
Ordered Home from West Indies	1	—	1
Vacant for Widow's Fund	—	15	15

	Officers	Non-Com. Officers and Men	Total
Old Establishment	—	2	2
In England	1	—	1
Wanting to Complete	2	51	53
Total of 15 Companies	105	1,430	1,535

5 Companies in West Indies.

	Officers	Non-Com. Officers and Men	Total
Present	17	460	477
Sick, Leave, etc.	4	—	4
Wanting to Complete	1	15	16
Total of 5 Companies	22	475	497

Vacant Officers.

Lieutenants S. Fitzgerald and E. Swayne Killed returning to Europe, September, 1798, in an engagement with a French Privateer.

DETAIL OF BRIGADES, BATTERIES, ETC., IN IRELAND.

Brigades.	Officers	Non-Com. Officers and Men	Total Artillery	Additional Gunners
East.				
Two at Island Bridge	6	87	93	8
One, Naas	3	36	39	4
One, Arklow	3	36	39	4
One, Wexford	2	31	33	7
North.				
Two, Charlemont	6	99	105	—
One, Belfast	3	39	42	—
One, Omagh	2	82	84	—

One, Enniskillen	2	36	38	—
Half, Coleraine	1	18	19	—
Half, Ballymena	1	19	20	—
Half, Dundalk	1	19	20	—
Half, Downpatrick	1	18	19	—

South.

One, Clonmel	4	52	56	85
Two, Cork	5	95	100	—
One, Bandon	2	36	38	—
One, Limerick	2	37	39	1
One, Tarbert	2	25	27	12
One Waterford	3	29	32	7
One, Kilkenny	2	27	29	26

West.

Two, Athlone	5	83	88	28
One, Athenry	2	36	38	—
One, Carrick-on-Shannon	3	19	22	—
One, Castlebar	1	18	19	—

Batteries, etc.

Londonderry, Strabane, etc.	2	59	61	—
Carrickfergus	—	12	12	—
Cork Harbour	4	75	79	—
Charles Fort	1	16	17	—
Duncannon Fort	1	11	12	—
Tarbert	—	12	12	12
Bantry	1	23	24	—
With Battalion Guns	—	16	16	—
Total	71	1,151	1,222	144

Militia Gunners Discontinued.

February.—The Additional Gunners from the Militia also, which at the period when the new organization* was determined on amounted to 213, were reduced by its operation in the February following (1799), to 76, which Number was gradually decreased, and in 1799 the use of Militia Gunners was altogether discontinued. —(*MSS. in R. A. Record Office.*)

Detachment to West Indies.

6th November.—A Detachment of the Royal Irish Regiment of Artillery consisting of 8 Officers and 100 Men, embarked at Dublin for the West Indies. They sail from hence to Cork, and from thence to Barbadoes and Martinique.—(*Dublin Journal.*)

---

* See Formation of Regiments into Brigades, 1798.

1800

DETACHMENT TO WEST INDIES.

15th January.—In the Monthly Return of the Regiment for January, 7 Officers and 89 Non-Commissioned Officers and Men is shown as having embarked from Cork Harbour on the 15th of that month, to complete the five Companies serving in West Indies.

APPOINTMENT OF BRIGADE MAJOR.

31st May.—Captain Joseph Maclean from the Royal British Artillery to be Brigade Major, *vice* Stewart.—(*Dublin Gazette.*)

Captain Maclean was the only Officer of the British Artillery placed on the strength of the Irish Artillery since April, 1756, when "The Artillery Company in Ireland" was organised.

APPOINTMENTS OF COLONEL IN CHIEF AND COLONEL *en Seconde*.

29th August.—Royal Irish Regiment of Artillery.

The Hon. Thomas Pakenham to be Colonel in Chief, *vice* the Earl of Carhampton, dated 29th August, 1800.—(*Dublin Gazette.*)

24th October.—Ordnance.

Letters Patent have passed the Great Seal of this Kingdom, constituting and appointing Lieut. Colonel Marcus Beresford, Lieut.-General of His Majesty's Ordnance in this Kingdom, in the room of Hon. T. Pakenham.—(*Freeman's Journal.*)

1st October.—MONTHLY RETURN OF THE ROYAL IRISH REGIMENT OF ARTILLERY FOR SEPTEMBER, 1800.

2 *Battalions*—20 *Marching Companies and Staff.*	Officers	Non-Com. Officers and Men	Total
15 Companies in Ireland	104	1,430	1,534
5 Companies in West Indies	23	475	498
Total	127	1,905	2,032
Invalid Company	3	50	53
Total Establishment	130	1,955	2,085

15 *Companies in Ireland.*	Officers	Non-Com. Officers and Men	Total
Present at Head Quarters, Pigeon House Fort	10	111	121
Island Bridge	4	23	27
Magazine Fort	1	26	27
Residing in Dublin	4	5	9
Sick,—Absent	2	18	20
Absent by Leave	7	1	8
In Custody with the Civil Power	—	4	4
Recruiting	3	13	16
Brigades and Batteries*	69	1,210	1,279
Not joined	1	—	1
Vacant for Widow's Fund	—	15	15
Old Establishment	—	1	1
Wanting to Complete	3	3	6
Total of 15 Companies	104	1,430	1,534

* The Total on page 330 is 68 officers and 1,211 men.

Detail of Brigades, Batteries, etc., in Ireland.

East. *Brigades.*

	Officers	Non-Com. Officers and Men	Total
Two at Island Bridge	5	95	100
One, Naas	2	35	37
One, Arklow	1	36	37
One, Wexford	2	36	38

North.

Three, Charlemount	7	136	143
One, Belfast	2	38	40
One, Derry	2	36	38
One, Coleraine	2	37	39
One, Dundalk	2	35	37
One, Enniskillen	2	37	39

South.

Two, Cork	6	99	105
One, Clonmel	3	57	60
One, Bandon	1	39	40
One, Limerick	2	38	40
One, Tarbert	2	35	37
One, Waterford	2	37	39
One, Kilkenny	1	36	37

West.

Two, Athlone	7	83	90
One, Galway	2	37	39
One, Carrick-on-Shannon	1	18	19
One, Castlebar	1	18	19

Batteries, &c.

Charlemount	—	13	13
Lough Swilly	1	22	23
Carrickfergus	—	13	13
Cork Harbour	6	80	86

Charles Fort	.	1	14	15
Duncannon	.	2	16	18
Bantry	.	1	20	21
Tarbert	.	—	15	15
Inspecting Brigades	.	1	—	1
Aide-de-Camp	.	1	—	1
Total	.	68	1,211	1,279

5 Companies in West Indies.	Officers	Non-Com. Officers and Men	Total
Effective	19	352	371
Wanting to complete	4	123	127
Total of 5 Companies	23	475	498

OFFICERS OF THE FIVE COMPANIES IN THE WEST INDIES.

Rank	Names	Remarks
Captain	G. Lindsay	—
,,	W. Galbraith	—
,,	S. Benson	—
Captain Lieut.	H. Lawson	—
,,	T. Porter	—
,,	J. J. Dunkin	On his Passage out
,,	J. Campbell	Sick in England
,,	C. Keane	—
,,	R. S. Brough	—
,,	A. Bredin	—
,,	F. Power	Ordered to Ireland
First Lieut.	J. Fellowes	—
,,	J. Armstrong	—
,,	G. R. Perdrian	—
,,	M. Roe	—
,,	J. C. Dennis	—

First Lieut.	E. Smyth	—
	H. Madden	Ordered to join in W. Indies
,,	W. Fuller	—
,,	G. Sturrock	—
,,	G. Armstrong	—
,,	H. Van Scharke	Ordered to Ireland
Second Lieut..	J. D. Blundell	—

INVALID COMPANY.

		Officers	Non-Com. Officers and Men	Total
On Command	Duncannon Fort	—	12	12
	Charlemont	—	5	5
	Buncrana	—	1	1
Sick—absent		1	—	1
Employed in the Line		1	—	1
Serving in the Militia		—	2	2
At the Gunpowder-mills		—	2	2
Totally unfit for any duty		—	21	21
In and about Head-quarters		—	7	7
Wanting to complete		1	—	1
Total		3	50	53

INVALID COMPANY AUGMENTED.

The Establishment remained unchanged from 1795 until the 1st October, 1800, when the Invalid Company being increased from 53 to 100, the strength of the Regiment became 2,132.

This is the greatest force the Royal Irish Regiment of Artillery ever arrived at.—(*MSS. in R. A. Record Office.*)

1801

UNION OF GREAT BRITAIN AND IRELAND.

1st January.—Dublin Castle.

This Day the Union of the Kingdoms of Great Britain and Ireland having taken Place, the Guns at the Salute Battery in the Phœnix Park were fired, and the Royal Standard of the United Kingdom was displayed upon Bedford Tower.—(*Dublin Gazette.*)

UNION OF IRISH ARTILLERY WITH BRITISH ARTILLERY.

From this measure arose the Incorporation of the Royal Irish Artillery with the Royal British Artillery.

3rd February.—His Excellency the Lord Lieutenant submitted a Plan for the reduction of ten Companies of the Irish Artillery, and for the remaining ten Companies to become an additional Battalion of the Royal British Regiment of Artillery.

The text of the Plan* referred to, is as follows:—

Copy of the Instructions for the Union of the Irish Artillery with the English Artillery, and the Terms granted to all the Irish Officers.

DUBLIN CASTLE, 8 *February*, 1801.

MY LORD,

After much consideration and reflection on a subject which is more complicated in execution than it appears in theory, I have the honour now to transmit to your

* Ordered by the House of Commons to be printed, 17th August, 1839.

Grace, to be laid before his Majesty, a detailed proposition for the eventual incorporation of the civil and military branches of the Ordnance departments of Great Britain and Ireland.

There is no great difficulty with respect to the civil line, as the principal officers who form the Board, and whose situations must naturally be done away, will receive compensation, in the same manner as all other persons whose employments may be abolished by the arrangement which his Majesty shall find it expedient to make in consequence of the Union of the two Kingdoms.

It will likewise be easy to provide for the small corps of Irish Engineers; but the incorporation of the regiment of Irish Artillery with that of Great Britain is a matter which deeply affects the interest of a great number of officers, several of whom have, from the length of their services, and the character they have supported, a strong claim to his Majesty's gracious attention, and to the justice and liberality of their country.

As the first step towards carrying his Majesty's commands into effect, I should propose the reduction of eight companies of the Irish Artillery, with a proportion of field officers; and in order to render this act more palatable, and perhaps more equitable, I should recommend that the field officers, in reference to their services, and in consideration of their having belonged to the Royal Irish Regiment of Artillery whilst it remained on its original and anciently instituted establishment, be permitted to retire upon full pay, and that the captains, captain-lieutenants, first and second lieutenants, be allowed half-pay, and be considered as having the same pretensions to be restored to full-pay in regiments of the line as the reduced officers of any other corps in his Majesty's service.

The non-commissioned officers and gunners of the reduced companies will either be attached as supernumeraries to the remaining companies of the two battalions of Irish, or be transferred to the British Artillery, as circumstances may require.

After this first arrangement shall have been completely carried into effect, I should recommend that two companies of the remaining twelve should be reduced, with the junior colonel commandant, and a proportion of officers, observing the same rule with respect to the terms of retirement for the respective ranks of officers as in the former reduction; and that the ten companies of which the Royal Irish Artillery will then consist, should be formed into one battalion, and become an additional battalion of the Royal British Regiment of Artillery, and be considered in every respect as forming a part of that regiment, the officers taking rank and having command according to their respective commissions; but as it would be highly injurious to the fair pretensions of the officers of the British Artillery, who have, from the first establishment of the corps, invariably risen by seniority from the lowest to the highest regimental commissions, to be deprived of those prospects of advancement to which, from ancient usage, they have been taught to look with confidence, and to be disappointed in their well-founded expectation by the introduction of officers who, from the dates of their first commissions, are by many years junior to them in the service, it would be expedient to inform the officers who are incorporated from the Irish Artillery that they cannot obtain further promotion until they shall become entitled to it in the line of seniority from their first entering into the service with those of the British Artillery; and as this just and necessary regulation may in some instances be a cause of discontent to the Irish officers, and abate their zeal, I should earnestly recommend, that not only the field officers, but likewise the captains, in this instance may, if they desire it, be permitted to retire upon their full pay.

With respect to the junior subalterns, at least, of each corps, they are in general so young, that, if it should not be objected to as a deviation from a general principle, there could be no material injustice to either if they should be placed in the list of the whole regiment, and rise afterwards according to the dates of their present commission.

The reduction of the whole corps of the Irish will by these means be progressive and gradual, which, for political as well as military reasons, may perhaps at present be thought most expedient; and if it should appear in the course of the business to be advisable to bring the complete execution of the measure to a more speedy termination, there is nothing herein proposed that will not tend to facilitate its final accomplishment.

I have, &c.,

(Signed)   CORNWALLIS.

His Grace the Duke of Portland,
   &c., &c., &c,

WHITEHALL, 16 *February*, 1801.

MY LORD,

I have had the honour to lay before the King your Excellency's despatch of the 3d instant, and I have the satisfaction to acquaint you, that his Majesty fully approves the detailed proposition which you have submitted to his consideration for the eventual incorporation of the civil and military branches of the Ordnance Department of Great Britain and Ireland.

His Majesty has, however, graciously condescended to suggest one alteration, which I have no doubt your Excellency will consider as an improvement of the original plan, namely, that if the field officers and captains of the remaining ten companies that are to form a battalion of British Artillery should desire to retire on their pay, the junior officers of that subsisting corps should be placed as the youngest of each rank in the Royal Artillery.

I have, &c.,

(Signed)   PORTLAND.

His Excellency the Lord Lieutenant of Ireland,
&c., &c., &c.

COMPANIES OF BRITISH ARTILLERY FROM ENGLAND.

25th February.—His Excellency the Lord Lieutenant submitted a request for two Companies of the British Artillery to be sent to Ireland, to be replaced by a number of the Gunners of the Irish Artillery who will be immediately sent to England to be added to the British Artillery.

Disposal of Supernumerary N. C. Officers and Gunners.

26th February.—The Master-General of the Ordnance submitted the following detail with respect to the disposal of the Supernumerary Non-Commissioned Officers and Gunners:—

There will be required for the Five Companies in the West Indies to complete them to the present Establishment,

   60 Gunners.

To complete these Companies to the British Establishment,

   25 Non-Commissioned Officers,
   80 Gunners.

To complete the Five Companies in Europe to the British Establishment,

   25 Non-Commissioned Officers,
   80 Gunners,

There will then remain to be disposed of,

   49 Non-Commissioned Officers,
   604 Gunners,

of which the British Artillery will take about 300 Gunners.

The number of the Supernumeraries will then be,

   49 Non-Commissioned Officers,
   300 Gunners,

as Supernumeraries, from which may be deducted the servants of most of the Reduced Officers who are bad Soldiers and other Men not fit for the Artillery service about

   80 Gunners.

There remains, therefore, to be disposed of only
220 Gunners.

It is humbly suggested that a number of Gunners nearly equal to those may be allowed to enter into the British Artillery in the West Indies, and that 220 Gunners to fill up the vacancies in consequence, and a proportion of Officers to replace those reduced there be ordered from hence to the West Indies.

Should Your Excellency think fit to admit this proposal, one or more Companies will be wanted in Ireland : to keep complete the disposition which Your Excellency has made for the defence of the Country, and to furnish 50 Gunners which are called for by the Deputy Adjutant General of Artillery in England, to complete the Detachment at Jamaica.

FURTHER REDUCTION OF THE REGIMENT.

27th March.—The Master General of the Ordnance issued the following Orders on the subject of a further reduction of the Regiment.

OFFICE OF ORDNANCE,

DUBLIN, *27th March*, 1801.

His Excellency the Lord Lieutenant having been pleased in obedience to His Majesty's command, to direct that a further reduction of the Royal Irish Regiment of Artillery shall take place from the 1st day of April next, and that it shall be finally incorporated and become part of the Royal Regiment of Artillery, the following detailed plan for carrying this arrangement into effect, has been submitted to, and finally approved by His Excellency.

. . . . . .

The remaining Ten Companies to be immediately formed into a complete Battalion, upon the Establishment of the British Artillery, each Company to consist of

- 1 Captain
- 1 Captain-Lieutenant
- 2 First Lieutenants
- 1 Second Lieutenant.
- 4 Serjeants
- 4 Corporals
- 7 Bombardiers
- 3 Drummers
- 98 Gunners

Total 121 to each Company.

The Non-Commissioned Officers and Gunners that will remain, after completing the Battalion upon this Establishment, will be attached to the Companies in Ireland and mustered as Supernumeraries.

The Master General desires it may be notified to all the different stations of the Regiment, both Abroad and at Home, that His Excellency the Marquis Cornwallis is pleased to direct, that *Three Guineas* shall be paid to each Non-Commissioned Officer and Gunner who shall be approved of, and Incorporated into the British Corps.

And the Master General directs that 800 Gunners shall be immediately selected, and hold themselves in readiness, to proceed with a Proportion of Officers and Non-Commissioned Officers, to the Head Quarters of the Royal Regiment of Artillery at Woolwich, each of whom shall be thoroughly instructed in his Duty, and shall measure at least five feet seven inches in height.

The whole of the Non-Commissioned Officers and Gunners to be incorporated, will in future be entitled to the same allowances for altering their clothing, and to Shoe Money, which are received by the Non-Commissioned Officers and Gunners of the British Artillery.

The Invalid Establishment, hitherto upon that Pay, will in future be entitled to the full Pay and Allowances of the Effective Battalions;—And in order that no distinction of any kind whatever shall be made between the Irish and British Gunners, the two Corps, thus Incorporated, will in future be styled,

"*The Royal Regiment of Artillery.*"

By Order of the Master General.

J. MACLEAN,
Brigade Major.

THE SEVENTH BATTALION, ROYAL ARTILLERY.

The Ten Companies thus incorporated was numbered the "Seventh Battalion of the Royal Regiment of Artillery." The Officers transferred to the British Establishment were of the following grades:—

    1 Colonel Commandant
    8 Captains

9 Captain Lieutenants and Captains
 19 First Lieutenants
 16 Second Lieutenants
  1 Brigade Major
  1 Chaplain
  1 Surgeon
  1 Quarter Master
 ——
 52 Total

A Nominal List of the Officers who were incorporated, and a Statement of the Rank to which they afterwards attained, is given in Appendix B.

THE INVALID COMPANY.

The Invalid Company was also added to, and incorporated with the Battalion of Invalids of the British Artillery.

THE BAND.

The Band of the Regiment, numbering about thirty-five, were sent to Woolwich, and the best Musicians were absorbed into the Royal Artillery Band, those least proficient being discharged.—(*England's Artillerymen*, by J. A. Browne).

Such was the end of the Royal Irish Artillery, and thenceforward the Regiment found no place in the Army List.

Dress, Etc., of the Regiment.

An old MS. in Royal Artillery Record Office states that the dress * of the Royal Irish Artillery was as follows :—

Blue coat with scarlet facings, cuff and collar gold embroidered : long button holes for the Officers, Serjeants and Corporals, and yellow worsted lace for the other Ranks : gold-laced cocked hat, black leather cockade, white cloth breeches, with short gaiters and white stockings in summer, and long gaiters in winter. The Non-Commissioned Officers and Men wore their hair powdered and clubbed. In 1798 the Non-Commissioned Officers and Privates were clothed in jackets, according to the form adopted by the Army, and the cocked hats were retained, but without lace.

The Arms of the Regiment at the incorporation were cavalry carbines—the bayonet and pouch (which was of black leather, and contained sixteen or eighteen rounds) were carried on the same belt. A cross belt was also worn to which a great coat was suspended that rested on the left hip. At an earlier period the Regiment was armed with long (or Queen Anne's) fusils, which, as worn out, were replaced by arms of various patterns, until the cavalry carbine was adopted.

* The National Museum, Dublin, contains an Irish Artillery Officer's blue cloth double-breasted coat, with scarlet facings, silver lace and ten gold buttons (period about 1780). The buttons bear the device of three balls, the Harp and Crown with a gun.

APPENDIX A

Succession of Colonels in Chief.

- 1760 James Marquis of Kildare
- 1766 Richard Earl of Shannon.
- 1770 Charles Marquis of Drogheda.
- 1797 Henry Earl of Carhampton.
- 1800 Hon. Thomas Pakenham.

Succession of Colonels *en Seconde*.

- 1760 Bernard Hale.
- 1789 Henry Earl of Carhampton.
- 1797 Hon. Thomas Pakenham.
- 1800 Marcus Beresford.

Succession of Colonels Commandant.

- 1783 John Straton.
- 1795 Richard Bettesworth.

Succession of Second Colonels.

- 1795 William Brady.
- 1795 Lucius Barber.
- 1800 John Pratt.

Succession of Lieut.-Colonels Commandant.

1760 John Rutter.
1762 Daniel Chenevix.
1776 John Straton.
1788 Richard Bettesworth.
1795 William Wright.
1795 John D. Arabin.
1795 William Buchanan.
1797 John Bourchier.
1800 Joseph Walker.

Succession of Lieut.-Colonels.

1793 William Brady.
1793 Lucius Barber.
1795 John Pratt.
1795 William Wright.
1795 John D. Arabin.
1795 Charles Moore.
1795 William Buchanan.
1795 Richard Legge.
1795 John Bourchier.
1795 Joseph Walker.
1800 Henry Sneyd.
1800 Hugh Swayne.

APPENDIX B

Roll of Officers who entered the Royal Irish Artillery from 1756 to 1801, giving the Dates of their Commissions at such Entry, and a Statement of the Rank to which they afterwards attained.

Names	Entered Irish Artillery		Rank afterwards attained	Dates of Retirements and Casualties
	Year	Rank		
Allen, Hans	1794	Lieutenant	Captain	Retired, 1801
Arabin, John D.	1773	Fireworker	Lieutenant-Colonel	Retired, 1801
Armstrong, Alexander	1783	Lieutenant	Major	Retired, 1801
Armstrong, Elliot	1794	Lieutenant	Lieutenant	To 23rd Light Dragoons, 1794
Armstrong, George	1797	Lieutenant	Lieutenant	Retired, 1801
Armstrong, Henry	1793	Lieutenant	Captain	Died, 1798
Armstrong, James	1795	Lieutenant	Lieutenant	To British Artillery, 1801
Armstrong, John	1794	Lieutenant	Lieutenant	Died, 1795
Armstrong, John	1795	Lieutenant	Lieutenant	To British Artillery, 1801
Armstrong, Nenon	1778	Lieutenant	Lieutenant of Invalids	Died, 1789
Atkinson, Thomas	1760	Fireworker	Lieutenant	Resigned, 1773
Atkinson, Thomas	1776	Lieutenant	Lieutenant	To Invalids, 1780
Baggott, John	1792	Lieutenant	Captain	Resigned, 1799
Baillie, Henry	1765	Fireworker	Fireworker	Retired, 1771
Baldwin, Henry	1794	Lieutenant	Captain	Died, 1801
Barber, Lucius	1763	Fireworker	Colonel	Retired, 1801
Benning, Conway	1795	Lieutenant	Lieutenant	Retired, 1801
Benson, Stawell	1793	Lieutenant	Captain	Retired, 1801
Beresford, Marcus	1800	Colonel *en Seconde*	Colonel *en Seconde*	Retired, 1801

Names	Entered Irish Artillery		Rank afterwards attained	Dates of Retirements and Casualties
	Year	Rank		
Bettesworth, Richard	1760	Captain	Colonel Commandant	Died, 1801
Bettesworth, Richard	1778	Lieutenant	Lieutenant	Resigned, 1781
Birch, Robert H.	1795	Lieutenant	Lieutenant	British Artillery, 1801
Blake, Walter	1793	Lieutenant	Captain	Resigned, 1798
Blake, Walter	1798	Lieutenant	Lieutenant	Died, 1800
Blaquiere, Thomas	1793	Lieutenant	Captain	Died, 1801
Blundell, Dixie	1782	Lieutenant	Captain	Died, 1797
Blundell, John D.	1797	Lieutenant	Lieutenant	British Artillery, 1801
Bourchier, John	1781	Lieutenant	Lieut. Colonel	Retired, 1801
Bourke, Palmer B.	1795	Lieutenant	Lieutenant	Resigned, 1799
Bowen, Stephen C.	1795	Lieutenant	Lieutenant	Retired, 1801
Brady, William	1756	Fireworker	Colonel	Died, 1800
Brady, William	1760	Lieutenant	Captain	Died, 1788
Bredin, Andrew	1794	Lieutenant	Captain Lieutenant	British Artillery, 1801
Briscoe, John	1799	Lieutenant	Lieutenant	British Artillery, 1801
Brough, Richard S.	1794	Lieutenant	Captain Lieutenant	British Artillery, 1801
Brownrigg, Henry	1756	Major	Major	Resigned, 1758
Buchanan, Andrew	1760	Fireworker	Captain	Resigned, 1779
Buchanan, William	1778	Lieutenant	Lieut. Colonel	Retired, 1801
Buchanan, William	1793	Lieutenant	Captain	Died, 1797
Burgh, Thomas	1760	Lieutenant	Captain	Resigned, 1781
Burrowes, Alexander	1760	Fireworker	Fireworker	Retired, 1771
Campbell, John	1794	Lieutenant	Captain Lieutenant	Retired, 1801
Carhampton, Earl of, Master General of the Ordnance	1789	Colonel *en Seconde*	Colonel in Chief	Succeeded by H. T. Pakenham, 1800
Carr, John	1794	Lieutenant	Captain Lieutenant	Retired, 1801
Cavendish, Henry	1794	Lieutenant	Captain	Retired, 1801
Charlton, George	1794	Lieutenant	Lieutenant	Resigned, 1796

Names	Entered Irish Artillery		Rank afterwards attained	Dates of Retirements and Casualties
	Year	Rank		
Chenevix, Daniel	1758	Major	Lieut. Colonel Commandant	Died, 1776
Church, James	1795	Lieutenant	Lieutenant	Died, 1796
Chute, Falkiner	1794	Lieutenant	Lieutenant	Resigned, 1794
Clibborne, William	1800	Lieutenant	Lieutenant	British Artillery, 1801
Clifford, Thomas	1798	Lieutenant	Lieutenant	Retired, 1801
Colclough, Dudley	1794	Lieutenant	Captain Lieutenant	Died, 1795
Coulson, Forster	1793	Lieutenant	Captain	Retired, 1801
Cowell, George	1779	Lieutenant	Captain Lieutenant	Resigned, 1792
Cowley, Edward W.	1799	Lieutenant	Lieutenant	British Artillery, 1801
Cradock, Richard H.	1760	Fireworker	Lieutenant	Retired, 1770
Crawford, Robert	1793	Lieutenant	Captain	Retired, 1801
Cullen, Edward	1799	Lieutenant	Lieutenant	Retired, 1801
Dawson, George	1793	Lieutenant	Lieutenant	Died, 1794
Dennis, John C.	1795	Lieutenant	Lieutenant	Retired, 1801
Desbrissey, Thomas	1760	Captain	Captain	Resigned, 1771
Devenish, Godfrey	1799	Lieutenant	Lieutenant	Resigned, 1800
Douglas, Wadel C.	1795	Lieutenant	Lieutenant	Retired, 1801
Drogheda, Earl of, Master General of the Ordnance	1770	Colonel in Chief	Colonel in Chief	Succeeded by E. of Carhampton, 1797
Du Bordieu, Saumarez	1798	Lieutenant	Lieutenant	British Artillery, 1801
Dunkin, John J.	1794	Lieutenant	Captain Lieutenant	British Artillery, 1801
Dyas, Richard	1795	Lieutenant	Lieutenant	British Artillery, 1801
Egan, Charles	1794	Lieutenant	Lieutenant	British Artillery, 1801
Ellison, Thomas	1794	Lieutenant	Lieutenant	British Artillery, 1801
Fairtlough, Francis G.	1794	Lieutenant	Captain Lieutenant	Retired, 1801
Faulkner, William	1797	Lieutenant	Lieutenant	Resigned, 1799

Names	Entered Irish Artillery		Rank afterwards attained	Dates of Retirements and Casualties
	Year	Rank		
Fellowes, James	1795	Lieutenant	Lieutenant	British Artillery, 1801
Fisher, John P.	1798	Lieutenant	Lieutenant	British Artillery, 1801
Fitzgerald, Stephen	1794	Lieutenant	Lieutenant	Died, 1798
Fleming, Arthur	1799	Lieutenant	Lieutenant	British Artillery, 1801
Fleming, Thomas B.	1793	Lieutenant	Captain	Retired, 1801
Francis, Robert S.	1793	Lieutenant	Captain	Retired, 1801
Fry, Oliver	1794	Lieutenant	Lieutenant	British Artillery, 1801
Fuller, William	1795	Lieutenant	Lieutenant	Retired, 1801
Galbraith, William	1793	Lieutenant	Captain	Retired, 1801
George, Delany	1760	Fireworker	Lieutenant	Died, 1771
George, Joshua	1790	Lieutenant	Captain Lieutenant	Died, 1794
Gildea, Andrew	1782	Lieutenant	Lieutenant	Died, 1787
Glubb, Frederick	1795	Lieutenant	Lieutenant	British Artillery, 1801
Goff, Thomas	1798	Chaplain	Chaplain	Retired, 1801
Graham, Robert	1756	Fireworker	Lieutenant	Died, 1764
Gray, William	1756	Lieutenant	Captain	Retired, 1776
Grey, William	1783	Lieutenant of Invalids	Lieutenant of Invalids	Died, 1787
Griffith, William	1800	Lieutenant	Lieutenant	Retired, 1801
Hall, Bernard	1760	Colonel *en Seconde*	Colonel *en Seconde*	Retired, 1789
Hall, Charles R.	1783	Lieutenant	Lieutenant	To half pay, 1783
Hall, Gervas R.	1783	Lieutenant	Captain Lieutenant	Retired, 1799
Hall, John T.	1777	Lieutenant	Lieutenant	Resigned, 1783
Hamilton, John	1794	Lieutenant	Captain Lieutenant	Retired, 1801
Handcock, John	1760	Fireworker	Captain	Died, 1786
Hanna, Joseph	1799	Quarter Master Lieutenant	Quarter Master Lieutenant	Retired, 1801
Hare, James	1782	Lieutenant	Lieutenant	Retired, 1789

Names	Entered Irish Artillery		Rank afterwards attained	Dates of Retirements and Casualties
	Year	Rank		
Harpur, Singleton	1779	Chaplain	Chaplain	Resigned, 1787
Harris, Thomas C.	1778	Lieutenant	Captain	Died, 1794
Hazard, Richard	1794	Lieutenant	Lieutenant	Retired, 1801
Hemmings, Matthew	1794	Lieutenant	Lieutenant	Retired, 1801
Heron, Thomas	1794	Lieutenant	Captain Lieutenant	Retired, 1801
Hickman, Henry	1794	Lieutenant	Lieutenant	British Artillery, 1801
Hill, Thomas	1776	Lieutenant	Lieutenant	Resigned, 1778
Hillas, John	1794	Lieutenant	Captain Lieutenant	Retired, 1801
Hunt, Arthur	1798	Lieutenant	Lieutenant	British Artillery, 1801
Irving, James	1794	Lieutenant	Captain Lieutenant	Retired, 1801
Irving, St. George	1793	Lieutenant	Captain	Retired, 1801
Jackson, Oliver	1794	Lieutenant	Captain	British Artillery, 1801
Jarratt, Thomas	1760	Lieutenant	Lieutenant	To Engineers, 1762
Jones, Hon. Benjamin	1793	Lieutenant	Lieutenant	Died, 1794
Keane, Charles	1794	Lieutenant	Captain Lieutenant	British Artillery, 1801
Kelly, William	1794	Lieutenant	Captain	Died, 1799
Kelly, William	1794	Lieutenant	Lieutenant	Retired, 1801
Kettlewell, John W.	1799	Lieutenant	Lieutenant	British Artillery, 1801
Kettlewell, Peter	1793	Lieutenant	Captain	Retired, 1801
Kildare, Earl of, Master General of the Ordnance	1760	Colonel in Chief	Colonel in Chief	Succeeded by Earl of Shannon, 1766
King, Gilbert	1763	Fireworker	Lieutenant	Retired, 1772
Lamiellere, Alexander	1760	Chaplain	Chaplain	Resigned, 1774
Lawson, Henry	1794	Lieutenant	Captain	Resigned, 1801
Legge, Richard	1779	Adjutant	Captain	Retired, 1801
Legge, Richard	1780	Lieutenant	Lieutenant Colonel	Died, 1800

Names	Entered Irish Artillery		Rank afterwards attained	Dates of Retirements and Casualties
	Year	Rank		
Lindsay, Alexander	1781	Surgeon	Surgeon	Resigned, 1798
Lindsay, George	1793	Lieutenant	Captain	British Artillery, 1801
Lowe, Charles	1796	Lieutenant	Lieutenant	Resigned, 1797
Lowe, Thomas	1795	Lieutenant	Lieutenant	Died, 1798
Lyster, Henry A.	1797	Lieutenant	Lieutenant	Retired, 1801
Macartney, Arthur C.	1799	Lieutenant	Lieutenant	British Artillery, 1801
Maclean, Joseph	1800	Brigade Major	Brigade Major	British Artillery, 1801
Madden, Henry	1795	Lieutenant	Lieutenant	Retired, 1801
Massey, George	1794	Lieutenant	Lieutenant	British Artillery, 1801
McGlezy, George	1795	Quarter Master	Quarter Master	British Artillery, 1801
McWilliam, David	1793	Lieutenant	Lieutenant	Resigned, 1794
Minchin, William	1795	Lieutenant	Lieutenant	Exchanged 1795 to 18th Foot
Moloney, Edmund	1793	Lieutenant	Captain	Died, 1794
Montgomery, John	1795	Lieutenant	Lieutenant	Retired, 1801
Moore, Charles, Lord	1788	Lieutenant	Captain	Resigned, 1800
Moore, Charles	1778	Lieutenant	Lieutenant Colonel	Resigned, 1797
Moore, William	1781	Lieutenant	Lieutenant of Invalids	British Artillery, 1801
Morton, John	1798	Surgeon	Surgeon	British Artillery, 1801
Napier, William	1800	Lieutenant	Lieutenant	62nd Regiment, 1801
Nash, Matthew	1778	Lieutenant	Captain	Resigned, 1790
Newall, George	1794	Lieutenant	Captain	Retired, 1801
Nixon, Henry	1794	Lieutenant	Captain	Retired, 1801
Nugent, Edmund	1789	Lieutenant	Captain Lieutenant	Died, 1794
Nugent, Nicholas	1793	Lieutenant	Lieutenant	Resigned, 1794
Nugent, Richard	1760	Fireworker	Fireworker	To 31st Foot, 1761
O'Neale, Hugh	1795	Chaplain	Chaplain	British Artillery, 1801
Ormsby, George	1794	Lieutenant	Lieutenant	British Artillery, 1801

Names	Entered Irish Artillery		Rank afterwards attained	Dates of Retirements and Casualties
	Year	Rank		
Pakenham, Hon. Thomas, Master General of the Ordnance	1797	Colonel en Seconde	Colonel in Chief	Retired, 1801
Pakenham, Edward M.	1800	Lieutenant	Lieutenant	British Artillery, 1801
Parkes, Robert	1760	Lieutenant	Lieutenant	Resigned, 1763
Paterson, Andrew	1798	Lieutenant	Lieutenant	Resigned, 1799
Patterson, Thomas	1794	Lieutenant	Lieutenant	To Londonderry Regiment, 1794
Pentland, William	1774	Chaplain	Chaplain	Resigned, 1779
Perdrian, George R.	1795	Lieutenant	Lieutenant	Retired, 1801
Porter, Thomas	1794	Lieutenant	Captain Lieutenant	British Artillery, 1801
Power, Francis	1794	Lieutenant	Captain Lieutenant	British Artillery, 1801
Power, James	1794	Lieutenant	Captain Lieutenant	British Artillery, 1801
Power, William	1800	Lieutenant	Lieutenant	British Artillery, 1801
Poynton, Samuel	1795	Lieutenant	Lieutenant	Died, 1798
Pratt, John	1771	Fireworker	Colonel	Retired, 1801
Purcell, Ignatius	1794	Lieutenant	Lieutenant	British Artillery, 1801
Ratcliff, John	1756	Fireworker	Lieutenant	Died, 1768
Richman, Daniel	1793	Lieutenant	Lieutenant	Resigned, 1794
Robinson, George St.G.	1778	Lieutenant	Lieutenant	Exchanged, 1782, to 96th Foot
Robinson, John	1771	Fireworker	Lieutenant	Resigned, 1781
Robison, David	1760	Adjutant	Captain of Invalids	Died, 1796
Roe, Marcus	1795	Lieutenant	Lieutenant	British Artillery, 1801
Rutter, John	1760	Lieutenant Colonel Commandant	Lieutenant Colonel Commandant	Retired, 1763
Salt, John	1760	Fireworker	Lieutenant	Retired, 1772
Semple, John	1794	Lieutenant	Lieutenant	Retired, 1801
Shannon, Earl of Master General of the Ordnance	1766	Colonel in Chief	Colonel in Chief	Succeeded by M. of Drogheda, 1770

Names	Entered Irish Artillery		Rank afterwards attained	Dates of Retirements and Casualties
	Year	Rank		
Sharman, Charles	1794	Lieutenant	Lieutenant	Retired, 1801
Sheckleton, Thomas	1794	Lieutenant	Captain	Resigned, 1798
Shenley, William	1795	Lieutenant	Lieutenant Lieutenant	British Artillery, 1801
Shettick, Barry V.	1800	Lieutenant	Lieutenant	Retired, 1801
Shewbridge Joseph	1778	Lieutenant	Captain	Died, 1794
Shortall, James	1793	Lieutenant	Captain	Retired, 1801
Sillery, Charles D.	1794	Lieutenant	Captain Lieutenant	British Artillery, 1801
Skipton, George	1756	Lieutenant	Captain	Resigned, 1771
Slessor, John	1794	Lieutenant	Captain Lieutenant	British Artillery, 1801
Smith, William	1772	Fireworker	Captain	Died, 1794
Smyth, Edward	1795	Lieutenant	Lieutenant	Retired, 1801
Smyth, Francis	1794	Lieutenant	Lieutenant	British Artillery, 1801
Smyth, John	1799	Lieutenant	Lieutenant	British Artillery, 1801
Sneyd, Henry	1782	Lieutenant	Lieutenant Colonel	Died, 1800
Stewart, Robert	1782	Lieutenant	Major	Retired, 1801
Stewart, William	1795	Lieutenant	Lieutenant	British Artillery, 1801
Straton, John	1756	Captain	Colonel Commandant	British Artillery, 1801
Straton, Robert J.	1778	Lieutenant	Lieutenant	Died, 1781
Stuart, Henry J.	1794	Lieutenant	Lieutenant	Retired, 1801
Sturrock, George	1795	Lieutenant	Lieutenant	Retired, 1801
Sturrock, Robert C.	1794	Lieutenant	Lieutenant	Retired, 1801
Swayne, Edward	1795	Lieutenant	Lieutenant	Died, 1798
Swayne, Hugh	1782	Lieutenant	Lieutenant Colonel	Retired, 1801
Taylor, John	1799	Lieutenant	Lieutenant	British Artillery, 1801
Thornhill, Richard	1787	Lieutenant	Captain Lieutenant	Died, 1794
Thornhill, Robert	1783	Lieutenant	Captain	British Artillery, 1801
Thwaites Frederick	1794	Lieutenant	Lieutenant	To Dublin Regiment, 1794

Names	Entered Irish Artillery		Rank afterwards attained	Dates of Retirements and Casualties
	Year	Rank		
Tisdall, Thomas	1794	Lieutenant	Lieutenant	British Artillery, 1801
Tomkins, Frederick	1794	Lieutenant	Captain Lieutenant	Retired, 1801
Tomkins, Luke G.	1794	Lieutenant	Captain	Retired, 1801
Trocke, Thomas	1787	Chaplain	Chaplain	Died, 1798
Tucker, William J.	1794	Lieutenant	Captain Lieutenant	Retired, 1801
Tyrell, Arthur	1781	Lieutenant	Captain	Died, 1794
Uniacke, Richard	1793	Lieutenant	Captain	Retired, 1801
Van Schaike, Henry	1797	Lieutenant	Lieutenant	Retired, 1801
Walker, Joseph	1781	Lieutenant	Lieutenant Colonel	Retired, 1801
Walker, William	1801	Lieutenant of Invalids	Lieutenant of Invalids	British Artillery, 1801
Walsh, Blaney	1795	Lieutenant	Lieutenant	British Artillery, 1801
Warburton, Peter	1794	Lieutenant	Captain	Died, 1800
Westropp, Poole	1793	Lieutenant	Captain	Died, 1798
Wigmore, Giles	1795	Lieutenant	Lieutenant	Died, 1799
Wilford, Ernest C.	1799	Adjutant	Lieutenant	British Artillery, 1801
Wilson, James	1763	Fireworker	Captain Lieutenant	Died, 1784
Winder, John	1799	Lieutenant	Lieutenant	British Artillery, 1801
Winter, Arthur	1760	Surgeon	Surgeon	Resigned, 1781
Wright, William	1772	Fireworker	Lieutenant Colonel	Retired, 1801
Young, Matthew	1770	Fireworker	Captain of Invalids	British Artillery, 1801

APPEN

LIST OF OFFICERS OF THE IRISH ARTILLERY WHO ENTERED THE
DATED 8TH APRIL, 1801, GIVING THE DATES OF THEIR COM-
TO WHICH THEY AFTERWARDS ATTAINED.

Names	Rank at entry to English Artillery	Rank Attained
John Straton	Colonel Commandant, 1783	—
George Lindsay	Captain, 1794	—
Robert Thornhill	Captain, 1795	Colonel, 1825
Oliver Jackson	Captain, 1800	—
John Slessor	Captain Lieutenant and Second Captain, 1795	—
Thomas Porter	Captain Lieutenant and Second Captain, 1795	—
John J. Dunkin	Captain Lieutenant and Second Captain, 1795	—
Charles Keane	Captain Lieutenant and Second Captain, 1797	Brevet Major, 1810
*Richard S. Brough	Captain Lieutenant and Second Captain, 1798	Colonel Commandant, 1846
Charles D. Sillery	Captain Lieutenant and Second Captain, 1798	Captain, 1804
*Andrew Bredin	Captain Lieutenant and Second Captain, 1798	Colonel, 1834
*James Power	Captain Lieutenant and Second Captain, 1799	Colonel Commandant, 1846
Francis Power	Captain Lieutenant and Second Captain, 1800	Major, 1823
Thomas Tisdall	First Lieutenant, 1794	Captain Lieutenant and Second Captain, 1801
George Ormsby	First Lieutenant, 1794	Captain Lieutenant and Second Captain, 1801
Oliver Fry	First Lieutenant, 1794	Captain, 1805
Thomas Ellison	First Lieutenant, 1794	Captain Lieutenant and Second Captain, 1801

* These Officers were serving in 1839, when the above List was furnished by
deaths, were obtained from "List of Officers of the Royal Regiment of Artillery,
services were taken from the same excellent compilation.

DIX C

ENGLISH ARTILLERY UNDER THE ORDER FOR INCORPORATION, MISSIONS AT SUCH ENTRY AND A STATEMENT OF THE RANK

Remarks	Services
Died in Ireland, 1803	—
Retired on his pay, 1804	—
Died at Jamaica, 1825	Salamanca, Corunna, rearguard ; Jamaica, 1825
Retired on half pay, 1804	—
Retired on his pay, 1801	—
Retired on his pay, 1801	—
Retired on his pay, 1804	—
Died at Barbadoes, 1813	Barbadoes, 1813
Died in London, 1859	Capture of St. Lucia ; Campaign under Sir Ralph Abercrombie, 1796 ; Capture of Guadaloupe under Sir James Leith, 1815 ; West Indies, 1796-1807 and 1813-20 ; Commanding Royal Artillery, Mauritius, 1824-29; Nova Scotia, 1833-7
Died in Spain, 1809	Spain, 1809
Died at Plumstead, 1845	Peninsula, 1812-14 ; Salamanca ; Capture of Granada, St. Vincent and St. Lucia under Sir Ralph Abercrombie ; West Indies, 1795-1805 ; Gibraltar and Peninsula, 1808-14 ; Upper Canada, 1819-24 ; Halifax, 1828-33
Died at Dover, 1851	Barbadoes and Martinique, 1797-99 ; Barbadoes and Demerara, 1806-08 ; St. Helena, 1816-21; Jamaica, 1826-29 ; Mauritius, 1834-40
Sold his Commission, 1823	Cape ; South America, 1806 ; Peninsula and Waterloo
Retired on First Lieutenant's pay, 1802	—
Retired on First Lieutenant's pay, 1802	—
Retired on full pay, 1819	—
Retired on First Lieutenant's pay, 1803	—

the Board of Ordnance, and the dates of their subsequent promotions and of their 1716 to 1899," collected by General W. H. Askwith, R.A. The notes on Officers

Names	Rank at entry to English Artillery	Rank Attained
Francis Smith	First Lieutenant, 1794	Colonel, 1837
Ignatius Purcell	First Lieutenant, 1794	—
Charles Egan	First Lieutenant, 1794	Lieutenant Colonel, 1825
George Massey	First Lieutenant, 1794	Captain, 1805
Henry Hickman	First Lieutenant, 1795	Lieutenant Colonel, 1825
Blaney Walsh	First Lieutenant, 1795	Lieutenant Colonel, 1826
*Robert H. Birch	First Lieutenant, 1795	Colonel Commandant, 1849
*James Armstrong	First Lieutenant, 1795	Colonel Commandant, 1849
James Fellowes	First Lieutenant, 1797	—
John Armstrong	First Lieutenant, 1797	—
Richard Dyas	First Lieutenant, 1798	Brevet Major, 1814
William Stewart	First Lieutenant, 1798	Captain, 1808
Marcus Roe	First Lieutenant, 1798	Captain, 1808
Frederick Glubb	First Lieutenant, 1799	Captain, 1808
William Shenley	First Lieutenant, 1799	Captain, 1808
John D. Blundell	First Lieutenant, 1800	Captain Lieutenant and Second Captain, 1805
Saumarez du Bourdieu	Second Lieutenant, 1798	Captain, 1813
John P. Fisher	Second Lieutenant, 1798	First Lieutenant, 1801
*Arthur Hunt	Second Lieutenant, 1798	Colonel, 1841

Remarks	Services
Died in London, 1837	Gibraltar, 1806-21; Peninsula, Cadiz, 1808; commanded a battery of 9 pounders on march from Ostend, but did not arrive in time for battle of Waterloo; Ceylon, 1828-34
Retired on his pay, 1802	
Sold his Commission, 1828	—
Died at Canterbury, 1812	Walcheren, 1809
Sold his Commission, 1828	Sicily, 1810
Sold his Commission, 1828	West Indies, 1809
Died at Dublin, 1851	Irish Rebellion, 1798; secret expedition to Mediterranean, 1805; under command of Sir James Craig; Sicily under General Fox; Walcheren, 1808-09; Peninsula, at Cadiz and Seville, 1810-13; West Indies, 1829-33 (no medals.)
Died at Hollymount, Ireland, 1853	St. Lucia, Tobago, 1803, under Lieut.-General Greenfield Surinam, 1804, under Lieut.-General Sir Charles Green, Bt.; St. Domingo, 1809, under Major-General Carmichael; Gibraltar, 1801-2; West Indies, 1802-5; Jamaica, etc., 1807-15; Ionian Islands, 1830-5; Comg. R. Artillery, Corfu, 1830-34
Retired on half pay, 1801	—
Retired on his pay, 1802	Egypt, 1801
Retired on half pay, 1817	—
Died at Barbadoes, 1809	Barbadoes, 1809
Died at Jamaica, 1810	Jamaica, 1810
Retired on full pay, 1819	Portugal, Ciudad Rodrigo, Almeraz, siege of Burgos, Salamanca, Badajoz, San Sebastian
Died at Cadiz, 1813	Cadiz, 1810-13
Retired on his pay, 1809	—
Died at St. Sebastian, 1813	Siege of St. Sebastian, 1813
Died at Antigua, 1802	Antigua, 1802
Died at Woolwich, 1853	Irish Rebellion; 1798; siege of Cadiz; Carthagena; Tarragona; joined army in Belgium, 1814; C.R.A. at defence of Tournay; served in small fortified town of Rocroi near Waterloo on 18/6/15, under fire on that morning; received prize money for Waterloo (no medal), with army in Paris between 1815-18; West Indies, 1800-06; Gibraltar, 1807-10; Cadiz, 1810-12; Carthagena, 1812-14; Belgium and France 1814-18; Newfoundland, 1827-31; Gibraltar, 1832-35

Names	Rank at entry to English Artillery	Rank Attained
John Briscoe	Second Lieutenant, 1799	Brevet Major, 1819
John Taylor	Second Lieutenant, 1799	Brevet Major, 1819
Edward W. Cowley	Second Lieutenant, 1799	Captain Lieutenant and Second Captain, 1806
John Winder	Second Lieutenant, 1799	Captain Lieutenant and Second Captain, 1806
Arthur Macartney	Second Lieutenant, 1799	Captain Lieutenant and Second Captain, 1806
John Smythe	Second Lieutenant, 1799	Captain Lieutenant and Second Captain, 1806
Arthur Fleming	Second Lieutenant, 1799	Captain Lieutenant and Second Captain, 1806
John W. Kettlewell	Second Lieutenant, 1799	Lieutenant Colonel, 1835
William Clibborne	Second Lieutenant, 1800	Brevet Major, 1821
*Sir William G. Power, K.C.B., K.H.	Second Lieutenant, 1800	Colonel Commandant, 1856
Edward M. Pakenham	Second Lieutenant, 1800	Captain Lieutenant and Second Captain, 1807
Ernest C. Wilford	Second Lieutenant, 1800	Major, 1821

Remarks	Services
Sold his Commission, 1825 .	—
Died at Woolwich, 1830	West Indies, 3 years; Peninsula, 1808-9; Talavera (W.); prisoner in France till end of war
Retired on his rank and pay, 1812	Peninsula, 1808; Cadiz, 1810
Retired on his rank and pay, 1813	—
Retired on his pay, 1811	West Indies, 1803; Walcheren, 1809; dismantling the works under Captain S. G. Adye
Retired on his rank and pay, 1812	—
Retired on his rank and pay, 1812	—
Retired on full pay, 1836	Copenhagen, 1807; allied armies, 1815; Rebellion in Ceylon, 1817-18; mentioned in G.O.'s; Island of Zealand, 1807; France, 1815; Ceylon, 1816-20
Died at Trinidad, 1834	Taking of Island of Martinique, 1809 (thanked in G.O.'s); Continent, 1805-12; West Indies, 1807-12; France, 1815-16; Canada, 1823-24; West Indies, 1832-34
Died at Shanklin, I. of Wight, 1863	Spain, Portugal and France, 1808-14, including battle of Talavera, sieges of Ciudad Rodrigo (wounded) and Badajoz; capture of French works at Almeraz; reduction of forts at and battle of Salamanca; siege of Burgos (wounded); siege of San Sebastian; passage of the Bidassoa Nive and Adour. Sir W. Power led the reserve to the assaulting party of Fort la Picurina during the last siege of Badajoz, and the commandant surrendered to him personally; America, 1814-16; Ceylon, 1839-44
Retired on his rank and pay, 1811	—
Retired on half pay of his army rank, 1826	—

INDEX

	PAGE
Accidents, in Firing	26, 56, 92, 94
Accounts, Irish and British kept distinct	8
America, North, Drafts for	186-7
—— Gallant behaviour of Drafts	191-3
Ammunition, proportion of, for Artillery and Infantry	50, 222
Appendices	343-59
Arms and Accoutrements, for Officers	42, 48, 65
—— for N.C. Officers and Men	43, 49, 107-8, 137, 139, 169, 189
Army in Ireland, Riots between Soldiers and Civilians	88-9
—— in a state of licentiousness	311-13
Arsenal Yard, Dublin Castle	307
Artillery, British, arrival in Ireland of Detachment	6, 9, 302
—— Arrival of Horse Artillery in Ireland	307-8
—— Irish, "Company of in Ireland" formed	29-33
—— A Regiment of four Companies raised	63-69
—— (See under Augmentations.)	
—— Formation of Regiment into two Battalions	288
—— —— into Heavy and Light Brigades	322
—— Regiment incorporated into British Artillery	339-40
—— —— numbered "Seventh Battalion of British Artillery"	339-41
—— Officers—List of who entered British Artillery	354-9
—— —— Roll of who entered Irish Artillery	345-53
—— Pay (see under Pay).	
—— Repository of	307
—— Train of (see under Train).	
Augmentations, in 1778, to 6 Companies	205, 210
—— in 1783, an Invalid Company added	230-1
—— in 1793, to 10 Companies	269
—— in 1794, to 12 Companies	276
—— in 1794, to 20 Companies	282
Ballinamuck, French Troops at	319-20
Ballynahinch, Battle of	318
Band of the Regiment	94, 105, 137, 149, 253, 341
Bantry Bay, the French Fleet off	298
Barracks, Dublin	37
—— (See under Chapel-Izod and Maynooth.)	
Battalion Guns to Regiments of Foot	34, 36, 62, 93, 104, 163
Batteries, Floating in Dublin Harbour	206-8, 211-17, 223
—— Salute in Phœnix Park	102, 124, 147
—— (See under Forts and Fortifications.)	

	PAGE
Beating Orders to raise Men (see under Recruiting).	
Board of Ordnance (see under Ordnance Board).	
Bombardiers, Warrant of Appointment (see under Train of Artillery).	
Bounty Money for Recruits (see under Recruits).	
Bread Money Allowance	61, 264-7
Bridge Master, Warrant of Appointment	99
British Artillery (see under Artillery, British).	
Bullocks for drawing Field Guns	304-6
Burial Expenses	237
Butt for Artillery Practice, at Kilmainham	10
—— at Phœnix Park	71, 82, 85, 92, 93, 118, 165
Cadets	91-2, 95, 116, 125, 127, 138
Cadet Gunners and Cadet Mattrosses	33
Cantonments at Chapel-Izod and Maynooth	73
Captains, Extra Expenses of their Companies	243-9
Captain Lieutenant, the Senior First Lieutenant of the Regiment given rank of	201
—— six First Lieutenants given rank of	234
Castlebar attacked by the French	319-20
Catholics not permitted to "take the shilling"	28
Chapel-Izod, Barracks at	1, 93, 97-8, 103, 106-13 146, 166-70, 261
—— Cantonments at	73
—— Ground belonging to Crown at	152
—— Head Quarters of Regiment at	1, 73-4
—— Infirmary at	112, 114, 117
—— King's House at	72, 78-80
—— Laboratory at	114
—— Robberies on the high roads in Village of	137
—— Village of	1, 2, 101, 150
Chatham, Companies at	308, 313-14
Clothing for Officers	138
—— for N.C. Officers and Men (see under Dress)	38, 42-4, 65-6, 71, 80-1, 94, 110, 115, 123, 139, 147, 151, 168, 186
Colonels in Chief	67, 76-7, 124, 150, 303, 327, 343
—— en Seconde	67, 261, 303, 327, 343
—— Commandant	234, 260, 288, 343
—— Second Colonels	288, 343
—— Lieut.-Colonels Commandant	67, 87, 180, 234, 288, 344
—— Lieutenant Colonels	269, 288, 344
Companies on Foreign Service	269, 274, 287, 314
—— Gallantry of	270-3
—— Extra Expenses of Captains	243-9
Courts Martial, Mattross tried by	2, 140-3
—— Officer tried by	303-4

	PAGE
Demonstrations, Political	122
Deserters	53, 90, 110
Detached Commands 70, 153-4, 164, 184, 194-5, 200, 203, 205, 210, 212, 218, 220, 223, 226-7, 230, 294, 299, 307	
Discharged Men	123, 133-4, 179, 181, 234-6
Distribution of the Regiment 197, 225, 279, 291, 294, 309, 323, 328	
Disturbances, Civil, suppression of by Troops	320-1
Dress of the Regiment	138-9, 151, 342
Driver Corps, formation and organisation	304-6
Drums, Kettle, at Funeral of Lord Lieutenant.	255
Dublin, Pieces of Ordnance at	104
—— Press (The)	3, 180
Dublin Castle, Armoury	164
—— Arsenal Yard	9, 307
—— Laboratory	109
—— Ordnance Office	16
—— Proof House	174, 176
—— Storehouses	164
Dunkirk, Companies on Service at	270-3

East India (see under Indies East).
Englishmen enlisted for Irish Artillery . . . 96
Enlistments, Irishmen not permitted to "take the shilling" 28
—— Ulster Protestants permitted to enlist in Irish Artillery 29
—— for the "Artillery Company in Ireland" . . 45, 48
—— for Regiments on the British Establishment . 50, 51
—— for Royal Irish Artillery . . 68, 81-2, 188, 241, 269
—— Englishmen enlisted for Irish Artillery . . . 96
—— in Cork by Major Boyle Roche . . . 177
—— Discharged Artillerymen enlist in E. India Co. Service 236
Enniscorthy (see under Vinegar Hill).
Establishment British (see under Foreign Service).
—— Irish (see under Irish Establishment).
—— of the Regiment (see under Artillery, Irish—Augmentations—last page of each year's events).
—— reduction of in years 1766, 1783, 1801 . 126, 135, 233, 333-9

Field Days and Reviews	144-5, 171-3
Fireworkers Lieutenant, appointment of	32-3
—— number reduced	129
—— rank abolished, and appointed Second Lieutenants	175
Firing (see under Accidents).	
—— improvement in the method of	221
Flag Howitzer at Funeral of Lord Lieutenant	254

	PAGE
Flanders, Companies on service in	271-4
Foreign Service, Companies on	4, 269, 275, 287, 313-4
Formation of Artillery Company in Ireland	6, 9, 29-33
—— Regiment of Royal Irish Artillery	63-9
—— Invalid Company	230-1
—— Corps of Drivers (see under Artillery, Irish)	304-6
Forts and Fortifications in Ireland (see under Batteries)	10-12, 103-4, 162-3, 214
France, Companies on service in	270-3
French Fleet off Carrickfergus	70
French Fleet off Bantry Bay	298
French Troops at Killala	319
French Cannon captured at Castlebar (see under Rebellion, 1798)	320
Funeral of the Duke of Rutland, Lord Lieutenant	253-8
—— Regimental Band, Flag Howitzer, and Kettle Drums at	253-5
Furlough, Regulation Form of	54
Garrisons and Magazines in Ireland	10-12, 110, 118, 164, 250
Gorey, battle near	318
Guards Regimental, detail of	127-8
—— Light House	190-1
—— Magazine Fort	181, 212, 250
—— Pigeon House Fort	190-1
—— Salute Battery	181
—— Allowance to Officers on Guard	190-1
Gun-yard at Kilmainham	10
Gunners reduced to Mattrosses pay	131
Gunpowder, no stated allowance of, for Artillery practice	219
Head Quarters of Regiment at Chapel-Izod	1, 73, 97-8
Honours to Master General of the Ordnance	82-3
Horse Allowance	60-1, 80
Horse Artillery, British, arrival of in Ireland	307-8
Hospitals (see under Infirmary).	
Indies, East, Discharged Artillerymen enlisted in Company's Service	236
Indies, West, Companies serving in	279-81, 289-90, 302, 314, 326-7, 330
Infirmary, Chapel-Izod	112-14, 117
—— Dublin	55, 117, 130
Invalid Company	6, 218, 228-31, 238, 248, 250, 331, 340-1
Ireland, French Invasion of	70, 298, 319-20
Irish Artillery Regiment (see under Artillery, Irish).	
—— Establishment, Mr. Fortescue's account of the	51-2

                                                                    PAGE
Irish House of Commons, Journals of 4, 6
—— Rebellion (see under Rebellion).

Kettle Drummer, Warrant appointing a . . . 256
Kettle Drums, state at Funeral of Lord Lieutenant . 255
Kilcullen, engagement at 317
Kildare, Curragh of, cabins built on 294
—— Earl of, Master of the Ordnance 57-9
—— Colonel-in-Chief 76-8
Kilkenny, Camp near 33
Killala, French Troops at 319
Kilmainham Hospital, Admission of Discharged Men to . 133
—— Butt for Artillery practice at 10
—— Gun-yard at 10
—— Repository of Artillery at 307

Laughlinstown, Camp at . . 288-9, 297-8, 306, 314
Leixlip, Company quartered at 81
Lieutenant-General of the Ordnance (see under Colonels,
    en Seconde).
—— (see under Ordnance).
Limerick, Temporary Batteries on the River Shannon . 214
Lodging Money to Officers and Men . 76, 149, 153, 178

Magazines (see under Garrisons and Magazines).
Masters-General of the Ordnance (see under Colonels in
    Chief).
—— (see under Ordnance).
Master Gunners (see under Train of Artillery).
Mattrosses, Gunners reduced to rank and pay of . . 131
—— Augmentation of 13 to each Company . . . 213
—— Appelation of abolished 234
Maynooth, Barracks at . 73, 86, 95, 98-9, 103, 112, 114
Militia, Additional Gunners from, discontinued . . 326
—— Officers raising Men for their Commissions . 276-8, 282
Muster of the Regiment 105
—— Invalid Pensioners 161
—— Detachments 164

Naas, battle at 318

Office, Regimental, allowance for 162
Officers, Commissions to . . . 32, 67-9, 76-77, 87
—— Education and qualifications 220
—— Orders to in writing 102
—— Warrants to 99, 156
—— List of who entered British Artillery . . . 354-9

	PAGE
Officers, Roll of, who entered Irish Artillery	345-53
(See under Succession of Officers.)	
Ordnance, Hon. Board, Establishment of	5, 13, 50, 143, 219, 336, 343
——— Lieuts.-General of	327, 343
——— Masters-General of	57-9, 82-3, 124, 143, 150, 327, 343
——— Office of, Dublin Castle	16
——— Warrants of Appointment	16-20, 99, 156
(See under Train of Artillery.)	
——— Cannon cast in Ireland	26, 36, 102-3, 209
——— Number of Pieces in Ireland	104, 155, 226-7
——— a new Piece tried	85-6
——— a Flying 6-Pounder	273
——— Guns drawn by bullocks	304, 306
——— Stores from England	8, 297
Oulart, Battle of	318-9

Parliamentary Papers, Union of Irish Artillery with British Artillery	332-6
——— List of Officers who entered the British Artillery	354-9
Pay of the Army in Ireland	264-7, 299-302
——— Artillery Train in Ireland	13, 22-3
——— Royal Irish Artillery	30-1, 38-9, 64-5, 68, 82, 136, 183, 233, 260, 264-7
Pay Lists	3, 101
Paymaster, Allowance to	251-2
Pensions	150, 161, 185
Pigeon House Fort, Dublin, stores at	189-190
Pontoon Boats	171-6
Press, Dublin (The)	3
Proof House, Dublin Castle	174, 176
——— Salute Battery	176, 184
Quarter Masters	61, 99
Rebellion in Ireland, 1798	314-5, 317-22
——— Artilleryman executed for Disloyalty	320-2
Records, Regimental, Dublin Castle Library	3, 4
——— Public Record Office	3
——— London, Public Record Office	3
——— Woolwich, Artillery Institution	3, 5
——— Artillery Record Office	3, 4
——— Royal Military Repository	9, 297
Recruiting, Beating Orders to raise Men	276-8, 282
——— in 1756-7	46-48
——— in 1774-7	186-7, 191
——— in 1778	202
——— Levy Money	186, 205, 209, 244, 284

	PAGE
Recruits—Drafts to England	283-4
Reductions in 1766, 1783, 1801 (see under Establishment).	
Riots and Disturbances	88-9, 120-2
Sick, Sedan chair for carrying the	135
St. Patrick, Knights of	227
Stationery, Allowance for	237
Straton, Captain Lieutenant, from British Artillery, 1755	9, 29, 32
—— Colonel Commandant to 7th Battalion Royal Artillery, 1801	340, 354-5
Strength of Regiment (see under Artillery, Irish).	
Subscription from Officers and Men to carry on the War	310-11
Succession of Colonels and Lieut.-Colonels	343-4
Tara, battle near	318
Test Act of 1673	28
Thurles, Camp at	25
Tower of London, Ordnance Stores from, on payment	8, 9
Train of Artillery in Ireland, in 1684, Gun-yard and Butt at Kilmainham	10
—— in 1687, Establishment and rates of Pay	13-4
—— in 1718-9, Instructions to march a Field Train	14-5
—— in 1734, Inferior Officers and Artificers purchased Employments and appointed by Warrant	16-20
—— in 1745, Warrant of Appointment to Bombardiers	23-4
—— in 1754, The *Material* provided for a new Field Train	20-2
—— in 1755, Establishment and rates of Pay	22
—— in 1756, Train Reduced on formation of the "Artillery Company in Ireland "—Gunners and Mattrosses incorporated with the new Company—Firemasters, Master Gunners and Bombardiers placed upon Half Pay	22-3
Union of Great Britain and Ireland	332
Union of Irish Artillery with British Artillery (see under Parliamentary Papers)	332, 340, 354-9
United Irishmen plan to take Dublin Castle and the Artillery at Chapel-Izod	314
Vinegar Hill, Battle of	318-9
Warrants, Master Generals of Appointment (see under Train of Artillery).	
West India (see under Indies West).	
Wexford, Iron Foundries in County of	103
Wicklow, Camp at	53

www.ingramcontent.com/pod-product-compliance
Lightning Source LLC
Chambersburg PA
CBHW031249230426
43670CB00005B/102